Spain Transformed

WITHDRAWN

Spain Transformed

The Late Franco Dictatorship, 1959–75

Edited by

Nigel Townson

palgrave
macmillan

First published in hardback 2007 and in paperback 2010 by
PALGRAVE MACMILLAN

Palgrave Macmillan in the UK is an imprint of Macmillan Publishers Limited,
registered in England, company number 785998, of Houndmills, Basingstoke,
Hampshire RG21 6XS.

Palgrave Macmillan in the US is a division of St Martin's Press LLC,
175 Fifth Avenue, New York, NY 10010.

Palgrave Macmillan is the global academic imprint of the above companies
and has companies and representatives throughout the world.

Palgrave® and Macmillan® are registered trademarks in the United States,
the United Kingdom, Europe and other countries.

ISBN-13: 978–0–230–00455–9 hardback
ISBN-13: 978–0–230–24888–5 paperback

This book is printed on paper suitable for recycling and made from fully
managed and sustained forest sources. Logging, pulping and manufacturing
processes are expected to conform to the environmental regulations of the
country of origin.

A catalogue record for this book is available from the British Library.

Library of Congress Cataloging-in-Publication Data
Spain transformed:the late Franco dictatorship, 1959–75/edited by
    Nigel Townson.
       p. cm.
    Includes bibliographical references and index.
    ISBN 978–0–230–00455–9 (hbk) 978–0–230–24888–5 (pbk)
    1. Spain—History—1939–1975. 2. Spain—Politics and government—
    1939–1975. I. Townson, Nigel.
    DP270.S627 2007
    946.082'6—dc22   2007018315

10   9   8   7   6   5   4   3   2   1
19 18 17 16 15 14 13 12 11 10

Printed and bound in Great Britain by
CPI Antony Rowe, Chippenham and Eastbourne

Contents

List of Tables

List of Figures

Equation

List of Abbreviations

AA.VV.	*Asociaciones de Vecinos* (Neighbourhood Associations)
AC	*Acción Católica* (Catholic Action)
ACF	*Asociaciones de Cabezas de Familia* (Association of Heads of Family)
ACNP	*Asociación Católica Nacional de Propagandistas* (Catholic Association of Propagandists)
ANEPA	*Asociación Nacional del Estudio de Problemas Actuales* (National Association for the Study of Current Problems)
AP	*Alianza Popular* (Popular Alliance)
APA	*Asociación de Padres de Alumnos* (Association of Parents of Pupils)
APF	*Asociaciones de Padres de Familia* (Association of Parents of Families)
CC.OO.	*Comisiones Obreras* (Workers' Commissions)
CCPF	*Confederación Católica de Padres de Familia* (Catholic Federation of Parents of Families)
CD	*Centro Democrático* (Democratic Centre)
CEISA	*Centro de Enseñanza e Investigación, S.A.* (Centre for Education and Investigation Ltd)
CSIC	*Consejo Superior de Investigaciones Científicas* (Superior Council of Scientific Research)
DNA	*Delegado Nacional de Asociaciones* (National Commission of Associations)
DNF	*Delegado Nacional de Familia* (National Family Commission)
DP	*Delegado Provincial* (Provincial Commissioner)
EEC	European Economic Community
ETA	*Euskadi ta Askatasuna* (Basque Land and Liberty)
FEDISA	*Federación de Estudios Independientes* (Federation of Independent Studies)
FET y de las JONS	*Falange Española Tradicionalista y de las Juntas de Ofensiva Nacional Sindicalista* (Spanish Traditionalist Falange of the Juntas of National Syndicalist Offensive)
GF	*Guardia de Franco* (Franco's Guard)
GODSA	*Gabinete de Orientación y Documentación, S.A.* (Orientation and Documentation Study Centre Ltd)

HOAC	*Hermandad Obrera de Acción Católica* (Workers' Brotherhood of Catholic Action)
INI	*Instituto Nacional de Industria* (National Institute of Industry)
JOC	*Juventudes Obreras Católicas* (Workers' Catholic Youth)
OEEC	Organization for European Economic Co-operation
OS	*Organización Sindical* (Official Trade Unions, otherwise known as the *Sindicatos verticales* or Vertical Trade Unions)
PCE	*Partido Comunista de España* (Spanish Communist Party)
PNV	*Partido Nacionalista Vasco* (Basque Nationalist Party)
PP	*Partido Popular* (Popular Party)
PSOE	*Partido Socialista Obrero Español* (Spanish Socialist Party)
RD	*Reforma Democrática* (Democratic Reform)
SEU	*Sindicato Español Universitario* (Spanish University Union)
SF	*Sección Feminina* (Female Section)
STV	*Solidaridad de Trabajadores Vascos* (Basque Workers' Solidarity)
UCD	*Unión de Centro Democrático* (Union of the Democratic Centre)
UGT	*Unión General de Trabajadores* (General Union of Workers)
UN	United Nations

Acknowledgements

Due to the fulsome financial and organizational backing of the *Fundación Carolina* (Carolina Foundation) in Spain, I was able to hold an international congress on the late Franco regime in November 2005 at the *Casa de América* in Madrid. This congress, and its participants, was the origin and inspiration for this collective work. I am therefore extremely grateful to Maira Herrero at the *Fundación* for accepting the congress proposal, to Alfredo Moreno for seeing it through, and to Piedad Martín for her invaluable preparatory work and sage advice. I should also like to thank the *Casa de América* for housing the congress and for its organizational input.

The comments and criticisms of Susana Aguilar Fernández, Zira Box, Elisa Chuliá, Geoffrey Jensen, Tim Rees, and my father, Duncan Townson, on parts or all of the introduction have been a great help. *Muchas gracias* to you all. None, of course, is responsible for the remaining errors and omissions.

I would also like to take this opportunity to express my gratitude to the many people who have shared their knowledge and understanding of the Franco dictatorship with me over the years, particularly Edward Malefakis, Pamela Radcliff, and Tim Rees for their generous and stimulating company.

At Palgrave-Macmillan, I have much appreciated the patient guiding hand of the commissioning editor, Michael Strang, and the unfailingly helpful advice and guidance of editorial assistant Ruth Ireland.

Finally, I would like to thank Belén Baniandrés for her active support and encouragement throughout the preparation of this book.

NIGEL TOWNSON

1
Introduction

Nigel Townson

Over the last 15 years of the Franco dictatorship, between 1960 and 1975, Spain underwent the greatest period of economic upheaval in its history while experiencing vast social and cultural changes. The ossified nature of the political system, crystallized in the dictator's famous conceit that 'all is tied down and well tied down', contrasted starkly with the fact that political attitudes and values, within the regime as well as within Spanish society as a whole, were changing too. Change, whether economic, social, cultural or political, was therefore the defining characteristic of these years.

Historians have none the less tended to disregard the social and cultural transformation of the later Franco regime, preferring instead to dwell on the economy and above all the politics of the dictatorship's opening decade, the 1940s, or on those of the transition to democracy that followed the demise of the dictator in 1975. As a result, the 1960s and early 1970s have been largely ignored. Indeed, there has been no wide-ranging, research-led study of the latter years of the Franco regime in English since Paul Preston's edited volume *Spain in Crisis* of 1976.[1] There are also remarkably few monographs on the period. Accordingly, general accounts of the dictatorship devote little attention to the social and cultural upheavals of the regime's final decade and a half. Still, the late Franco regime is of unquestionable interest not only because of the sheer magnitude of the all-encompassing changes that took place but also because the transition from dictatorship to democracy – and, to a lesser extent, the subsequent development of democratic Spain – is inexplicable without taking into account the transformative tumult of these years.

Consequently the rationale behind this book is that the period 1960–75 has been unjustifiably neglected, that it is as worthy of scrutiny as the one that followed it, and that, while the transition to democracy in Spain of 1975–78 has been widely lauded as a paradigmatic process, the late Franco regime is highly instructive with regard to the relationship between socio-economic and cultural change and the making of democracy. *Spain Transformed* aims to shed new light on the 1960s and early 1970s by drawing on unpublished research while simultaneously engaging with the variegated work of sociologists and political scientists, who have devoted much more attention to the period than historians. This interdisciplinary intent is enhanced by the endeavour to place the changes in Spain within a comparative context. The history of modern Spain is rarely placed within such a framework, but the alterations undergone during the late Franco regime simply cannot be dissociated from the wider ones emanating from Western Europe and the United States. As a result, *Spain Transformed* presents original research on the 1960s and early 1970s while exploring novel approaches to a watershed period in modern Spanish history that has hitherto received too little attention for too long.

The Franco dictatorship was not unchanging but went through a number of distinct stages.[2] Following the Civil War of 1936–39, the regime appeared to seek the construction of a totalitarian State along fascist lines, aligning itself with Nazi Germany and Mussolini's Italy during the Second World War in the conviction that Spain would benefit from an Axis triumph. The simultaneous neotraditionalist cultural and religious revival illustrated the hybrid nature of the dictatorship from the outset. The implacable nature of the New State was reflected in the wide-ranging repression of the vanquished from the Civil War, with the execution of around 50,000 political prisoners and the maintenance of martial law until 1948, as well as in the relentless pursuit of economic self-sufficiency (or autarky), the result of which was to condemn much of the populace to hunger and despair, while greatly enhancing the State's sway over society.[3] For most Spaniards, the 1940s were bleak and harrowing years, a 'time of silence' when the dictatorship was at its most oppressive and opprobrious.

With the end of the Second World War, the Franco regime, confronted with the defeat of the Axis and the hostility of the Allies, sought to flee its pariah status within the Western world by casting its fascistic trappings aside for the more acceptable ones of 'National-Catholicism' and the doctrinal subterfuge of 'organic democracy'. Moral condemnation by the United Nations in 1946, however, highlighted the regime's isolation. None the less, the fissured front of the anti-Francoist opposition, the Allies' search for stability in Western Europe, and the fortuitous unfolding of the Cold War eventually allowed Franco, now zealously promoting himself as 'the sentinel of the West' in the crusade against Communism, to break the international quarantine by 1948. Catholic ascendancy within the regime resulted in the latter being defined in the Law of Succession of 1947 as a 'Catholic, social and representative State, which, in accordance with its traditions, declares itself a kingdom', which mollified those foreign powers, such as Britain, that advocated a monarchist solution to the 'Spanish problem', as well as much Catholic opinion, both at home and abroad. Not surprisingly, the first international agreement of note to be secured by the Franco regime after the Second World War was the Concordat of August 1953 with the Vatican. More importantly still, anti-Communism persuaded the Truman administration to back the Franco regime as early as 1948, this culminating in the Bases Agreement of September 1953, which, in turn, paved the way for Spanish membership of WHO, UNESCO, the International Labor Organization, and, in 1955, of the United Nations' General Assembly itself. Meanwhile, the adversities of autarky were being sloughed off as the economy became somewhat less protected and more competitive, growth rising – albeit starting from a very low threshold – to 4.35 per cent p.a. between 1951 and 1958. Opposition groups now emerged that were not directly linked to the Civil War and which aimed to supersede the paralysing polarization induced by the conflict of 1936–39 through the advocacy of reconciliation rather than revenge. This was reflected in mounting intellectual and artistic dissent from the early 1950s onwards, the appearance of a new working class movement (involved in the strikes of 1956 and embodied in the first *Comisión Obrera*, or workers' commission, in 1957), and in the Madrid student revolt of 1956, which brought together – for the very first time – opponents of the regime from the camps of the victors and the vanquished alike.

In response to the economic crisis of the late 1950s, technocratic ministers of the secretive lay Catholic organization, Opus Dei, carried out a rationalization and liberalization of the Spanish economy that, together with the reform of the State bureaucracy, launched the unprecedented economic growth of the 1960s and early 1970s. Between 1960 and 1973, indeed, only Japan's national economy grew faster. Entry into the IMF, the World Bank, and the Organization for European Economic Cooperation signalled the further internationalization of the dictatorship, but the doors of political international bodies, above all the EEC – which the regime had initially approached in 1962 with a view to opening negotiations – remained firmly shut. Spain's tardy industrial revolution also ushered in far-reaching social and cultural change. Mass emigration, both within Spain and beyond, resulted in an exodus from the countryside, that, along with large-scale foreign and domestic investment, transformed rural and urban societies alike not only in class terms but also in terms of their values, mentalities and culture, as well as greatly altering the physical landscape as cities sprawled and the *pueblos* shrank. In most respects, the increasingly prosperous and pluralistic Spain of the 1960s and 1970s was a far cry from the impoverished, grimly conformist society of two decades earlier. Moreover, regime ideology, now shaped to an important degree by the modernizing lexicon of 'development', had become so diffuse that the dictatorial elites were no longer effectively welded together by a Francoist orthodoxy. Another sign of the times was that the repression had become much more selective and, in many respects, more lenient. The protests of students, intellectuals, progressive clergy, and workers, of which the latter was the most redoubtable opposition force from the early 1960s on, did much to erode the legitimacy of the dictatorship while fostering a collective conviction that change was inevitable. Still, the opposition was too weak and too divided to actually overthrow the dictatorship, though a broader, if more inchoate, social and cultural resistance to the regime grew steadily throughout these years. By the time of Franco's death in 1975, the political and institutional carapace of the dictatorship may have remained overwhelmingly intact, but the society within it had been transformed.

The very longevity of the Franco dictatorship, the substantial shifts in policy that took place under it, the deliberate ambiguity and dilatoriness that characterized Franco's leadership, and, above all, the synchronization of differing right-wing political cultures and ideologies, accounts for the protracted debate over the political nature of the regime. Was it, for example, a totalitarian construct, a military dictatorship, a fascist one, an authoritarian regime of limited pluralism, or a modern despotism?[4]

The origins of the debate over the nature of the Franco dictatorship lie in the Civil War. Some contemporary observers regarded the Nationalist State in-the-making as a brutal variant on the traditional military dictatorship, such as that of General Primo de Rivera in the 1920s. They rejected the term 'fascist' in part because of the country's relative socioeconomic backwardness and in part because they perceived that the interests of Spain's dominant classes would be more effectively served by established institutions such as the army and the Catholic Church rather than by new ones such as the fascist single party. 'You can have all the fascists you want in Spain', judged republican president Manuel Azaña in late 1937, 'but there will never be a fascist regime. If a violent movement triumphs over the Republic, we will relapse into a military and ecclesiastical dictatorship of the traditional type, whatever slogans are adapted and whatever mottos are adopted'.[5]

For most of the Spanish and European left, however, 'Francoism' was indeed 'fascism'. To an extent, this was a question of ideological stigmatization, much as the Nationalists demonized their opponents as 'reds'. More persuasively, Francoism was equated with fascism not so much because of the political similitudes with Mussolini's Italy or Hitler's Germany but because of its violent defence of the traditional oligarchy in the face of the twin threats of parliamentary reformism and working-class revolution. The stress on fascism's socio-economic (as opposed to its political) dimension was of Marxist inspiration, the Communist International describing it as 'the open and terrorist dictatorship of the most reactionary, most chauvinistic, and most imperialist elements of financial capital'.[6] None the less, the most resounding international denunciation of the Franco dictatorship as 'fascist' was the resolution of the United Nations' General Assembly of 12 December 1946.[7]

So overpowering was the identification of Francoism with fascism that it was not until the 1960s that a widely discussed alternative vision of the regime emerged. US-based Spanish sociologist Juan Linz elaborated the concept of the 'authoritarian regime' precisely in order to define the Franco dictatorship. According to Linz,

> authoritarian regimes are political systems with limited, not responsible, pluralism: without elaborate and guiding ideology (but with distinctive mentalities); without intensive or extensive political mobilization (except at some points in their development); and in which a leader (or occasionally a small group) exercises power within formally ill-defined limits but actually quite predictable ones.[8]

While Linz's Cold War-inspired paradigm has been widely adopted by historians such as Stanley Payne and Javier Tusell, sociologists such as Amando de Miguel, and political scientists such as Guy Hermet and Richard Gunther, it has also generated a protracted and polemical debate of an undeniably ideological hue. Opponents have lambasted Linz on the grounds that he focuses on the regime's formal political features to the detriment of its social, and above all its class, ones. Moreover, his contention that the regime exhibited a 'limited pluralism' has been severely criticised for lending the dictatorship a certain democratic legitimacy, if not actually exonerating it.[9]

An alternative interpretation to the Linzian vision did not emerge, however, until the dictatorship was spluttering to its end. The timing was no coincidence given that opponents of the regime, now able to express their opinions within Spain with greater liberty than before, were understandably eager to denounce the dictatorship – and thereby consign it to the past – while implicitly putting the case for democracy. Sociologists Salvador Giner and Eduardo Sevilla Guzmán attempted to supplant Linz's thesis by proposing that the regime be regarded as a 'modern despotism': that is to say, 'a mode of class domination in which power is exercised on behalf of the dominant class, and in its name, by a despot or small elite'. Clearly Giner and Sevilla Guzmán's Marxist-inspired formulation attached far more weight to the regime's class dimension than did Linz's thesis, but it nevertheless incorporated many aspects from the latter. [10]

Other critics of Linz did not so much rework his thesis as reject it altogether. During the two decades following the death of Franco, historians such as Manuel Tuñón de Lara, Paul Preston and Julián Casanova have signalled their discrepancy with Linz by postulating a recasting of the Marxist model of the 1930s. Francoism must be identified with fascism, contends Casanova, because 'it fulfilled the same historic mission, pursued the same ends, and, above all, achieved the same "benefits" as the fascist regimes of Italy and Germany'. In all three cases, he insists, 'the social function of fascism was to stabilize and strengthen capitalistic property relations and secure the social and economic domination of the capitalist class'. [11] Other scholars, however, have objected that such aims have not distinguished fascism alone but have characterized numerous other regimes, including military, oligarchical–liberal, and even democratic ones. Fault has also been found with the Francoism-as-fascism school for contending that the dictatorship's fundamental features were forged during its first decade, thereby denying – in stark contrast with Linz and others – that the regime evolved in any meaningful way. A further criticism of the revisionist Marxist school is that, as Michael Mann argues, fascism cannot be defined solely in terms of its social function. Further, Mann maintains that the Franco dictatorship, along with many other non-democratic right-wing regimes, cannot be satisfactorily explained in terms of a single typology. On the contrary, Francoism can only be properly understood as an amalgam of differing political and ideological currents. Thus for Mann the Franco regime was, at least until the 1960s, a 'semi-reactionary corporatist regime', in which the pillars of the ancien régime – the monarchists, military, and Catholic Church – overcame the challenge of the masses through a mixture of outright repression and the incorporation of modernist features such as 'organic nationalism', a strengthened State and 'borrowings' from fascism. Neither does Robert O. Paxton, in *The Anatomy of Fascism*, regard the Franco dictatorship as fascist. He contends that the regime exhibited 'a minimum of fascist excitement ... certainly after 1942, and probably before'. By 1970, he concludes, Francoist Spain 'had long become an authoritarian regime ... with almost no visible fascist coloration'.[12]

What is indisputable is that the coalition that made up the Franco dictatorship was bound together by a fundamental set of beliefs. On the one hand, all the forces of Francoism shared a common hostility to democracy, liberalism, Communism (and 'its accomplices and hirelings'), materialism and atheism. On the other hand, all defended a strongly centralized State, authoritarian government, a prepotent national identity, a profoundly conservative social order, and the centrality of the Catholic Church to Spanish cultural and social life. In addition, few would dispute that Franco's pivotal role in the foundation and subsequent unfolding of the regime made it, in the last instance, a personal dictatorship (as its very definition as 'Francoist' indicates, as does usage of the generic term 'Francoism').[13] As Head of State, Prime Minister, Commander-in-Chief, and Head of the Movement (or single party), Francisco Franco regarded himself as being responsible not to an electorate, the Cortes, the Cabinet, the Army, the Falange, the Catholic Church, or, indeed, to any other body, but only 'to God and to History'. Power, as Santos Juliá insists, ultimately lay not with the institutions or other entities but with Franco, and Franco alone, which explains why, from the outset of his rule to the very end, the dictator was able to appoint and dismiss generals, Falangists, Catholics, and other individuals much as he pleased, without ever facing an institutional or organizational revolt.[14] None the less, the dictatorship was not merely a personal regime. Franco himself always appreciated that defections and divisions within the ruling coalition would undermine, and could even imperil, the dictatorship, and that, as a result, the communion and collaboration of all its leading forces was required. Nor did the regime appear to stand still. Broadly speaking, the dictatorship can be divided into a quasi-totalitarian or semi-fascist phase from 1939 to 1945, a National–Catholic, corporativist one up to the late 1950s, and, finally, a period defined above all by its technocratic, developmental nature, which lasted up until the demise of the dictator in 1975.[15] In short, the regime was not in thrall to a single ideology or doctrine from beginning to end. Nor was any one phase of the dictatorship dominated absolutely by a particular ideology or doctrine.

From this perspective, it can be postulated that neither the Franco dictatorship in its totality nor a single part of it is encapsulated entirely by any one of the political typologies usually applied to the non-democratic regimes of the twentieth century. On the contrary, the regime should perhaps be seen as one that welded together different typologies in an amalgam that, moreover, changed its composition over time. In other words, the Franco dictatorship can be viewed not as a static construction cast in concrete, but as one that evolved between its foundation in the 1930s and its fall in the 1970s.

The debate over the nature of the Franco dictatorship will doubtless acquire greater authority and nuance the more the regime is subjected to first-hand research. However, the only period of the 37-year dictatorship that has been fairly extensively researched is its opening decade. In large measure this is because the 1940s can be regarded in many ways as a continuation of the central, watershed trauma of twentieth-century Spain: the Civil War. Indeed, the dictatorship's founding myth was the Nationalist triumph in the war of 1936–39. The regime's manichean vision of the conflict as a Catholic Crusade against atheistic, Communist hordes, along with the post-war division of Spanish society into victors and vanquished, was deliberately designed to keep the memory of the Civil War alive in order to legitimize a dictatorial power whose origins lay in military revolt.[16] A further continuity was the Nationalist repression of the defeated Republicans. During the Transition, the crimes committed during the hardline repression of the 1930s and 1940s were never addressed in political terms as a result of the overriding quest for consensus, but during the last decade or so a considerable effort has been made by historians, civil associations, and private individuals to locate and identify the victims of the repression, the outcome being the digging up of impromptu graves and the uncovering of concentration camps, jails, and detention centres, along with a flood of books, press articles and television reports on all aspects of the repression, including the post-war purges of the professions and the experiences of republican women.[17] Consequently the reconstruction of the repression has further underscored the linkage between the Civil War and the early Franco regime, and, in the process, revived research on the 1940s.

Another important continuity between the two periods was the Francoist alignment with Nazi Germany and Fascist Italy. During the Civil War, the German and Italian fascist regimes backed the Nationalists with massive, arguably decisive, material support, while during the Second World War, Franco, having signed up to the Anti-Comintern Pact in 1939 while abandoning the League of Nations, returned the

Axis's favour with covert material and logistical support and the dispatch of the Blue Division to the Eastern Front. He was even prepared, in late 1940, to enter the war on the German side, but Hitler was then unwilling to meet the *Caudillo*'s terms. Interest in Spain's history at this juncture is consequently enhanced not only by its merger into the wider drama of the Second World War, but also through its association with fascism. That Franco's future between 1936 and 1945 appeared to depend on the fortunes of the Axis powers only adds to the allure. At no moment was this more evident than at the end of the Second World War, when the very existence of the Franco dictatorship, following the Axis defeat, appeared to hang in the balance. The uniformed, authoritative Franco of the 1940s is also a somewhat more arresting historical protagonist than the ageing, civilian-attired figure of the later years. Finally, the 1940s have also generated interest because a good many historians regard these years as the quintessence of the regime. Francoism is herein regarded as a Spanish variant of European fascism, not so much in terms of its formal political and institutional aspects as in terms of the social function fulfilled by its use of repression and in particular violence. From this perspective, violence was deployed in order to protect elite interests during a period of capitalist crisis, above all from the revolutionary working class. The contention is that the dictatorship's repressive features did not, in essence, change. In this vein, Michael Richards writes that between 1939 and 1945 the regime executed thousands of opponents and 'continued to put its enemies to death until... the 1970s', thereby obscuring the reality of the changes that the dictatorship underwent between the 1930s and the 1970s.[18]

By contrast with the 1940s, the last quarter century of the Franco regime has received relatively short shrift from historians. A basic problem of access has bedevilled research into the dictatorship's last decade or so. A 30-year rule governs general access to the Spanish archives, but in the case of a document that relates to an individual's 'privacy' this can be withheld for 25 years following the latter's death (or, if this is unknown, for 50 years from the date of the document), thereby limiting greatly the scope of research on the 1960s and 1970s.[19] Furthermore, much archival material has simply been destroyed in order to avoid the incrimination of individuals and organizations alike. The Falange, Civil Guard, and police, for example, have all shredded a great deal of material from this period. There has also been a major historiographical handicap to the study of the late Franco regime. The history of twentieth-century Spain has been skewed by a bias towards political history, which to an important extent has been a result of the enormous attention paid to the politically charged history of the Civil War and its origins. None the less, the social and cultural history of the twentieth century has been sorely neglected not only in comparative terms but in absolute ones, too – significant stretches of the social and cultural history of the last century have received scant attention. Given this bias towards political history, the salient shortcoming of the last two-thirds of the dictatorship is that it lacks the high drama and high profile of the first third. In reality, by the 1950s the regime was consolidated, the opposition not representing a threat to its existence right up until Franco's death. In the meantime, regime politics was distinguished by a stifling lack of public debate and an equally manifest lack of political reform. The declining personal protagonism of the dictator himself during the 1960s, governmental affairs being increasingly left to his dour and dogmatic right-hand man, Luis Carrero Blanco, also detracts from interest in the period.

Indeed, greater attention has been paid to opposition politics in the 1960s and 1970s than to the politics of the regime. Here, too, the subject has its limits, as the relative gains of the anti-Francoist opposition have been emphatically overshadowed by the absolute triumph of democracy during the Transition. Moreover, the political drama and public debate of the post-Franco period are inherently more appealing than the circumscribed, often dreary politics of the Franco era itself. Accordingly, the sweeping economic and social changes of the 1960s and 1970s have frequently been overlooked as the mere backdrop to, or at best the required context for, the momentous political events of the Transition. The fact that the Transition was made possible by collaboration between Francoists and anti-Francoists might also have inhibited research on the period for fear of stirring up politically divisive – even democratically damaging – debates over the past activities of those that served the dictator. A final, overarching reason for the neglect of the late Franco regime is that perception of this period has been greatly distorted by the prism of the Transition. Hindsight has made the very success of the transformation of the dictatorship into democracy appear not only as inevitable in its own right but also as the natural outcome of the economic and social changes of the previous two decades. The 'political miracle' of the Transition has thereby been converted into the unavoidable corollary of the 'economic miracle' of the late Franco regime. The insoluble shortcoming of this explanatory model, championed above all by the functionalist school and modernization theorists, is that it is too mechanistic. Few contemporary observers took it for granted that the socio-economic metamorphosis of the 1960s and early 1970s made

it inevitable, or even likely, that dictatorship would give way to democracy. On the contrary, many opponents of the dictatorship regarded *el desarrollo* (development or, more broadly, modernization), and the consumerism to which it gave rise, as a cunning strategy elaborated by the regime in order to depoliticize and demobilize the disgruntled masses. During the post-Franco era, analysts such as José Amodia denied that a genuine transition had taken place at all as both State and society allegedly remained in the thrall of the Francoist oligarchy.[20] Only with the consolidation of democracy in Spain did scholars – now armed with the inestimable advantage of hindsight – identify a linear link between the 'economic' and the 'political' miracles. It can be argued, however, that this represents a retrospective reading of a process that was both more complex and more contingent than the determinists would allow.[21] The impact of the functionalist and modernization paradigms have also deflected attention from the late Franco period by ascribing to it a mere supporting role within the greater drama of the Transition.

Change during the late Franco period was due above all to the transformation of the economy. At the outset of the 1950s the Spanish economy began to crawl out from the protectionist shell of the autarkic regime that had characterized – and inhibited – it ever since 1939. Limited liberalizing measures along with administrative adjustments helped Spain take advantage of the unprecedented boom of the Western economies, then just under way. Between 1951 and 1958, the Spanish economy grew at the impressive rate of 4.35 per cent p.a., though starting from a very low threshold: the GNP for the year before the Civil War broke out, 1935, was not surpassed until 1951, while the renta *per capita* for 1935 was not matched until 1953. There were also severe shortcomings to the upsurge of the 1950s, such as high inflation, a huge public deficit and extensive underemployment, along with continuing restrictions on the importation of goods, technology and capital.[22] Indeed, the dictatorship found itself in 1959 on the verge of suspending payments on the international debt. The Opus Dei technocrats who entered the government during the late 1950s therefore took liberalization a step further by pushing through a series of administrative and economic reforms that culminated in the Stabilization Plan of July 1959.

In many ways, as Pablo Martín Aceña and Elena Martínez make clear in their chapter on 'The Golden Age of Spanish Capitalism', the term 'stabilization' was something of a misnomer. Certainly, the Plan was designed to 'stabilize' economic growth, but this was to be achieved not by 'stabilizing' the autarkic model but by undertaking a 'radical change of direction in economic policy'. The principal goals of the Plan were to bring inflation under control, eliminate numerous restrictions within the domestic market and integrate the Spanish economy more fully into the international one, thereby harnessing Spain more effectively than ever to the thrusting Western economies (though State intervention remained prominent, as shown by the Development Plans of 1964–73). Drawing on the very latest data, Martín Aceña and Martínez reveal the sheer magnitude of the 'economic miracle': between 1959 and 1974 real growth averaged 6.9 per cent p.a., Japan being the only developed nation to surpass this performance. This rate of growth, seven times that for the previous century, affected all sectors of the economy, but above all industry, which grew at nearly 10 per cent p.a. In short, Spain took a mere 15 years to make the leap from a largely agrarian-based economy to an industrial one. At the time of Franco's death, as Martín Aceña and Martínez underline, 'Spain stepped into the First World and joined the exclusive club of those countries with a p.a. income of $2000 or more'.

The most polemical aspect of Spain's industrial revolution has been the degree to which this can be attributed to the initiative of the dictatorship itself. To what extent, in other words, should the Franco regime take credit for the 'economic miracle'? Apologists have insisted that an overriding objective of Franco from the outset was the creation of an ample and prosperous middle class that would bring social and political peace to Spain, and that, as a result, the transformation of the economy should be regarded as one of the dictatorship's greatest legacies. By contrast, detractors of the dictatorship have viewed such self-congratulatory triumphalism as a cynical claim that owes more to hindsight than to foresight, while attributing the 'miracle' more to the unparalleled strength of the international economy than to the intervention of the dictatorship.

From the perspective of Martín Aceña and Martínez, the regime's programme of liberalization was doubtless responsible for Spain's greater international integration, for a more orthodox monetary policy and for a balanced budget. On the other hand, they contend that the Spanish economy, despite the restrictions of autarky, was already growing strongly in the 1950s as a consequence of the post-Second World War boom in the West. Thus the 'greatest virtue' of the dictatorship was not so much to activate or sustain the 'economic miracle' as to allow it to follow its course. Moreover, the authors insist that the very form which modernization took in Spain diverged greatly from that in Western Europe. The refusal of the Francoist State to implement a fiscal reform that would have injured the interests of its social base together with its rejection of the type of 'social pact' that characterized the European democracies had far-reaching consequences. The dictatorship not only eschewed many of the economic reforms typical of the European democracies, such as the development of infrastructure and the streamlining of an unwieldy and inefficient public sector, but it also failed to undertake leading social reforms such as the expansion of the Welfare State and the redistribution of national wealth. Spain's route to modernization was therefore profoundly conditioned by the regime's dictatorial priorities.

The principal pillars of the 'economic miracle' were foreign investment, emigration and tourism. Geographical proximity to the booming economies of Western Europe, along with Cold War-induced proximity to the US, facilitated massive foreign investment in Spain once the protectionist barriers were lowered, while huge labour shortages in Western Europe sucked in millions of immigrant workers from Southern Europe. The over 1.5 million Spanish workers that emigrated abroad between 1960 and 1972 reduced domestic unemployment, strengthened the bargaining power of workers back home, and sent back remittances sufficient to cover over 50 per cent of the foreign debt.[23]

The third pillar of the 'economic miracle', tourism, was a leading focus of both foreign and domestic investment, as well as of internal migration, but it has so far been subjected to little research. A major revaluation of the role played by tourism in reshaping not only Spanish society but also the Franco dictatorship is offered by Sasha Pack. The upgrading of tourism to ministerial status in 1951 reveals that the dictatorship was far from oblivious to the emergence of the 'leisure civilization' as an essential part of the post-war European experience. The very strength of the industry's upsurge in the 1950s allowed the regime to survive a number of economic crises while permitting it to undertake greater policy experimentation. Accordingly, and in contrast to the prevailing wisdom, Pack affirms that the growth of tourism in Spain was not a consequence of the 1959 Stabilization Plan, but a *cause*. Vertiginous growth of the tourist trade in the 1960s and early 1970s – briefly converting Spain into the world leader – not only helped shift European wealth southwards but also turned Spanish tourism into a paradigm for countries in Europe, South America and elsewhere.

While previous studies have highlighted the impact of foreign tourists on the outlook of ordinary Spaniards – although Pack insists that this involved the transmission of social and moral values rather than political ones – far less attention has been paid to that on the dictatorship itself. Within the regime, the moral imperatives of the old guard clashed with the economic priorities of the new, the latter being determined to demonstrate that Spain was a 'modern' country not only in material terms, but also in attitudinal and behavioural ones. At heart, this was an eminently nationalistic enterprise as the modernists were eager to counter 'anti-Spanish slander'.

By drawing on tourism as a means of regeneration from above, as epitomised by the exertions of Manuel Fraga at the Ministry of Information and Tourism between 1962 and 1969, the aim of the modernists was also to show the outside world that Spain was modern in a political sense. As a result, State tourism embraced the promotion of certain liberal values and attempted to offer an image of Spain that was more pluralistic than the Andalusian stereotype. In the short term, Sasha Pack concludes, tourism buttressed the dictatorship by generating prosperity and by enhancing the regime's legitimacy, but in the medium term it undermined the dictatorship by making both State and society more liberal and more pluralistic. Furthermore, the spectacular success of the tourist industry served to bring Spain and Western Europe closer together not only in material and social terms, but also in terms of shared mentalities. Tourism in Spain may be associated with the slogan 'Spain is Different', but the paradox is that tourism probably did more than anything else to make Spain more 'normal'.

The alterations in social attitude and values to which tourism contributed formed part of a much broader and deeper change within Spanish society. The massive movements of money, goods and peoples is unquestionably linked to the emergence of new aspirations, ideas and values. Enormous internal emigration, generated in large part by tourism, was one facet of this process. During the 1960s, 4.5 million Spaniards moved from the countryside to the city or from one locality to another. Demographic mobility, along with the mass arrival of foreign tourists, helped spread different ideas and values, whether intentionally or not. More importantly still, emigration to countries such as France, Germany and Switzerland not only brought Spanish workers into greater contact with the anti-Francoist opposition, but often furnished them with an apprenticeship in democratic and in particular trade union practices. More generally, the experience of emigration acquainted many Spaniards with different lifestyles, social environments and political cultures. The very freedom with which Spanish workers could travel to and from their homes, together with the frequency with which they did so, meant that emigration arguably left a greater imprint on Spanish society than anywhere else in Southern Europe.[24]

Exposure to new values was also facilitated by the rapid urbanization of the 1960s and 1970s and by the greater accessibility to media outlets such as cinema, radio and the press – all of which had had a limited diffusion following the Civil War – and above all to the new medium of television. The prosperity generated by development did not benefit the upper reaches of society alone, but was widely distributed. As a result, the extreme poverty and injustice that had previously characterized Spanish society were largely exorcised as living standards rose and people joined the consumer revolution. In 1960, only 4 per cent of households had a car and 1 per cent a television, but by 1975 the figures had soared to 40 and 85 per cent, respectively. Spanish society of the 1960s and 1970s thereby became both more consumerist and secular: more in tune, in sum, with the 'Western life-style'.[25]

The unprecedented socio-economic changes of the 1960s and early 1970s influenced the whole gamut of attitudes and values – everything from societal relations and expectations to sexual mores and moral prerogatives – that collectively made up what can be described as the 'mentality' of Spaniards during this period. In analysing the change in mentalities that took place during the late Franco regime, Walter Bernecker regards the Spanish experience as being more profound than that of other contemporary industrial societies as it constituted not just a series of adjustments or modifications in outlook but a veritable revolution. This transformation in mentalities did not, however, involve a wholesale exchange of 'old' attitudes and values for 'new' ones, but an ambivalent process of assimilation in which some attitudes and values were accepted or integrated, while others were rejected or reformulated. Indeed, Bernecker judges that the traditional account of the differing reactions of people to modernization simply does not do justice to the complexity of the Spanish case. He also insists that new mentalities were not adopted in a linear fashion as the process of adaptation could retreat as well as advance, sometimes being reversed altogether. Neither can the transformation in mentalities be seen as a straightforward outcome of economic change. On the contrary, Bernecker rejects this reductionist paradigm on the grounds that *desarrollo* was at once a cause and a consequence of evolving mentalities; in other words, the relationship between modernization and mentalities was of a reciprocal, not unilateral, nature. For instance, the massive extension of higher education in the 1960s can be seen not only as a consequence of economic growth but also as a cause, given the new expectations fostered by greater educational opportunities. The upshot was that Spaniards rapidly adopted many of the attitudes and values commonly associated with the 'modern' world. At the same time, they also imbibed ideas and ideologies that clashed directly with the dominant doctrinal discourse of the dictatorship. Marxism was foremost, the diffusion of which was widespread amongst students, workers, artists and intellectuals, as well as amongst progressive sectors of the clergy. The overall shift in mentalities of the 1960s and early 1970s, Bernecker concludes, was of a revolutionary magnitude that contradicted and confounded the eternal aspiration of the dictatorship to a depoliticized and deferential society.

Such sweeping change notwithstanding, Spanish exceptionalism during this period – 'Spain is different' – is often taken for granted; in other words, that dictatorial Spain lagged far behind democratic Europe. But was this really the case? Few scholars, especially historians, have taken the trouble to place Spain's trajectory during the 1960s and the early 1970s within a comparative context. Tom Buchanan therefore undertakes the unusual, but necessary, task of examining to what extent, and in what ways, the Spanish experience mirrored that of Western Europe. Politically speaking, the Franco regime was far from exceptional within Southern Europe given the existence of the Salazar dictatorship (1932–74), and that of the Greek colonels (1967–74). Furthermore, Buchanan warns that the divergences in the 1960s between 'democratic' Europe and the Franco dictatorship should not be overdrawn, given the relatively restricted number of democratic States, the somewhat limited nature of contemporary European democracy and the major upheavals suffered by mainstream democratic States such as France and Italy. None the less, the reconfiguration of European democracy in the early 1970s, rooted largely in the extension of political and social rights and the forging of a stronger sense of a common democratic identity, meant that 'the gulf between Franco's Spain and democratic Western Europe became unbridgeable', a gulf that became virtually unsustainable with the fall of the Portuguese and Greek dictatorships in 1974. More broadly, many of the developments that characterized Western Europe during the 1960s and early 1970s, such as the momentous changes brought about by modern industrial capitalism and the emergence of new social movements and forms of protest, were also experienced by Spain. The difference between Spain and its democratic neighbours lay in the manner in which the Franco regime responded to these challenges. Moreover, Spain remained far removed from democratic Europe with regard to certain issues such as gender relations.

By placing the dictatorship within a comparative context, Tom Buchanan is able to highlight the divergences between Franco's Spain and Western Europe, but also the points of convergence. He concludes that the two were not nearly as different as is often assumed.

Comparative analysis, however, also enables the author to delineate the unquestionable limitations of a regime that ultimately aspired to integration within Western Europe. Spain was not so much 'different' as 'the same but different'.

While the literature on the political opposition to the dictatorship is quite substantial, we know far less about how the dictatorship itself perceived the opposition and the rapidly evolving society from which it emerged. There is no question that the socio-economic and cultural changes of the 1960s and early 1970s not only profoundly reshaped Spanish society but also effected the State. It is otherwise impossible to explain why the Francoist Cortes, by means of the Law of Political Reform of 1976, dismantled the dictatorship's political system and replaced it with a democratic one, or that the three key figures of the Transition – King Juan Carlos, Premier Adolfo Suárez, and Cortes President Torcuato Fernández Miranda – had all been faithful servants of the old regime. In order to understand this transformation, contends Antonio Cazorla, one has to go beyond politics at the highest national level (about which a good deal has been written) and scrutinize the political *culture* of the Franco regime. He does this by reconstructing the authorities' perception of social change and political protest in 1962, a year of major strikes, and then again in 1972, as the regime drew to its close, before assessing how the State responded to these challenges.

Cazorla's research reveals that, on the one hand, the overwhelming bulk of Spaniards were more concerned with their personal economic welfare – not least as a result of the deprivations of the previous two decades – than with the uncertain rewards of political militancy. Accordingly, protest often involved material issues rather than political ones. Indeed, in most of Spain the level of anti-Francoist political activity was strikingly limited, people being inclined to accommodate themselves to the dictatorship without necessarily identifying with it. In this light, conventional accounts of the political opposition to the regime tend to exaggerate both the presence and the impact of dissenting students, workers, and so on. On the other hand, Cazorla shows that the regime did not assume that all protest was inherently political, but distinguished between the economically motivated and that of a more ideological hue. Moreover, the authorities were well aware of the widespread disenchantment with, or indifference to, the dictatorship. Still, they had no idea how to overcome this popular alienation, limiting themselves to reflecting on the need for 'new compromises' in order to guarantee 'social harmony', while failing to take any purposeful initiatives.

Antonio Cazorla therefore rejects the traditional view of a hardline regime that was impervious to the society around it. Rather than a bipolar battle between State and society, he perceives a reciprocal relationship between the two: the State conditioned society but the latter also influenced the State. Indeed, without taking into account the way in which Francoist political culture was tempered in the 1960s and 1970s by a society in transformation, Cazorla concludes, the subsequent transition from the dictatorship to democracy is inexplicable.

One notable consequence of the evolving political culture of Francoism was the emergence of heterodox currents. Given the ban on political parties and the failure of the 1964 Law of Associations to embrace political entities, groups from within the dictatorship created alternative channels for the discussion and dissemination of political issues. Cristina Palomares analyses the appearance, nature, and goals of these groups, which ranged from private gatherings and clubs to seminars, research centres, and publications, as well as embracing economic and cultural associations. Broadly speaking, these nonconformists can be divided into *aperturistas* and *reformistas*, the former favouring a cautious opening-up of the regime from above, while the latter advocated the wholesale replacement of the dictatorship by a democratic regime. Both tendencies, however, were united by the conviction that reform of the dictatorship had to come about by means of the regime's very own institutional and judicial mechanisms. The ambiguous attitude of the dictatorial rulers, at once aware of the need for some sort of *apertura* but afraid of the consequences, allowed for a limited degree of debate. The authorities, for example, knew full well that political matters were discussed within the confines of supposedly non-political organizations. More importantly, the Press Law of 1966, despite its many restrictions, did permit greater public debate. As Palomares stresses, these discordant voices never represented more than a small minority within Francoism's political class, they never constituted a unified alternative to the regime and they never represented a serious threat to the dictatorship. None the less, these non-conformist circles helped pave the way to the Transition by opening up spaces for political discussion, by fomenting public debate and by channeling demands for change. In common with Antonio Cazorla, Cristina Palomares maintains that these fissures within the dictatorial elites can be seen as a response to the wider socio-economic and cultural changes of the 1960s and 1970s. Similarly, she concludes that this shift in perspective within the political class of Francoism was of fundamental importance to the subsequent transition from dictatorship to democracy.

Clearly the emergence of reformist currents within the upper echelons of the dictatorship indicated that it could not afford to stand still in the face of the fast-changing society of the 1960s and early 1970s. The regime itself did in fact undertake policy initiatives in this direction, but they have received remarkably little attention from scholars. Pamela Radcliff's chapter on the opening up of the channels of popular participation in public affairs through the revival of associational life thereby permits a radical reappraisal of this scarcely noticed dimension to the dictatorship. The tensions generated within Spanish society by modernizing developments such as economic liberalization, university expansion and the urban crisis prompted workers, students, and local residents alike to seek solutions to their daily problems by means of new forms of collective representation, not least because the remote and inadequate Francoist State was more of a problem than a panacea. Pressure from below thereby produced an opening from above as the State sought to contain popular protest by augmenting participation in the public arena. The upshot was the Law of Associations of 1964, which spawned a whole new generation of voluntary organizations: by 1967 twice as many associations had been founded as in the previous 23 years. Although created within a dictatorial framework, these groups developed basic democratic practices such as mutual tolerance, negotiation, the holding of elections and the lobbying of public authorities. Consequently associational life – albeit under the watchful eye of the dictatorship – encouraged the emergence of a more participatory and pluralistic civil society.

The associational current generated by the 1964 Law converged with that created by the *Movimiento* (the Movement, or state-sponsored single party), which from 1958 onwards sponsored a whole range of family-centred groups that allegedly embraced a million members by 1972. Unlike the 1964 Law, this was a purely top-down initiative, designed to arrest the *Movimiento*'s decline within the regime through popular mobilization. Like the 1964 Law, this promoted democratic practices within a dictatorial context. Still, the *Movimiento*'s undertaking has been largely ignored, partly due to the refusal of Franco to approve the *Movimiento*'s project for *political* associations and partly as a result of the perception that this was the last, desperate fling of a reactionary, retrograde organization that had nothing to offer in terms of the construction of a democratic Spain. None the less, as Radcliff stresses, both the voluntary and *Movimiento* associations undermined the demobilization and deference that had characterized associational life under the Franco regime by fomenting greater participation and empowerment. The irony is that by doing so the State strengthened not only civil society but also the burgeoning opposition movement. To paraphrase E.P. Thompson, Pamela Radcliff thereby rescues many ordinary men and women of the Spain of the 1960s and early 1970s from the condescension of the modernization theorists, for whom the masses were swept along pre-determined paths by impersonal forces, and from that of the transition theorists, for whom the masses were peripheral to the political process. She thereby demonstrates how socio-economic and institutional change during the late Franco period translated into the democratic realities of the post-Franco era since the citizens' movement of 1977–79, which did so much to shape the Transition, was the heir to the Francoist associations. As Radcliff persuasively argues, the social history of the Transition, which is yet to be written, cannot be divorced from that of the late Franco regime.

The emergence of a pre-democratic civil society within Franco's Spain was not limited to the development of democratic practices within local communities, family associations and the workplace, but also included the unfolding of a liberal, non-authoritarian culture. Originally, the Franco dictatorship had pursued a largely fascistic cultural policy, but following the defeat of the Axis powers in 1945 this gave way to one that was decidedly more National Catholic. According to the dominant interpretation of cultural change under the regime, as exemplified in the work of Juan Pablo Fusi, and, more recently, that of Jordi Gracia, by the mid-1950s this policy too had failed. By then, the regime, in the words of Fusi, had lost the 'battle of culture' to liberalism. This is not to deny the existence of an official mass culture, but this was merely a 'subculture' that highlighted 'the failure' of the dictatorship's cultural policy. Worse still, from the mid-1950s a critical current emerged from within the regime, a further – and serious – blow to its legitimacy.

This prevailing interpretation is challenged by Elisa Chuliá in her chapter on culture under the late Franco regime. She rejects the contention that the dictatorship responded to the ascendancy of liberal and other dissident currents through a mixture of repression and, in Fusi's words, an 'evasive and escapist subculture', on the grounds that this does not account adequately for the regime's longevity. From her perspective, official culture during the late Franco regime must be seen in terms of a new legitimizing discourse. In the late 1950s, the discourse rooted in the origins of the regime (victory in the Civil War) gave way to one based on the exercise of power, above all the consolidation of Franco's 'peace' and the capacity of the newly modernized State to satisfy the material needs of ample sectors of the population. According to Chuliá, this discourse of 'peace' and prosperity profoundly shaped the official culture, to which end, it should not be forgotten, the regime could count not only on the principal sources of political, economic, cultural and social information (through its control of television, radio, the press and publications), but also on the *Movimiento* and the Catholic Church, both of which still wielded considerable cultural influence.

In reality, the dictatorship never gave up the 'battle for culture'. On the contrary, it competed vigorously with liberalism and other cultural offerings, achieving widespread success, as reflected in the films of Lazaga, the comedy works of Alfonso Paso, and the radio novels of Guillermo Sautier Casaseca. This process, nevertheless, was subject to an inbuilt tension between ideological orthodoxy and commercial considerations, the regime's own Press Law of 1966 doing much to boost the latter at the expense of the former. The upshot was a variegated cultural landscape in which a regime-sponsored culture competed with alternative, non-official ones. However, the more commercial the official culture became, the less evident became its ideological content. This evolution in Francoist culture meant that it became increasingly compatible with other forms of government. Thus many of those citizens that voted for the democratic Constitution of 1978 had previously identified themselves with the official culture of the dictatorship, not with that of the anti-Francoist alternatives. That Francoist popular culture is little appreciated today does not diminish its historical importance. Still, Chuliá concludes, the regime's search for legitimacy through the pursuit of a commercial, competitive culture eventually proved its undoing, an ironic, and unintended, consequence.

Of the three founding pillars of the dictatorship, the one which possessed the greatest social and cultural influence, and yet which was to change the most during the 1960s and early 1970s, was the Catholic Church. During the 1950s there was mounting theological, generational and political discord within ecclesiastical circles, but, as William Callahan underlines in his chapter on the Catholic Church, this 'did not form by any stretch of the imagination a coherent movement of change'. Indeed, the turning point in the relationship between the church and the Franco regime was not the result of reform from within Spanish Catholicism but from without – the Second Vatican Council of 1962–65. The Council's teachings on religious liberty, human rights and the role of the church in an increasingly secular and pluralistic society, all of which was designed to adjust the church to the modern world, unleashed a prolonged debate within the Spanish Church that in the end was to erode the very ideological underpinnings of the alliance between church and State that had served both so well since 1939. The ageing cohort of bishops may not have formed a homogenous ideological block – in 1965 the Cardinal of Seville went so far as to urge Franco in person to embrace democracy – but the conservative majority was slow to react to Vatican reform. Generational change within the upper echelons (accelerated by the arrival of a new papal nuncio in 1967), together with the clamour of a much more radical rank-and-file – now mobilized around causes such as human rights, social inequality and regional nationalism – generated a generalized discontent with the dictatorship from within the Catholic Church. The unremitting pressure from below resulted in the unprecedented holding of a Joint Assembly between the bishops and the clergy in September 1971, this marking the first occasion on which the Catholic Church publicly questioned its relationship with the Franco regime. Two years later, the statement 'On the Church and the Political Community' made explicit the church's acceptance of political change within a pluralistic society. Thus, by the time of Franco's death, the Catholic Church accepted the need not only for a radical revision of its relationship with the State but also for the establishment of a new political system, yet, as William Callahan stresses, the church defended an emphatically gradual transformation of the political landscape while remaining profoundly suspicious of the Left. Still, the disengagement of the Catholic Church from the dictatorship – manifest at the rank-and-file level long before the hierarchy embraced change – was a critical blow to the regime, as the church had furnished the Francoist State with its principal source of social and cultural legitimation. Further, the very fact that an institution as deeply conservative as the Spanish Catholic church had divorced itself from the dictatorship was indicative of the limits to the regime's ability to accommodate a fast-changing society.

As the chapters by Pablo Martín Aceña and Elena Martínez, Sasha Pack and Tom Buchanan have made clear, by the 1970s the international context set distinct limits to the continuity of the Spanish dictatorship, especially as the latter's legitimacy was by now tightly bound up with the fruits of modernization and the goal of 'Europeanization', this including membership of the hitherto unsympathetic EEC. Indeed, the creation of an international climate hostile to the Franco dictatorship, along with external support for the anti-Francoist opposition, owed much to Western European actors such as the European Community, the Council of Europe, certain states (most prominently Germany), as well as numerous political parties, trade unions and party foundations. Much less evident, though, is the contribution of the US to the democratization of Spain. New light is shed on this critical question by Charles

Powell. He maintains that US government priorities were shaped above all by the Cold War and in particular by the question of the further renewal of the military Bases Agreement of 1953, which was due to expire in September of 1975. The overriding importance of this geo-strategic issue for the US meant that its support for democratization in Spain was never more than 'modest'. International developments in the early 1970s, such as the oil crisis of 1973–74, the Yom Kipper War of 1973 and the collapse of the Portuguese and Greek dictatorships a year later, merely accentuated Spain's strategic value for the US, thereby making the Americans even more reluctant to become involved in Spanish domestic affairs. There is no doubt that the US could have done a very great deal more to back the movement for democracy in Spain, but, Powell contends, from 1971 the US did at least encourage and support Prince Juan Carlos in his quest for a third way between the Francoist hardliners and the anti-Francoist opposition. In overall terms, however, the US's commitment to the democratization of Spain was distinctly tepid, especially when set against the explicitly pro-democratic stance of Western Europe. Powell therefore concludes that Samuel Huntingdon's much-quoted thesis, according to which there was a major shift by the US 'toward the promotion of human rights and democracy in other countries' from 1974 onwards, simply does not apply to the Spanish case.

Wariness of assuming an automatic or even significant linkage between the modernization of the 1960s and 1970s and the subsequent transition to democracy is underlined by Mariano Torcal's examination of the emergence and consolidation of democratic opinion in Spain. Since the Transition, the country has registered consistently high levels of support for democracy, which have evolved not only into majority *unconditional* support for democracy, but also into what political scientists term an attitudinal 'safety area', or the point at which support for democracy is sufficiently strong and stable that it is largely unaffected by the vicissitudes of politics or economic crises. Only once the 'safety area' has been reached does a new-found democracy, such as that of post-Franco Spain, become finally consolidated. Torcal analyses these trends by means of statistical models which evaluate not only the different political generations since the Civil War but also the development of an attitudinal safety area in the Spanish case. His statistical findings lead him to the conclusion that the transformation of Spanish society in the 1960s and early 1970s was responsible neither for majority unconditional support for democracy nor for the emergence of an attitudinal safety area in post-Franco Spain. On the contrary, Torcal contends that support for democracy grew vertiginously not in the last decade-and-a-half of the dictatorship but only once the Transition itself was under way. From this perspective, the transformation in support for democracy was a highly instrumental choice that was shaped above all by the political events of the Transition. In other words, the best school for democracy was democracy itself. On the other hand, the limited growth of democratic sentiment under the Franco dictatorship does not mean that the latter enjoyed overwhelming support. The dominant reality was that of a 'great, silent majority' that did not identify strongly with the regime, but for whom peace, justice, and law and order were the priorities rather than democracy. None the less, Torcal argues that the dictatorship's legitimizing discourse of peace and prosperity during its later years contributed both to the Transition and the subsequent consolidation of democracy. In this sense, he concludes that the Transition cannot be understood or explained without taking into account the later Franco period.

In an overview of the period, Edward Malefakis highlights the extraordinary longevity of the Franco dictatorship, not just in terms of the European experience, but in relation to Asia, the Americas and Africa; that is to say, the rest of the world. The key to this exceptional durability, he argues, lay in its capacity for change. 'There has *never* been', he insists, 'a personal dictatorship which has changed as much as Franco's did'. Of crucial importance in regard to its continuity throughout the 1960s and during the early 1970s was its wide-ranging administrative reforms, the radical shift in the economy, the transformation in labour relations and the cultural revolution. Even the repressiveness of the regime mutated over time – during its last 15 years less than one person a year was executed for political reasons – though it was still capable of 'flashes' of the old 'brutality'. In opposition to the 'essentialists', Malefakis therefore maintains not only that the Franco dictatorship changed, but also that this facet of the regime was fundamental to its longevity. Indeed, such was the extent of the evolution of the dictatorship – 'a truly unique historical case' – that by its end Spain was able to undertake 'perhaps the most successful transition from dictatorship to democracy that the world has ever witnessed'. Still, the 'sad truth' is that Spain's level of socio-economic development in 1975 was probably similar to that which it would have achieved had the dictatorship never existed, which makes the latter, in Malefakis's judgement, merely 'a parenthesis, however awful, in Spain's history'.

The aim of *Spain Transformed* has been not only to suggest new approaches to the study of the late Franco dictatorship but also to make available a considerable amount of new research on the period. The resulting emphasis has been on the vital importance of social and cultural change during this period – both of which have been greatly neglected – while political change has been approached not so much in terms of high politics as in relation to the broader themes of the emergence of civil society and evolving political mentalities. At the same time, the collection has stressed that many of the alterations within Spain cannot be divorced from wider ones that proceeded from without. The endeavour to place events and processes within a comparative context has also permitted a more nuanced analysis of the extent to which, and the ways in which, Spain under Franco was indeed 'different'. The fact that many of the contributors have drawn on different disciplines, or are themselves from fields other than history, has undoubtedly suggested new lines of inquiry and provided new insights, thereby facilitating a richer and more rounded vision of the period.

Spain Transformed can be said to look two ways at once. On one hand, the book looks back at the Franco dictatorship as a whole insofar as it contributes to an understanding of how the regime survived from 1939 right up until 1975. The dominant view to emerge from this collective work is that the dictatorship evolved over time and that this capacity for change was quintessential to its longevity. On the other hand, the book looks forward to the transition from the dictatorship to democracy. Prevailing interpretations of the Transition tend to highlight its political and elitist features, but many of the contributors to this volume stress that study of the late Franco regime reveals neglected social, cultural and popular dimensions to the transitional process. In this regard, *Spain Transformed* helps us to understand not only *why* the Transition took place, but also the *form* which it finally adopted. Accordingly, the 1960s and early 1970s can be regarded as the bridge between the dictatorship and democracy, or as the transition to the Transition. Finally, *Spain Transformed* also underlines that the late Franco dictatorship is worthy of study in its own right. The very enormity, multiplicity and rapidity of the changes undergone by Spanish society during the 1960s and early 1970s, and the myriad ways in which they shaped or played off one another, make it an inherently fascinating period. The political straitjacket of the dictatorship notwithstanding, Spanish society was transformed between 1959 and 1975, with far-reaching consequences that were at once intended and unintended.

Notes

1. Paul Preston, ed., *Spain in Crisis: Evolution and Decline of the Franco Regime* (Hassocks: Harvester, 1976).
2. The most comprehensive general account of the dictatorship is Stanley G. Payne's *The Franco Regime 1936–1975* (Wisconsin: University of Wisconsin Press, 1987), while Raymond Carr and Juan Pablo Fusi's *Spain: Dictatorship to Democracy* (London: George Allen and Unwin, 1979) is very lucid and lively. The best brief account in English is Jean Grugel and Tim Rees' *Franco's Spain* (London: Arnold, 1997). *Spanish History Since 1808* (London: Arnold, 2000), edited by José Álvarez Junco and Adrian Shubert, contains succinct overviews by Antonio Cazorla, 'Early Francoism, 1939–1957', pp. 259–76, and Sebastian Balfour, 'The *Desarrollo* years, 1955–1975', pp. 277–88. See also the essays in Helen Graham and Jo Labanyi, eds, *Spanish Cultural Studies: An Introduction. The Struggle for Modernity* (Oxford: Oxford University Press, 1995) as well as those in Barry Jordan and Rikki Morgan-Tamosunas, eds, *Contemporary Spanish Cultural Studies* (London: Arnold, 2000). Three articles by Edward Malefakis are essential reading on the dictatorship: 'Spain and its Francoist heritage', in John H. Herz, ed., *From Dictatorship to Democracy* (Connecticut: Greenwood Press, 1982), pp. 215–30; 'Cambio estructural y transición a la democracia', in Javier Tusell and Álvaro Soto, eds, *Historia de la Transición (1975–1986)* (Madrid: Alianza, 1996), pp. 349–62; and 'La dictadura de Franco en una perspectiva comparada', in José Luis García Delgado, ed., *Franquismo: El juicio de la historia* (Madrid: Temas de Hoy, 2000), pp. 11–55. For general works in Spanish, see in particular Carlos Barciela et al., *La España de Franco, (1939–75): La economía* (Madrid: Síntesis, 2001); José Luis García Delgado, ed., *Franquismo*; Jordi Gracia and Miguel Ángel Ruiz Carnicer, *La España de Franco, (1939–75): Cultura y vida cotidiana* (Madrid: Síntesis, 2004); Jesús A. Martínez, ed., *Historia de España. Siglo XX. 1939–1996* (Madrid: Cátedra, 1999); Enrique Moradiellos, *La España de Franco, (1939–75): Política y sociedad* (Madrid: Síntesis, 2000); and Javier Tusell, *La dictadura de Franco* (Madrid: Alianza, 1987).
3. Julius Ruiz, *Franco's Justice: Repression in Madrid after the Spanish Civil War* (Oxford: Oxford University Press, 2005), p. 7. See also Paul Preston, *The Politics of Revenge: Fascism and the Military in 20th Century Spain* (London: Unwin Hyman, 1990), pp. 41–3, 151–7, 181–2 and Michael Richards, *A Time of Silence: Civil War and the Culture of Repression in Franco's Spain, 1936–1945* (Cambridge: Cambridge University Press, 1998), passim. The best starting point in Spanish is Santos Juliá, ed., *Víctimas de la Guerrra Civil* (Madrid: Temas de Hoy, 1999).
4. On the debate over the nature of the dictatorship, see Malefakis, 'La dictadura de Franco', in José Luis García Delgado, ed., *Franquismo*, pp. 11–55; Payne, *The Franco Regime*, pp. 622–41; Eduardo Sevilla Guzmán and Manuel González de Molina, 'Política social agraria del primer franquismo', in José Luis García Delgado, ed., *El primer franquismo* (Madrid: Siglo XXI, 1989), pp. 135–48, 180–7; as well as the historiographical overviews in Moradiellos, *La España de Franco*, pp. 11–23, 209–25 and Tusell, *La dictadura*, pp. 86–106.
5. Manuel Azaña, *Obras Completas IV: Memorias políticas y de guerra* (Madrid: Giner, 1990), p. 813, cited by Moradiellos, *La España de Franco*, p. 210.

6. Cited by Moradiellos, *La España de Franco*, p. 212.

7. The resolution in full is published in José María del Valle, *Las instituciones de la República española en exilio* (Paris: Ruedo Ibérico, 1976), p. 223. The resolution of the Political Commission was even more explicit, declaring that 'in origin, nature, structure and general conduct, the Franco regime is a fascist regime', p. 221.

8. Juan J. Linz, 'An Authoritarian Regime: Spain', in Eric Allardt and Yrjö Littunen, eds, *Cleavages, Ideologies and Party Strategies: Contributions to Comparative Political Sociology* (Helsinki: Westermarck Society, 1964), pp. 291–341. The article was subsequently published in Erik Allardt and Stein Rokkan, eds, *Mass Politics: Studies in Political Sociology* (New York: The Free Press, 1970), pp. 251—83, 374–81. Linz's other articles on Francoism are also of fundamental importance. See 'From Falange to Movimiento-Organización: The Spanish Single Party and the Franco Regime', in S.P. Huntington and C.H. Moore, eds, *Authoritarian Politics in Modern Society: The Dynamics of Established One-Party Systems* (New York: Basic Books, 1970), pp. 128–203; 'Continuidad y discontinuidad en la élite política española: De la Restauración al régimen actual' in Linz et al., *Estudios de ciencia política y sociología. Homenaje al profesor Carlos Ollero* (Madrid: Gráficas Carlavilla, 1972), pp. 361–423; 'Opposition in and under authoritarian regimes: the case of Spain', in R.A. Dahl, ed., *Regimes and Oppositions* (New Haven: Yale University, 1973), pp. 171–259; 'The Party System of Spain: Past and Future', in S.M. Lipset and S. Rokkan, eds, *Party Systems and Voter Alignments: Cross National Perspectives* (New York: Free Press, 1967); 'Totalitarian and authoritarian regimes', in F.I. Greenstein and N.W. Polsby, eds, *Handbook of Political Science*, vol. 5 (Reading, MA: Addison-Wesley, 1975), pp. 175–412. See also Juan J. Linz and Amando de Miguel, *Los empresarios ante el poder público* (Madrid: Instituto de Estudios Políticos, 1966) and 'La élite funcionarial española ante la reforma administrativa', *Sociología de la Administración pública española. Anales de Moral Social y Económica*, 17 (1968). Finally, see J.J. Linz and J.M. de Miguel, 'Las Cortes Españolas 1943–70. Un análisis de cohortes. Primera parte: Las cohortes', in *Sistema*, no. 8 (January 1975), pp. 85–110 and 'Las Cortes Españolas 1943–70. Segunda parte: Las élites', in *Sistema*, no. 9 (April 1975), pp. 103–23.

9. For the debate over Linz's interpretation see José María Maravall, *Dictatorship and Dissent: Workers and Students in Franco's Spain* (London: Tavistock, 1978), Chapter 1, as well as *Papers. Revista de Sociología*, no. 6 (1977) and no. 8 (1978).

10. The quote is from Salvador Giner, *Sociología* (Barcelona: Península, 1985), p. 141, cited by Moradiellos, *La España de Franco*, p. 217. See Eduardo Sevilla Guzmán and Salvador Giner, 'Absolutismo despótico y dominación de clase. El caso de España', *Cuadernos de Ruedo Ibérico*, no. 43–45 (January–June 1975), pp. 83–103, as well as their articles, 'From despotism to parliamentarianism: class domination and political order in the Spanish State', in R. Scase, ed., *The State in Western Europe* (London: Croom Helm, 1980), pp. 197–229, and 'Spain: from corporatism to corporatism', in Allan Williams, ed., *Southern Europe Transformed: Political and Economic Change in Greece, Italy, Portugal and Spain* (London: Harper & Row, 1984), pp. 113–41. Sevilla Guzmán and Manuel González de Molina, in 'Política social agraria', in José Luis García Delgado, ed., *El primer franquismo*, pp. 135–87, revised the concept originally coined by Sevilla Guzmán and Giner.

11. See his essay 'La sombra del franquismo: ignorar la historia y huir del pasado', in Julián Casanova et al., *El pasado oculto: Fascismo y violencia en Aragón (1936–1939)* (Madrid: Siglo XXI, 1992), pp. 1–28. The quotes are from pp. 5 and 25. See also the essay by Casanova on 'La dictadura de cuarenta años', in Julián Casanova, ed., *Morir, matar, sobrevivir: La violencia en la dictadura de Franco* (Barcelona: Crítica, 2002), pp. 1–17. For a recent defence of the Franco regime as 'fascist', see Vicenç Navarro, 'Tergiversaciones de nuestro pasado. Una visión republicana de nuestra historia', *Cuadernos Republicanas*, no. 62 (Autumn 2006), pp. 11–45.

12. Michael Mann, *Fascists* (Cambridge: Cambridge University Press, 2004), Chapter 2 (especially pp. 45–8), in addition to pp. 4–5, 345–7, 350–2; Robert O. Paxton, *The Anatomy of Fascism* (London: Penguin, 2004), pp. 149—50, p. 217. Stanley Payne insists in *Revista de libros*, no. 120 (December 2006), pp. 23–5 that a 'long and slow process' of 'defascistization' of the Franco regime began in 1943.

13. The most comprehensive biography in English is Paul Preston's monumental *Franco* (London: HarperCollins, 1993). There are a number of much briefer, but very good, biographies: Sheelagh Ellwood, *Franco* (Essex: Longman, 1994); Juan Pablo Fusi, *Franco: A Biography* (London: Unwin Hyman, 1987) [With an updated version in Spanish: *Franco: Autoritarismo y poder personal* (Barcelona: Suma de Letras, 2001)]; Geoffrey Jensen, *Franco: Soldier, Commander, Dictator* (Washington, DC: Potomac Books, 2005); and J.W.D. Trythall, *Franco: A Biography* (London: Hart-Davis, 1970). Gabrielle Ashford Hodges, *Franco* (New York: Thomas Dunne, 2000), provides a psychological profile.

14. Santos Juliá, *Un siglo de España: Política y sociedad* (Madrid: Marcial Pons, 1999), pp. 156–60.

15. Few, if any, scholars would dispute that the Civil War period (1936–39) was fundamental to the configuration of the Francoist State, while many historians regard the years 1969–75 as a separate phase, defined by the regime's final crisis. On the periodization of the regime, see Elisa Chuliá, *El poder y la palabra: prensa y poder político en las dictaduras. El régimen de Franco ante la prensa y el periodismo* (Madrid: Biblioteca Nueva, 2001), pp. 18–20; Moradiellos, *La España de Franco*, pp. 24–7; Payne, *The Franco Regime*, pp. 622–3; Tusell, *La Dictadura de Franco*, pp. 247–64.

16. Paloma Aguilar Fernández, *Memory and Amnesia. The Role of the Spanish Civil War in the Transition to Democracy* (Oxford: Berghahn Books, 2002). The original Spanish version is *Memoria y olvido de la Guerra Civil española* (Madrid: Alianza, 1996).

17. An immense amount has been published on the repression over the last two decades. See the bibliographies in Juliá, ed., *Víctimas de la Guerra Civil*; Richards, *A Time of Silence*; and, in particular, Ruiz, *Franco's Justice*, the most recent. See also Javier Rodrigo, 'La bibliografía sobre la represión franquista: hacia el salto cualitativo', *Spagna Contemporanea*, 19 (2001), pp. 151–69. Of the more than 100 'personal accounts' registered in the catalogue of the *Biblioteca Nacional* [National Library] in Madrid since 2000, a great many concern the memoirs of victims of the Francoist repression. On the contributions and limitations of these accounts, see Hugo García, 'Los testimonios sobre la represión franquista: la mirada de las víctimas y la judicialización de la victoria', in *Historia y Política*, 14, 2 (2005), pp. 283–90.

18. Richards, *A Time of Silence*, p. 30. In a similar vein, Pere Ysàs contends that in interpreting Francoism 'one cannot forget nor minimize the centrality of repressive violence throughout its trajectory from its bloody origins until the last executions in September 1975'. See Pere Ysàs, *Disidencia y Subversión: La Lucha del Régimen Franquista por su Supervivencia, 1960–75* (Barcelona: Crítica, 2004), p. x. For further criticism of this approach, see Ruiz, *Franco's Justice*, pp. 226–7.

19. Ruiz, *Franco's Justice*, pp. 11–12, footnote 57. For recent complaints regarding archival inaccessibility, see the letter published in *El País* 4 May 2006 by Francisco Espinosa Maestre, Francisco Moreno Gómez and 64 others, 'Memoria histórica y archivos', as well as the article by Julián Casanova in *El País* 13 September 2006, 'Sin archivos, no hay historia'.

20. José Amodia, *Franco's Political Legacy: From dictatorship to Façade Democracy* (London: Allen Lane, 1977).

21. See, for example, Charles Powell, *España en democracia, 1975–2000* (Barcelona: Plaza & Janés, 2001), pp. 17–22.

22. Payne, *The Franco Regime*, pp. 464–6, and Albert Carreras and Xavier Tafunell, *Historia económica de la España contemporánea* (Barcelona: Crítica, 2004), p. 278.

23. The remittances, which refer to the period 1960–74, are in Juliá, *Política y sociedad*, p. 185. See also Malefakis, 'Spain and its Francoist heritage', in John H. Herz, ed., *From Dictatorship to Democracy*, pp. 217–18 and 'Cambio estructural y transición', in Tusell and Soto, eds, *Historia de la Transición*, pp. 355–6.

24. Juliá, *Política y sociedad*, pp. 184–6. Also, Malefakis, 'Spain and its Francoist heritage', in John H. Herz, ed., *From Dictatorship to Democracy*, pp. 217–8, 222–3; and 'Cambio estructural y transición', in Tusell and Soto, eds, *Historia de la Transición*, pp. 355–6, 358–9.

25. The data is from Juan Pablo Fusi and Jordi Palafox, *España 1808–1996. El Desafío de la Modernidad* (Madrid: Espasa-Calpe, 1997), p. 311. Also, Malefakis' 'Spain and its Francoist heritage', in John H. Herz, ed., *From Dictatorship to Democracy*, p. 219 and p. 222, and 'Cambio estructural y transición', in Tusell and Soto, eds, *Historia de la Transición*, pp. 357–9, as well as the limpid comparative summary in Richard Gunther, José Ramón Montero and Joan Botella, *Democracy in Modern Spain* (New Haven and London: Yale University Press, 2004), pp. 68–78.

2
The Golden Age of Spanish Capitalism: Economic Growth without Political Freedom

Pablo Martín Aceña and Elena Martínez Ruiz

Fifteen years of rapid economic growth

From an economic standpoint, the period 1960–74 appears as one of the brightest ones in Spanish contemporary history. In 15 years the country underwent a remarkable structural transformation as well as an undeniable improvement in the standard of living and a profound social change. These were undoubtedly years of economic success, the authoritarian and antidemocratic nature of the regime notwithstanding. As a result, there was a stark contrast between the resistance of the political system to change (the superstructure) and the dynamism of its economy (the base). In other words, there was 'growth without political freedom', as stated in a recent overview of Franco's Spain.[1] Of course, such a statement is not new. A large number of scholars devoted to the economic history of Spain have highlighted the modernization of the Spanish economy during the 1960s and early 1970s. The classic surveys of Donges, Fuentes Quintana, García Delgado, Martínez Serrano, Rojo, and Viñas, amongst others, have revealed the timing and the essential keys to understanding the deep transformation undergone by Spanish society during the late Franco regime.

More recent works, published over the last 5 years, have quantified and explained more accurately the speed of this change and the technical factors which brought about or led to the referred transformations. According to the latest estimations made by Prados de la Escosura,[2] the rate of growth of the total real product was about 7 per cent annually (6 per cent in per capita terms), which was above that of all other industrial nations except Japan. The rate of growth of the Gross Domestic Product per inhabitant during the 15 years from 1960 to 1975 was seven times greater than that of the previous century and two times greater than over the last 25 years. Swift economic changes began in 1960. Scholars consider the starting point to be the 1959 Stabilization Plan, which corrected the macro-economic disequilibria accumulated over previous decades and introduced an array of reforms designed to reduce the number of regulations within the internal market, to liberalize the economy, and as to open it up to foreign competition.

Changes affected every sector, but they were especially intense in the industrial one, which grew at an average rate of 9 per cent. Thus industry became the true epicentre of modernization. It registered the highest productivity increases, thanks to the adoption of new technologies, intense capital investment, and a rapid substitution process of imports of both intermediate and final goods. Structural transformations were the other key element to growth. They contributed to the per capita output increase since resources shifted from agriculture, with low productivity levels, towards industry and services, which were high productivity sectors. In a decade the weight of primary activities (agriculture, fishing, and mining) fell from nearly 25 per cent of Gross Added Value in 1960 to 10 per cent in 1975.

Fuentes Quintana has summarized the variety of forces that explain the outstanding growth rate during these years: (i) a social desire to develop as an essential motor of change: what Michael Postan highlighted in relation to European growth during this period, namely a spirit of modernization which surpassed the requirements and sacrifices which such growth imposed, this argument being perfectly applicable to Spain; (ii) the relative underdevelopment of the country, the elimination of which opened up a vast array of opportunities given the prevailing gap between the available techniques and those applied to the Spanish productive processes; (iii) the introduction of technology through imports of capital goods, direct investments, and the acquisition of patents and registered trade marks, which permitted the renewal of industrial equipment and production processes; (iv) a sustained increase in consumer demand and in the investment rate – private and public– as compared to earlier periods; (v) the international openness which connected the Spanish economy to world markets, encouraged competition, and broadened its narrow internal market; (vi) the availability of resources for growth: internal saving (derived from output increases) and external saving (foreign investments), as well as unused labour (a large pocket of agrarian underemployment and young female labour which had not participated hitherto in the productive process). The rural exodus not only provided industry with cheap manpower, but it also permitted an increase in productivity in the countryside and the advance of agricultural mechanization, which broke down and eventually eliminated the traditional agricultural system, and (vii) during this period Spain enjoyed terms of trade which were favourable to industrial prices as compared to energy, raw materials, and food prices.[3] For their part, García Delgado and Jiménez, in their work of synthesis on Franco's economy, have enumerated four distinct factors which contributed to the rapid economic development of this decade-and-a-half: (a) the low prices of raw materials and energy; (b) the availability of external financial means; (c) easy access to modern international technology, and (d) an elastic supply of labour (agricultural, female, and that resulting from the high fertility rates registered during the 1960s).[4]

A more analytical explanation of the exceptional performance of the Spanish economy has been provided by Serrano Sanz and Pardos in a recent and excellent article.[5] As these authors explain, output may be expanded either by increasing the amount of resources devoted to productive activities or by improving factor returns or productivity. Most scholarship concerning the 1960s and early 1970s has concluded that the main engine of Spanish output expansion was the increase in 'total factor productivity'. In particular, the single most important contribution to growth was a significant improvement in the output per worker ratio, which increased by 6.4 per cent, which was well above the increase in the employment rate and almost as much as income growth. Its dominance was so overwhelming (labour productivity evolution was responsible for up to 95 per cent of per capita income growth) that it demands a detailed description (Table 2.1).

To understand why the evolution of labour productivity was so impressive during the late Franco period, we must turn to the theories of endogenous growth (a branch of neoclassical growth theory) which makes income per worker growth depend upon two elements. First, the level of capital per worker. Secondly, technical progress, that is, a more efficient use of the same amount of factors, which can be achieved by

Table 2.1 Long-term growth of the Spanish economy (%)

	PIB	PIB pc
1850–50	1.34	0.71
1951–74	6.35	5.23
1951–58	4.35	3.51
1959–74	6.92	5.86
1975–2000	2.40	1.71

introducing more advanced technologies (product and process innovations), by improved management, by human capital accumulation (as a result of education or learning), and by production externalities resulting from better infrastructures. Also, the contribution of structural change to productivity growth derived from workers shifting from low to high labour productivity sectors is also often stressed in the economic development literature.

Indeed, from the beginning of the 1960s, after the Stabilization Plan of 1959, the Spanish economy registered an intense process of capitalization. This was basically due to high investment rates (close to an average of 25 per cent of real GDP), to the technical progress incorporated through the importation of new capital goods, and to the growing presence of foreign-capital companies with great technology-creation capacity. As a result, net capital stock rose at an annual rate close to 7 per cent in real terms, almost exactly as much as the rate of growth of total domestic product. Figures relating to the composition of production and the distribution of employment by sectors demonstrate the economic transformation that took place. The share of industry and services increased to the detriment of agriculture, which went down by five points. At the same time employment in the primary sector declined by more than 10 points, while the other two sectors gained population. As Prados de la Escosura has underlined, 'labour productivity increased in the golden age at a rate more than eight times that of the preceding years and structural change was responsible for more than one third of such growth' (Table 2.2).

In short, Spanish development between 1960 and 1974 was due basically to an increase in labour productivity. This was possible thanks to three essential processes: (i) the substitution of old techniques by more modern ones, made possible by the importation of capital goods and the acquisition of technology and new managerial methods associated with foreign investment; (ii) the reallocation of resources (labour and capital) from low to high productivity economic activities, and

Table 2.2 Employment distribution by sectors (%)

Sectors	1950	1960	1974
Primary	48	40	23
Secondary	26	28	35
Tertiary	26	32	42

(iii) the intensification of capital accumulation, due to the increase in the investment ratio, facilitated by both favourable expectations (a vigorous domestic and foreign demand), relatively efficient financial markets, and government support of private investment by means of a variety of fiscal, financial, trade and tariff mechanisms.

Industry was one of the basic elements in the expansion process from the mid-1960s on. Industrial growth, faster than that of the economy as a whole, had powerful backward linkages, as it demanded intermediate inputs produced by other sectors. Industry also played an essential role by making technical transformations possible. Such transformations were characterized by a notable increase in the use of chemical, metallic, and energy inputs, and a reduction in traditional (transportation, general services), and primary (agriculture, mining, wood) inputs. The sectors which grew the most and whose total output share increased were chemical industries, basic metal industries, metallic processing, and the construction of transportation material: sectors in which technical-change diffusion was most intense. While in 1964 these sectors, which were producers of capital goods and basic industrial inputs, amounted to 39 per cent of total production, in 1974 their weight had increased to 46 per cent. Energy industries, such as electricity and oil refining, also showed significant growth. Structural changes reflected the advance of the so-called new sectors, as well as the introduction of modern inputs, such as petrol, electricity, and artificial fibres. In short, the distinctive performance of industry notably changed productive specialization within the country as well as altering its economic structure.

In 1975, the year Franco died, Spain could already be considered to have an industrial economy – quite different from the 1940 agrarian-based one – and a productive structure similar to that of the western economies. During the second part of the Franco years, bereft of democracy and political freedom, Spain stepped into the First World and joined the exclusive club of those countries with a per capita income of $2000 dollars or more.

Macro-economic stabilization and interventionism

Analysis of Spanish economic policy during the 1960s and 1970s must necessarily start with the Stabilization Plan of 1959. By the mid-1950s it was obvious that the growth model adopted at the end of the Civil War (1936–39) had become exhausted. Pressing disequilibria, such as strong inflationary pressure, an appalling public deficit, and a serious balance of payments' problem, threatened to block the Spanish economy's hitherto timid advance. Faced with this difficult situation, the Francoist economic authorities, after meeting some resistance, undertook a radical shift in economic policy: from an inward-looking to an outward-looking strategy. The array of measures designed by the ministries of Finance and Trade was intended to correct these desequilibria and to integrate the economy into the international market in order to ensure the continuity of the growth process.

The first step in this direction was the incorporation of Spain into the OEED (Organization for European Economic Co-operation), and into the economic organizations which had been created as a result of the Bretton Woods Agreements: the International Monetary Fund and the World Bank. Greater international co-operation, the reduction of protectionism, and the re-establishment of a multilateral payment system were at the top of these institutions' set of priorities. Spain's integration thus signalled its political willingness to abandon the autarkical model and to follow the liberalization trend which had been initiated in Europe at the end of the 1940s. Membership of the world's main economic forums also permitted the Spain of the Stabilization Plan to take advantage of the appropriate technical advice and important initial credits, which were required for the Plan to succeed.

The 1959 programme included a set of monetary and fiscal measures aimed to contain inflation, eliminate public deficits, devalue the currency, remove exchange rate controls, correct the negative balance of payments, and reduce the interventions and regulations of the domestic market. In order to control the rise in the price level, the Bank of Spain increased interest rates and imposed quantitative restrictions on the supply of bank credit. Simultaneously, the Ministry of Finance passed a fiscal reform intended to increase tax revenues and reduce budgetary expenditures. It also stopped the issue of government debt automatically pledged with the Bank of Spain, which had so far been the main source of money creation. On the international front, the inefficient multiple exchange rate system was removed and a new, realistic single exchange rate was introduced, while a notable devaluation from 48 to 60 pesetas per dollar was enforced. At the same time, different measures were taken to deregulate and to liberalize foreign commerce: in 1960 the licence system was substituted by a new customs tariff, with high rates initially, but then gradually reduced in subsequent years. New legislation was introduced to allow capital imports, so as to encourage direct foreign investment in Spanish firms and those industrial sectors which had until then been reserved only for national ones.

The results of the Stabilization Plan were impressive. Monetary expansion was curtailed in a few months, inflation was curbed, and the deficit disappeared from the budget. The results of the measures affecting the foreign sector were immediate too: the trade balance deficit was drastically reversed and a surplus on the current account had already emerged by 1960. Furthermore, that very same year Spain received a considerable flow of capital imports. Even more important was the change in the mood that followed the abandonment of autarky, the removal of the most excessive controls, and the elimination of the suffocating Statist interventionism. The Plan introduced greater freedom for corporate and individual firms and a new atmosphere for private investors. As Juan Sardá, then head of the Bank of Spain's research department and one of the Plan's architects, put it, the programme of 1959 was designed to open the economy to international competition and to lay the foundations of a free market economy. Interventionism had to be definitely abandoned and government guidance substituted by private initiative. Economic leadership had to be transferred to private hands and the allocation and distribution of resources left entirely to the forces of demand and supply. The Spanish economic system had to approach the type of economy prevailing in most Western European countries.

Although the Stabilization Plan laid the basis for the long-run development of the Spanish economy, the truth is that the initial advances soon slowed down and in certain areas came to a halt. Fiscal orthodoxy was respected and monetary restraint continued in order to ensure a stable macro-economic framework. However, the Franco regime was not prepared to relinquish control over the productive system and let market forces perform freely. Economic as well as political freedom was never a reality. Once autarky had been liquidated a renewed interventionism emerged with new targets and instruments. Although the authorities accepted that private entrepreneurship should play a larger role in the allocation of resources, the National Industry Institute (*Instituto Nacional de Industria*) (INI), a powerful holding company of public entities set up in 1941 and one of the backbones of State intervention in the economy under autarky, remained in place. INI's size was reduced and its activities had to abide by the subsidiary principle, but it continued to absorb a huge amount of physical resources and financial funds. Industrial policy adopted new forms. In 1963 the old-fashioned National Industry Act was replaced by the so-called Preferential Industry Act. Its purpose was to promote the development of firms that could best meet the economic and social objectives that were considered a priority for the government. According to this Act, aid would be granted to companies operating in sectors that were declared of 'preferential interest' or located in the so-called 'preferential industrial location' areas.

To coordinate the activities of public institutions and private firms, in 1964 the government introduced the Development Plans, a French-imported economic policy instrument. The Plan was a mechanism by which the government set its investment targets and its sectorial and territorial priorities. Three new industrial policy instruments were designed: the 'Concerted Actions', the 'Sector Restructuring Plans', and the 'Special Plans'. In order to promote a rapid rate of industrialization in all regions of the country, the government made use of a number of measures that included direct subsidies, tax advantages, tariff reductions, and, above all, privileged access to public and private financial funds. The most satisfactory results were achieved in sectors where the presence of public firms was significant (iron and steel, electricity, naval construction, and petrol refining). By contrast, in sectors where the presence of the State was negligible, achievements were relatively modest.

In 1962 a new Banking and Credit Act was passed. It established the basic rules which official credit entities, banks, and savings banks had to follow. The Bank of Spain was nationalized and the so-called official credit entities (the Industrial Credit Bank, Local Credit Bank, Mortgage Bank of Spain, Exterior Bank of Spain) reorganized. Furthermore, the 1962 Act made a distinction between commercial and industrial banks: the former would concentrate on short- and medium-term operations, while the latter would help finance long-term projects and investment in infrastructure and social capital. Although this legislation allowed financial institutions greater freedom, many regulations none the less were maintained. Expansion plans, such as the opening of new branches, were subject to government approval, interest rates and many other banking operations were also kept under Treasury control, while capital enlargement – the issue of new shares or bonds – also needed the approval of the monetary authorities. A cornerstone of the regime's interventionist network, banks and savings institutions had to fulfil two essential purposes. On the one hand, provide low-cost funding to cover the needs of the Treasury. The Bank of Spain was thereby called upon to play an essential role by maintaining low interest rates and by securing banks and saving banks easy access to their lines of credit. On the other hand, regulations were also put in place in order to guarantee that investment would be directed to the so-called priority sectors. Among the various mechanisms designed to accomplish this task, the two most widely used ones were the 'special rediscount lines of credit' and 'official credit' channelled via the government-controlled banks.

Through the 'special discount', the Bank of Spain committed itself to rediscount credits granted by banks and savings banks to certain sectors and firms (at preferential rates). Three sectors benefited from these low-cost funds: heavy industry, shipbuilding, and the export of manufactured goods. Credit granted by the official credit institutions aimed to promote investment in select sectors or in socially desirable activities. To finance the official credit entities, large amounts of so-called 'investment *cédulas*', a special type of bonds, were floated. Banks and savings banks were forced to take part in these operations by buying the largest part of each issue. This meant that a significant proportion of their resources were invested in government guided assets.

Labour relationships were exhaustively regulated. Non-official trade unions and the free association of workers were prohibited. The government intervened in the establishment of wages, salaries, and working conditions, negotiations between workers and entrepreneurs were undertaken under official supervision, lay-offs were strictly forbidden, and the government guaranteed near full employment by introducing complicated dismissal procedures. In compensation, increase in wages and salaries were kept below the rise in productivity. Labour mobility was restricted and in general the labour market was plagued with rigidities that impeded its adaptation to changes in economic activity and to the modifications that were taking place in the economic environment during these years.

The nature of the 'Spanish miracle'

The 'Spanish miracle' was to a certain extent the result of a natural catching-up process similar to that experienced by other Western European countries. A sustained flow of domestic and foreign investment pushed the economy vigorously upward. Imported techniques helped modernize obsolete firms. The reforms adopted in 1959 and the partial liberalization measures introduced thereafter facilitated the integration of the country into the international economy. Spain registered a new phase of convergence with the higher European standards of living. To what extent can the 'Spanish miracle' be attributed to the Spanish authorities? To what extent must the merit for the transformation of the country be attributed to the economic policy of the Franco regime? Should Franco and his regime be credited with the economic success of the country?

The most recent scholarship has suggested that the so-called 'Golden Age' of the European economy was the consequence of an extraordinary and sustained catching-up process that permitted Europe to close its productivity gap with the United States. American investment, American technology, and American managerial methods were adopted by European firms. Economic policy, institutional reforms, and international co-operation facilitated the process. During the Golden Age, Western Europe grew at unprecedented rates, well beyond its historical trend.

Catching-up is not an automatic process set in motion by the mere existence of a leader country from which one can learn and which can be imitated. The truth is that very few countries have managed such a smooth recovery process as that of Western Europe after the Second World War. To understand the European economic growth process, we must thus pay attention to the special circumstances at work in the postwar decades. Two factors are essential to understanding its success. First, the existence of what has been called 'social capability', which relates to the presence of an educated and disciplined workforce, capable of assimilating the technological and organizational advances imported from the US economy. Secondly, postwar international agreements created an institutional framework favourable to growth. The problems of legitimacy and the class conflicts that plagued the interwar period were overcome. Political stability and the participation of both entrepreneurs and workers in the decision-making processes facilitated the adoption of reforms that enhanced productivity. Rapid growth contributed to a more equal distribution of income and wealth.

Intra-European agreements and organizations, created under American guidance and protection, such as the European Payments Union, were of even greater importance than the initial financial aid channelled through the Marshall Plan. Confrontation was replaced by close co-operation amongst the nations of the continent. Across-the-border pacts between capital and labour reduced uncertainty and made it possible for all economic agents to harbour stable expectations and long-term investment perspectives. It was this new political and economic international environment that has been highlighted as one of the most important elements in explaining the Golden Age. Wage moderation was accepted in exchange for a continued investment effort on the part of the business community. In addition, governments committed themselves to providing public services and preferential goods, and introduced legislation in order to aid private investment. Permissive monetary policies ensured low real interest rates, while the fiscal system, distinguished by progressive taxes, had the role of improving the distribution of income. The institutions created as a result of the Bretton

Woods conference of 1944, such as the International Monetary Fund, established new forums of discussion and new ways to solve economic and financial conflicts. Exchange controls and national barriers to trade were partially removed. National markets were opened to competition. Business developed in a more friendly and favourable atmosphere. In this context, it is therefore not difficult to understand the remarkable investment rate achieved by the European economies from 1950 onwards.

No doubt, all these aspects were also at the heart of Spanish development during the 1960s. Catching-up was, as in the rest of Europe, the result of this new international economic environment. As has been mentioned, investors did not miss the opportunities opened up by the favourable international scenario described above. Workers moved to high productivity sectors, while entrepreneurs shifted their efforts towards the most profitable branches of industry. Specialization took place according to Spain's comparative advantages. Foreign capital and technology were attracted to relatively cheap labour-intensive and low-cost agricultural and manufacturing sectors. Spanish goods gained easy access to world markets. Many Spanish products increased their share in the export trade. Likewise, the buoyant tourist industry and substantial remittances from emigrants shored up the balance of payments. Income from exports, tourism, and emigrants financed a considerable part of the intermediate and final imports vital to maintaining high levels of economic activity. Permissive monetary policies assured low interest rates. If necessary, price stability was sacrificed on the altar of rapid economic growth. The exchange rate of the peseta was kept relatively unchanged, although it was devalued when needed in order to maintain the competitiveness of Spanish goods and services in foreign markets. Government expenditures and revenues increased, though the budget was balanced for most of the time. Regulations imposed on banks and savings banks ensured cheap funds for the public sector as well as for some protected sectors and companies that were allowed to raise capital at a lower rate than the actual market price. Entrepreneurs were free from trade union demands or from workers' claims. Franco's authoritarian regime assured full employment but at the same time prohibited the existence of any type of labour-class organization.

Because of the distinct non-democratic political features of the Franco regime, the 'miracle' occurred within an institutional framework different from that prevailing in most Western European nations. Apart from its terrible political and social results, the regime was also responsible for certain economic outcomes. In the Western European countries, the 'social pact' constituted a three-party agreement, explicit or otherwise. Workers accepted that wages would grow no more than productivity in exchange for a commitment from managers to employ most of their profits in productive investments. Workers also accepted the basic rules of the capitalist system in exchange for a State that would guarantee all citizens a minimum standard of living as well as the provision of social goods and services such as education and health insurance. The creation of the Welfare State was the counterpart of social stability. To the Welfare State was transferred the responsibility for distributing the benefits of economic growth amongst the entire social spectrum. It was, therefore, a system by which economic agents – owners, managers and workers – agreed on the means to distribute national income. The role of the government was to ensure that the agreements were respected. The governments were also responsible for smoothing the productive cycles, fighting unemployment, and providing a stable economic atmosphere. Most of all, they had to do everything possible to improve the distribution of income and wealth.

The Spanish economy grew as much as the European one, but lacked the creation of an efficient Welfare State. Franco's regime did not need a 'pact' in order to guarantee social peace, for repression rendered the agreements and redistributive measures unnecessary. The distinctive feature of Spanish growth within the European framework was the absence of a State that was responsible for wealth distribution. Education, health insurance, and the other elements typical of a Welfare State were undeveloped or entirely absent in Spain. The share of wages in Gross National Product increased, but income distribution remained very unequal. Workers benefited from the fruits of development but not to the same extent as their European counterparts. Economic policy was an important, albeit passive, actor in the play of the 'Spanish miracle'.

Pluralistic Spain: the regional distribution of wealth

In a recent work, Dobado describes very vividly the magnitude of the regional inequality of wealth within autarkic Spain. According to this author, 'the income gap between Vizcaya and Almeria was, in 1955, slightly greater than that between, for example, Belgium and Algeria or Brazil in 1960, that is to say, it was of an order of magnitude that we can very well refer to as *intercontinental'*. Such an illustrative comparison shows one of the most striking features of the Spanish developmental process: the interprovincial disparity of wealth, measured in per capita terms. In 1959 the main industrial areas of the Basque country and Catalonia were at the top of the regional rank, followed by Madrid, the Balearic Islands, Cantabria, Navarre, Valencia, La Rioja, Asturias, and Aragón. All of these areas enjoyed standards of living above the national average, which for the first three cases (the Basque country, Catalonia, and Madrid) amounted to nearly 80 per cent of the European average income. At the other extreme, Andalusia, Castile, and Extremadura fell below 40 per cent of the Western European level.[6]

The strong rate of expansion of the Spanish economy after 1960 put in motion a convergence process among the different geographical areas as the least-developed regions were also those that grew fastest. A ranking of regions according to their wealth in 1959 would be almost exactly the inverse of a classification according to their growth rates between 1960 and 1975 (see Table 2.3). Thanks to the new data provided by Domínguez Martín, it can be stated, for example, that Castile, Murcia, and Galicia, three of the poorest regions in Spain in 1959, registered the fastest GDP per capita growth rates between 1960 and 1975. As developmental theory explains, the potential for growth partly depends, among other things, on the initial level. Low-income countries can easily benefit from well-known technology and foreign entrepreneurial practices that allow them to obtain rapid efficiency gains. Capital accumulation can proceed

Table 2.3 Spanish autonomous regions ranked according to GDP per capita

	Position in 1959	Rate of growth, 1960–75	Position in 1975
Andalusia	15	5.8	16
Aragón	10	5.1	8
Asturias	9	4.7	10
Balearic Islands	4	5.9	1
Basque country	1	4.1	3
Cantabria	5	3.6	7
Castile-La Mancha	16	6.6	14
Castile-León	11	6.0	11
Catalonia	2	4.6	4
Extremadura	17	5.1	17
Galicia	13	6.1	15
Madrid	3	5.1	2
Murcia	14	6.3	12
Navarre	6	5.2	5
La Rioja	8	4.7	6
Valencia	7	4.4	9
Canary Islands	12	5.7	13

at high rates if labour mobility is not impeded and there is a reasonable supply of investment. Spain during the *desarrollismo* (development) years was an example of this kind of phenomenon. Structural change, that is, the shifting of resources from less to more productive sectors – for example, from dry land to irrigated land or from the primary sector to industry – was especially intense in the less-developed areas, thus producing a more homogenous economic structure throughout the country. Indeed, as a result of this process, the differences between the poorer and richer regions were reduced. However, it is also true that the less-developed regions' potential for growth was not fully exploited, so that, at the end of the Franco years, in 1975, the gap between the wealthiest region, the Balearic Islands, and the poorest, Extremadura, was still a substantial one. The per capita GDP of the inhabitants of the islands was 2.3 times greater than that of the people living in Extremadura. The four richest regions in Spain – the Balearic Islands, Madrid, the Basque country, and Catalonia – reached a GDP per capita level in 1975 close to or above the European average, while the three poorest regions at the time of Franco's death (Extremadura, Andalusia, and Galicia), were 60 per cent below the European average.[7]

Part of the convergence process was due to reductions in regional population. Migration served to equalize income across the board, as the excess agrarian labour supply was eliminated. In fact we know that internal migratory flows accelerated in this period, stimulated by the fast-growing demands of industry. Large areas of the country experienced a relentless loss of population, while others became the homeland of those searching for better jobs and new opportunities. Thus, hundreds of inhabitants from Andalusia, Extremadura, and Castile left their homes seeking to improve their standards of living in the urban and industrial agglomerations. It was so intense a movement that some regions, such as the two Castiles and Extremadura, registered negative demographic growth, while the population in Andalusia, Aragón, and Galicia hardly grew. By contrast, the population in Madrid, the Basque country, Catalonia, the Balearic and Canary Islands experienced the greatest population increases in their history. Even those regions that enjoyed a relatively rapid growth lost population during these years, such as Navarre, Aragón, and La Rioja. Furthermore, not only did per capita income disparities but also demographic size and density divergences remain.

What role did regional policy play during the *desarrollismo* years? One of the most publicized aspects of industrial policy during the later Franco years was its territorial achievements. Through the 'development poles' and the 'preferential location areas', the State tried to promote an industrialization process in different locations across the country. The purpose was to reshape the spatial distribution of industrial activity. Development poles were intended to produce social and economic changes in certain poor provinces, as well as aiming at the creation of new jobs in order to prevent emigration. To achieve this goal, firms with important forward and backward linkages were set up. The decision to establish a 'pole' in a particular province depended on the availability of natural and human resources as well as on a pre-existing level of economic activity. Areas were chosen if economic planners considered that they could become an industrial cluster in the near future. The so-called preferential locations were characterized by serious economic imbalances (high unemployment rates, low levels of education, poor infrastructures) that had to be corrected. The *polígonos industriales* (industrial estates) were designed for locations which did not qualify as development poles. In any case, firms set up under any one of these regional development programmes were granted special economic advantages, such as access to low-cost credit lines, long-term subsidies, and tax rebates.

Twelve 'poles' were created in Andalusia, Galicia, Castile, La Rioja, Aragón, and Asturias. And three areas within Castile and Extremadura were declared preferential locations. To stimulate the establishment of industries within these zones, regional and local authorities were prepared in many instances to provide financial aid. The results, however, were far from satisfactory. Although some locations experienced structural changes with an increase in manufacturing employment, the truth is that only those places which exhibited some kind of industrial pre-structure, and where new investment was concentrated in the automobile sector, as was the case for Valladolid or Vigo, did they undergo a remarkable and lasting change. In other cases, such as Córdoba, Oviedo, or Granada, the industrialization process did not really take off and came to a halt as soon as the financial aid ceased. Huelva provides another example of dubious success. A first-rate petrochemical plant was built there, which nevertheless failed to alter the area's economic structure. We can thus assert that regional policy during the *desarrollismo* years did not alter Spain's industrial map. Factory activity remained concentrated around Barcelona, Madrid, and the Basque country, and only some areas lying along the axes joining this triangle, such as Navarre and Zaragoza, benefited from the regional economic policy implemented during the *desarrollismo* period.

Conclusions

In the last 15 years of Franco's rule, the Spanish economy underwent a profound transformation. By 1975 the country was already amongst the group of the most-developed nations of the world. The rapid economic change described above is what permitted Spain to become closer to Europe, although significant differences still remained with the leading European economies. The roots of Spain's development are to be found in a notable labour productivity increase, greater investment, structural changes in productivity, and the incorporation of new technologies. The Spanish income level rose, consumption patterns improved, and the expectations of the population, which demanded a greater supply of social services such as education and health, rose. The stimuli provided by tourism and emigration also contributed. However, this remarkable transformation in the standard of living occurred within a non-democratic framework in which political freedom and democratic trade union rights were denied, two features that overshadow the economic conquests of these years. In fact, the role of the Francoist State and of the regime's economic policy in this story of success remains an object of heated historiographical debate. To what extent was economic policy responsible for the development achieved in the second half of the Franco regime? Was it a natural or an induced growth? Who was responsible: Franco or the market? Can we speak of an historic debt to Franco and his regimen for having taken Spain out of underdevelopment?

The economic policy of the Golden Age period should be interpreted as a partial correction of the excesses of autarky. The liberalization programme initiated with the Stabilization Plan permitted the integration of Spain into international markets at a time of great stability and strong growth in terms of the world economy. State-owned enterprise stepped back and the leading role of private initiative was favoured. Macro-economic stability was maintained thanks to fiscal authorities' orthodox behaviour and to a flexible monetary policy, which was accompanied by real product expansion. These factors contributed to economic growth by providing the ideal conditions for a continuous flow of both Spanish and foreign investment, which in turn ensured capital accumulation and productivity gains. However, a balanced judgement about the causes of the 'Spanish miracle' must not overlook the fact that the industrialization process, and the transformations undergone during these years, would have not been so profound, or even have existed at all, had they not coincided with an extremely expansionary phase of the European and world economies: to a certain extent, the 'Spanish miracle' was part of a common 'miracle' shared by the whole continent. The merit of the economic policy of the regime consisted in taking advantage of the so-called Golden Age of world capitalism. The precise ability of Francoist policy makers was *not* to oppose the influences emanating from abroad, but to take advantage of the exceptional winds blowing from the world economy. In sum, the development of Spain mirrored the rapid self-sustained growth of Western Europe.

Notes

1. C. Barciela, M.I. López, J. Melgarejo, and J.A. Miranda, *La España de Franco (1939–1975). Economía* (Madrid: Síntesis, 2001).
2. L. Prados de la Escosura, *El progreso económico de España (1850–2000)* (Madrid: Fundación BBVA, 2003).
3. E. Fuentes Quintana, 'Tres decenios de la economía española en perspectiva', in J.L. García Delgado, ed., *España. Economía* (Madrid: Espasa Calpe, 1988).
4. J.L. García Delgado and J.C. Jiménez, 'La economía', in *La época de Franco (1939–1975). Historia de España Menéndez Pidal* (Vol. XLI) (Madrid: Espasa Calpe, 1996).
5. J.M. Serrano Sanz and E. Pardos, 'Los años del crecimiento, 1959–1975', in F. Comín, M. Hernández, and E. Llopis, eds, *Historia económica de España, siglos XIX y XX* (Barcelona: Crítica, 2002).
6. R. Dobado, *Geografía y desiguldad económica y demográfica de las provincias españolas, siglos XIX y XX* (Madrid: Universidad Complutense de Madrid, 2004).
7. R. Domínguez Martín, *La riqueza de las naciones. Las desigualdades económicas regionales en España, 1700–2000* (Madrid: Alianza, 2002).

3
Tourism and Political Change in Franco's Spain

Sasha D. Pack

Few cases illustrate the potency of tourism as a form of international relations better than the experience of Franco's Spain. Historically shunned by all but the most intrepid travellers, Spain became a major hub of postwar European leisure, absorbing a massive current of vacationers in search of seaside pleasures and an escape from staid routine. The consequences for Spain were at once economic, cultural, and political. Foreign tourists strengthened the ostracized regime, providing by the mid-1950s both its largest source of foreign currency and compelling evidence of its acceptance by democratic Europe. They also posed challenges for the Franco regime and its foundational principles of moral and economic autarky. Far the greatest draw were the popular seaside resorts of the Mediterranean littoral, where resentment of Madrid's authority was generally higher. Local service economies soon became tied to international commercial networks and operated largely outside the official National–Corporatist structure. The postwar tourist boom reinforced the Franco dictatorship's sovereignty while simultaneously triggering significant institutional and cultural transformation.

Casual associations between tourism and the dynamism of the late Franco period have invited general conclusions about the former's role in political change. As early as 1971, the sociologist Amando de Miguel noted with irony that the famous slogan, 'Spain is Different' served to promote an industry that had rendered Spain 'less different' with respect to democratic Europe.[1] Historians similarly have reflected that tourism 'bred an unquenchable desire to live like Europe,' rather than promote Spanish exceptionalism.[2] Such observations are undoubtedly valid, but

47

the link between European leisure culture and Spanish democratization was neither inexorable nor overdetermined. It is widely known that the Franco regime, like numerous other authoritarian regimes, was capable of fostering and maintaining liberal economic policies without a political opening. The most dramatic social impact was, moreover, limited to a small portion of Spanish territory, usually in concentrated asphalt enclaves some distance from the major population centres. The influence of tourists was in any case demotic rather than democratic. In general, they demanded basic comforts and personal freedoms at an affordable cost; those with even subtly political agendas could have formed only a negligible minority among the hordes.

Tourism accumulated political and economic significance in Spain gradually over the course of the twentieth century, reaching a peak in the decades following Second World War. Postwar trends in international travel and leisure exerted considerable influence on the development of the Franco regime as it adjusted from its interwar and largely xenophobic origins to the main currents of the postwar European conjuncture. Scholarly treatments of the Spanish transition's international aspects have emphasized institutions rather than socio-cultural and economic trends – and quite rightly, considering that throughout the process institutional compromise outweighed social mobilization in the conventional sense.[3] Yet the blossoming of a 'leisure civilization' during the third quarter of the twentieth century was a major event of transnational social history with particular resonance in Spain. Its features included a strong consumer preference for warm seaside resorts, new distribution models for leisure, and the widespread belief that mass travel fostered international harmony. Famously apolitical in their preferences, Europe's leisure consumers formed a major aspect of the emerging postwar network of material and cultural exchange, reaching Franco's Spain at a time when conventional diplomatic and commercial relations were restricted. They might be considered emissaries of an incipient and irresistible European empire marked by consumerism, efficiency, mobility, and permissiveness.

These naive ambassadors became a massive spectacle in a country with a long-enduring peripheral identity and strong recent memories of isolation. As a political good, tourism chiefly served the strain of modern Spanish conservatism representing gradual reformism and 'regenerationist' nationalism.[4] The embodiment of this lineage was Manuel Fraga, who is widely recognized as a protagonist of pre-transition reformism and perhaps the godfather of post-Franco Spanish conservatism. Fraga served as Franco's Minister of Information and Tourism from 1962 to 1969, when he developed a political style blending pragmatic acceptance of social change and liberal influence with his conservative support for crown, Church, and a strong sense of national cohesion.[5]

The politics of tourism in modern Spain

The significance of foreign tourists to the politics of Spanish identity and 'conservative regenerationism' long predated the Franco regime. Spain's conflicted identity as a European nation in modern times has been conditioned by geographical marginality, imperial decline, and the singular hostility it faced from other European powers. The notorious 'Black Legend,' contrasting Spanish savagery, superstition, and idleness with European enlightenment and progress, was confirmed and amplified in countless travel diaries between the seventeenth and the nineteenth centuries.[6] Bourbon reformers of the eighteenth century first proposed that improvements in the quality of roads and inns might form part of a broader effort to improve Spain's international reputation and commercial ties.[7] Initiatives in this spirit continued throughout the nineteenth century, though any real progress was stunted by internal conflict, ineffective leadership, and a general poverty of resources available for infrastructural improvement.

Though leisure travel became commonplace in Europe during this period, Spain remained marginal to the main itineraries. Several coastal and spa resorts appeared and even thrived – the *veraneo*, or summer retreat to the coast or the sierra, became a defining custom of the Spanish middle classes – but only San Sebastián approached the international stature of the Atlantic resorts of France and Belgium. Towards the end of the nineteenth century, Europeans developed a taste for bronzed bodies and warm seawater. The elaborate contraptions designed to shield sea-bathers' skin from exposure while on land fell into disuse and bodies were increasingly on display.[8] The new preference for warmth and sun precipitated the rise of the French *Côte d'Azur* in the 1870s, and by 1900, numerous dusty enclaves, notably along Catalonia's *Costa Brava* and around Málaga in the South, were hoping to attract foreign clientele by appealing to similar appetites. The Spanish initiatives were limited in their success and drew nearly universal derision from Europe's major tourist guide books, which portrayed Spain as a destination for the adventuresome traveller rather than the pleasure tourist seeking status and comfort.[9]

Tourism first became the object of state attention in Spain during the early twentieth century. At the urging of numerous liberal and conservative elites, Alfonso XIII (1902–31) created the world's first state tourism bureau in 1905, charged with promoting Spain abroad and regulating the quality and prices of hotels. The bureau's activities were fleeting and generally ineffective, but indicated a growing appreciation for the power of 'consumer diplomacy' – the idea that tourism, particularly at hotels, formed a crucial form of commercial and cultural interaction whereby foreign travellers formed their judgements of Spanish civilization. Already by the dawn of the twentieth century, the Spanish state had given organized expression to the belief that tourism was a powerful tool to project a modern national image, to provide remote towns the opportunity to promote their attractiveness, and to foster important social and commercial engagement with other parts of Europe.[10]

Travel to Spain remained very limited during the 1920s and 1930s, never exceeding one-tenth of 1 percent of the GNP, but motives behind such precocious state involvement were not limited to economics. Successive governments expanded state involvement in the tourism industry, in the words of the pioneering promoter the Marqués de la Vega Inclán, 'not only for the wealth it can bring to Spain, but for the general aspect of its culture and international ties.'[11] An *esprit-de-corps* crystallized among state and private tourism promoters around the notion that they were engaged in the mutually reinforcing activities of national propaganda, infrastructural modernization, and commerce. The Primo de Rivera dictatorship invoked the interests of tourism to justify large highway and sewerage improvement projects, citing a need to increase 'positive impressions' and 'eliminat[e] any pretext for...unfavorable judgments' on the part of foreign visitors.[12] After 1931, the Second Republic conceived tourism as an auxiliary to its overarching foreign policy of internationalism, participating in League of Nations efforts to streamline customs procedures for pleasure travellers. Tourism attained its tightest connection to politics in 1938, when, in the midst of civil war, Franco established '*Rutas de Guerra*' tours to take foreigners to active battle zones while delivering overtly Nationalist commentaries. The impact on international opinion was probably negligible, but, as Sandie Holguín has demonstrated, the exercise of representing the insurgent cause to foreign tourists helped to shape the regime's formative myths.[13]

Tourism and democratic citizenship after 1945

The outcome of Second World War served to enhance the political significance of tourism in Franco's Spain and also more broadly in

Europe. The travel industry as it emerged in postwar Europe was strongly social–democratic in its ethos and increasingly organized along industrial models of mass distribution and efficiency. By the middle of the twentieth century, in the words of one social theorist, 'holidays had become almost a marker of citizenship, a right to pleasure.'[14] The extension of social citizenship to the realm of leisure, which had begun in the 1930s, was sanctified in the United Nations' Universal Declaration of Human Rights of 1948, which endorsed the right to 'periodic holidays with pay.'[15] Paid vacation allotments increased rapidly in the 1950s throughout Western Europe, and enterprising travel firms soon learned to exploit massive demand and modern distribution methods. Consumer costs dropped precipitously and volume expanded.

War-weary citizens did not immediately embark on foreign holidays *en masse*, but the speedy reestablishment of an accessible international travel system carried considerable economic and political weight. Alon Confino, a social historian of Germany, has remarked on the importance of recreational travel in restoring a semblance of normality to postwar European society.[16] Quickly restoring the southward flow of tourist revenue would go considerable distance to ameliorating the problem of grave trade imbalances, as it had done for several countries before the war. Britain's Labour government recognized in the tourism industry a twofold opportunity: (1) to appease a public eager for overseas travel, and (2) to use tourism as a means of transferring sterling to war-ravaged countries, enabling them to purchase British-made industrial products. At the same time, the Labourites wished to avoid the impression of permitting the wealthy to spend freely abroad while ordinary subjects continued facing shortages at home. They resolved the dilemma by imposing strict currency allowances on Britons leaving the sterling zone. This policy encouraged countries wishing to profit from tourism to develop large volumes of inexpensive accommodations rather than a few exclusive resorts. Other northern countries adopted similar policies, most significantly West Germany once the travel ban on its citizens was lifted in 1950. To resolve the problem of supply, travel firms eyed Spain's vast stretches of undeveloped coastline as an ideal destination for low-cost high-volume holidays.[17]

Tourism is largely absent from the familiar story of Spain's plight directly after Second World War. Owing to lingering associations with the defeated Axis, Spain was initially excluded from all the major postwar multilateral organizations and was denied aid from the Marshall Plan. For its part, the dictatorship made fierce appeals to the nation's moral and economic independence and regarded the liberal attitudes of modern

Europe to be a scourge of decadence. Efforts were directed towards expanding heavy industries, purging lingering opposition, ensuring the regime's security, and restoring conservative social norms. As Juan Pablo Fusi has observed, the dictatorship discarded creative revolutionary cultural programmes in favour of a cultural policy based on censorship. [18] Foreign tourism apparently fitted nowhere in this agenda. Accommodating it would require relatively more open borders and would compromise the regime's control over the international exchange value of the Spanish currency, a requirement of its chosen industrial policy. Tourists were recognized, moreover, to be an uncomfortably liberal social force. Conservative clergy had long warned that modern sea-bathing practices turned women into 'carnal goddesses.' [19] Foreign tour operators demanded to circulate freely through Spanish cities without official chaperone, fuelling authorities' anxieties that political agitators might slip past border control posing as tourists or that the more unsavoury aspects of Spain's post-Civil War repression and poverty might be exposed to impressionable travellers.

Yet despite the pretenses of Francoist ideologues on the one hand and the builders of postwar antifascist Europe on the other, Spain by no means was hermetically isolated from the postwar European system. All West European countries arranged to buy Spanish raw materials and agricultural produce, the sale of which kept Franco's industrial ambitions afloat. Spain played an essential part in postwar economic reconstruction because of its ability to provide such goods inexpensively, helping to contain inflation throughout Western Europe at a critical and fragile juncture. [20] Certain elements within the regime, in particular the relatively liberal Foreign Ministry and the currency-starved treasury, envisioned that tours and holiday packages might serve an economic purpose similar to other exports while also helping to mitigate the country's unenviable diplomatic predicament. They aimed to deploy foreign tourism in the service of the 'national resurrection' the regime boasted to have unleashed.

Affordable holidays were perhaps not as pressing for the European economy as tungsten and wheat, but several interests on both sides of the Pyrenees favoured the development of Mediterranean resorts. The development of low-cost resorts in Spain would expand Europe's supply of inexpensive holiday destinations while keeping afloat the Franco regime's industrial ambitions. A collection of British investors, travel agents, and wartime aviators looking to profit from their expertise in peacetime, began mining the coasts of Catalonia and the tranquil Mediterranean isle of Majorca. Local hoteliers, mostly neophytes, guaranteed the British travel firms low rates in exchange for guarantees of investment capital and a steady flow of clientele.[21] This kind of direct contracting violated the nominal legal structure of Francoist corporatism, but the Spanish government lacked both the will and the bureaucratic machinery to stifle it.

Some elements of the regime indeed harboured interest in encouraging this type of liberal commercial exchange. The Foreign Ministry viewed the prospect of opening the country to foreign travellers as a primary weapon in fighting 'anti-Spanish' slander. A Spanish diplomat in London predicted in 1948 that his country was ideally positioned to capture 'the new socialist tourism [sic] of travelers with budgets limited to modest amounts,' adding, 'The moral value is self-evident, considering that [Spain and Great Britain] scarcely know one another.'[22] The Ministry of Industry regarded tourism revenue as an ideal means to nourish national industries with foreign currency without subjecting them to open competition. The two ministries jointly established special exchange rates for pleasure travellers in 1947, revising the rates several times subsequently to tourists' further advantage.[23]

Spain's tourist boom

Interest in Spain as a holiday destination first began to accelerate around 1949. It was in that year that pre-1936 figures for foreign entries were surpassed. This first wave was largely directed towards the seaside resorts of the Costa Brava and Majorca, though cities and cultural sites also drew growing numbers. Volume grew steadily throughout the 1950s, first among French, British, and American clientele, then West Germans and Scandinavians. Total tourist entries approached 1 million in 1954, doubling by 1957 and again by 1960.[24] The religious and nationalist shrines which the regime might have hoped to promote receded in comparison with the 'sea–sex–sun' formula emblematic of postwar commercial tourism.

The unprecedented influx of foreigners soon penetrated the core of the regime's identity. Amid a general government restructuring in 1951, Franco found fit to elevate tourism to a cabinet-level portfolio. The new Ministry of Information and Tourism was so named in order to soften the nomenclature of what was essentially a censorship bureau, but there were indeed benefits to officially recognizing this increasingly important field of social and commercial activity. On occasion, official information media attempted to exploit tourism for domestic propaganda: Images of massive queues at border checkpoints, projected on cinema screens nationwide in a 1951 newsreel, provided apparent proof that the international ostracism of the 1940s was over.[25] Such publicity exercises were highly exceptional before 1962, however. The greater political challenge was to preserve this excellent revenue source without causing alarm among the regime's socially conservative constituency. Authorities issued stern warnings in the Spanish press promising 'the most exact enforcement' of laws designed to 'impede any unhygienic bathing practices that could threaten public decorum or attack the moral traditions of this country.'[26]

Language to appease the regime's moralist streak was at odds, however, with the two basic goals of obtaining foreign revenue and discrediting the antimodern reputation of the Franco regime and Spain generally. Legislation restricting exposure of the back and legs and separating the sexes at the beach constituted for many holidaymakers a paramount killjoy. Spanish tourism offices and northern European travel agents assured reluctant clients that the laws were rarely enforced. On the exceptional occasions when they were, however, banner headlines appeared in tabloids across Europe, provoking the sensation, in the words of an indignant Spanish diplomat, 'that Spain oppresses the tourist, a notion completely out of line with reality.'[27] Within Spain, as well, there was evidence that the moral autarky of the 1940s was loosening by the early 1950s. The leading Catholic daily opined that restrictive beach laws confirmed for many foreigners that 'Spain is the quintessential backward country, quaint and absurd, where even sun and sea-bathing become a moral problem.'[28] Named for an early nuclear test site, the bikini swimsuit rarely caused blistering blindness when exhibited at the beach, but a more serious affront occurred when tourists neglected to cover their bare skin upon rising to street level. To prevent this, authorities ordered the construction of dressing houses, but penalties were generally not levied on tourists who failed to use them. Indeed, though formally prohibited, the bikini was generally tolerated by the later 1950s, especially in the newer popular resorts of the Mediterranean. According to a West German travel writer, 'nobody causes a fuss about it, nor does the Civil Guard respond with a scalding bayonet.'[29] On the contrary, authorities in coastal locales were often so fearful of foreign tabloid accusations of Spain's 'inquisitorial customs' that affronted locals frequently denounced their failure to enforce the laws.[30]

Tourism revenue gave the regime the strength and confidence to implement major economic reforms. Annual increases in tourism were constant throughout the 1950s, and, although the phenomenon was not as visible to the general public as it would later become, it was not lost on economists. By 1954, government economists were exploring the possibility that tourism revenue might fully neutralize Spain's debilitating commercial deficit.[31] The main obstacle was a massive black market for the Spanish currency, as foreign (principally British) travel agencies had learned how to acquire pesetas at price well below even the preferential tourist rate. Possibly half of tourist revenue in 1954 failed to arrive through legal channels, with the effect of fuelling inflation without increasing national purchasing power for foreign goods. The situation only worsened. In 1957 and 1958, official statistics revealed a paradoxical situation whereby revenue fell dramatically even though the number of foreign visitors continued to rise.[32] None of this was lost on authorities: the Ministry of Information and Tourism routinely monitored the discrepancy between underground and official tourist exchange values and industry journals decried the illicit practices. The British ambassador acknowledged in 1958, 'To an increasing extent, peseta notes are being purchased at unofficial rates outside Spain.'[33] Meanwhile, as the country suffered an inflationary crisis, foreign currency reserves were rapidly depleting. A general devaluation in 1959 was necessary to stabilize the peseta and eliminate the black market, and the promise of increased tourism revenues as a result softened the pain of such a plan.

The 1959 devaluation coincided with deregulation of package-tour air charters across Western Europe, launching a second phase of acceleration in the European – and in particular the Spanish – tourism economy. This catapulted Spain past France in foreign tourist volume in 1960 and past Italy in 1964, briefly to the status, as the Franco regime's triumphalist publicists phrased it, of 'world's foremost tourist power.'[34] Over the 1960s, tourism extended to new coastal zones around Málaga, Alicante, the Canary Islands, and the pilgrimage route to Santiago de Compostela. The 2.8 million foreigners to arrive in 1959 became 19 million in 1969. Tourist revenue covered two-thirds of the Spanish trade deficit over that period.[35] The revenue also provided the most valuable collateral for obtaining loans from the World Bank and other international agencies to finance the decade's rapid development.[36]

Tourism and the politics of 'Neo-Regenerationism'

Although the economic aspects of this opening were generally welcomed, the regime was ambivalent about the political implications of the incipient tourist boom. The self-styled 'technocrat' clique of conservative bureaucrats who had engineered Spain's economic recovery after 1957 cautioned against 'El Dorados and get-rich-quick panaceas' like the tourism economy.[37] Many were members of the shrouded *Opus Dei* lay Catholic society and harboured close ties to leading Spanish industrialists. They regarded tourism as a 'highly worrisome' social force that undermined the regime's authority and diverted investment resources away from sounder projects.[38] As a revenue source, they frequently labelled tourism a 'temporary' [*coyuntural*] economic stabilizer and encouraged investors to concentrate on more conventional industries.[39]

The interests of tourism gained a powerful voice in 1962, when Franco appointed the eloquent young reformer Manuel Fraga to be the new Minister of Information and Tourism. Unlike many of his colleagues in the cabinet, Fraga considered the continued growth of Spain's tourism industry to be inexorable, and in any case beneficial to the country's economic and social vitality. Though loyal to the dictatorship, he believed that social, cultural, and economic change could not continue indefinitely without altering the regime's starchy political and institutional framework. Foreign tourism ought to be supported and channelled, as Restoration patriots once had imagined, to the broader ends of a controlled revolution from above. In a speech to the national assembly, Fraga characterized tourism as 'the foundation of the decisive failure of the recent derisive campaigns against our country,' while the sector also 'respond[ed] perfectly to the demands of every process of growth.'[40] He predicted that the presence of foreign tourism would provoke a 'qualitative change in the psycho-social panorama of the community,'[41] simultaneously projecting outward a modernizing ambition and engendering a mentality of progress and openness among Spaniards. To growing numbers of investors, coastal municipalities, and liberal reformers, Fraga offered a compelling alternative to the technocrats, who they feared would exploit tourist revenue in the short term while leaving the industry to languish and decay.

The main elements of the *Fraguista* tourism development strategy were classically indicative of conservative regenerationism. One goal was to mobilize the population to embrace a broadly pro-European understanding of Spanish identity. Fraga's speeches frequently declared that tourism was 'Spain's European vocation.'[42] Tourism became a central turbine driving 'Europeanization,' a vague but powerful abstraction that, as for other European nations, promised a definitive triumph over national historical problems and anxieties. In practical terms, this meant improving roads, municipal services, hotels, and restaurants to meet international standards. It also implied a tolerance and even an embrace of foreign attitudes and behaviours, and, perhaps of equal importance, official countenance of this tolerance.

The other goal was to engage a kind of managed decentralization of initiative and regulation. Tourism would need to reflect a plural Spain with variegated identities, cultural traditions, and modes of leisure. The ministry developed programmes to dole out albeit modest funds for municipalities to develop their own civic improvement and tourism promotion projects. A more controversial programme was the Law of Centers and Zones of National Tourist Interest, designed to submit major resort areas to central management. The idea was to preserve the attractiveness of tourist regions and limit the leverage of land developers, who often harboured little interest in the quality or sustainability of resorts and frequently ignored building codes. Despite these intentions, the proposed law drew criticism from all directions. Champions of municipal interests claimed that it concentrated too much power in the hands of Fraga's ministry, while advocates of centralized industrial policy considered the law a dangerous boost for an industry and a ministry so threatening to the regime's continuation. After considerable debate, the law was implemented in 1963 in a largely impotent and watered-down form.

Fraga possessed more leverage on other issues related to tourism development. All cabinet figures agreed on the need to eliminate all pretexts for 'anti-Spanish' impressions among foreign visitors. Roads and municipal services were generally inadequate to receive the quantities of visitors arriving in Spain each year. This was especially true in remote villages which in the span of a decade had become major international resorts accommodating threefold population increases during the summer months. Though many in the regime would have preferred to allocate state resources elsewhere, the demands of revenue and the nation's good image made infrastructural investment in many coastal areas a necessity. The situation's urgency – and with it Fraga's power – increased in 1962 after a World Bank mission cautioned that 'other Mediterranean countries are making very competitive efforts' to challenge Spain's dominance of the package holiday market.[43] The government proceeded to spend lavishly on roadway improvement, disproportionately so in insular and coastal areas heavily trodden by tourists. For 1965, 53 per cent of roadway funds were allocated for Mediterranean provinces, which comprised 30 per cent of the national population, while interior provinces, 48 per cent of the population, received 12 per cent of highway funds. Several new airports were built in a similarly centrifugal pattern, including one on a sparsely populated coastline untouched by tourism but owned by well-connected resort developers. [44]

The other crucial target of state attention was hygiene, perennially considered a Spanish deficiency vis-à-vis European refinement. The new and largely inexperienced class of hoteliers faced rigorous government inspection, received incentives for modernization, and received much didactic instruction in travellers' expectations of service and cleanliness. But many hygiene problems in hotels and restaurants were symptomatic of a wide gap between tourist and local standards which proved difficult to close without also raising the low prices so attractive to European tourists. The government was more effective in addressing broad infrastructural problems related to hygiene and sanitation. Concerns about contaminated water prompted even the *Caudillo*, who mentioned tourism almost never, to tell a confidant that he 'worr[ied] that the government would neglect sewage and public health, producing a case of typhoid...and that this would create a panic, causing a reduction in tourism difficult to overcome.' [45] This issue too rose above the cabinet struggle over investment priorities, resulting in the creation of an effective Central Sanitation Commission with close ties to tourist bureau officials. By 1968, prefects received fewer complaints of stomach illness and cleanliness from tourists than they had a few years earlier. Egregious violations of modern sanitation standards were isolated rather than commonplace. In interior regions beset with relatively few foreign tourists, however, municipal sanitation and communications languished. [46]

The political dividends to be earned from modernization – the 'staging' of growth, as Cold-War historians have labelled this worldwide epochal practice – were perhaps as transcendent as the growth itself. [47] The pastoral romanticism embodied in the 'Spain is Different' advertising slogan increasingly belied the message that state and private promoters preferred to convey. This was captured more accurately by a Madrid banker who predicted in 1959 that those who visit Spain 'will no longer believe that we all go around dressed as bullfighters' and 'will consider us as a serious country.' [48] State newsreels, screened before all feature films, featured numerous segments demonstrating in one way or another the link between tourism and national progress. One likened the Mediterranean island of Majorca to 'an aircraft carrier' that 'would not function if not for its expertly designed transport system.' [49] Another featured Benidorm, 'until a few years ago, a small Alicantine locale asleep in its own history...[but] today...an important population center...where we admire the liveliness of its streets and the splendor of its buildings.' [50] Tourism also was among the protagonists in a 1964 media campaign, directed by Fraga, commemorating 25 years of the Franco dictatorship. Brandishing the lingo of current international development economics, one radio message characterized tourism as 'a phenomenon of the masses, the keystone of the stage researchers...have christened with the name "mass consumption."'[51] Official media frequently displayed photographs of large international resorts at Torremolinos and Benidorm, in the words of a Spanish tourism office director, 'to express the expansion and creative potential of our tourism.' A leading travel agent noted, 'In order to demonstrate our progress to the Spanish public...[we] emphasize repeatedly that 200 planes per day land in Majorca,' spawning impressions at home and abroad 'that Majorca is no longer a tranquil island, [but rather] a giant construction site.'[52]

A final aspect to staged growth was rising tourist movement among Spaniards themselves – a potent sign of national progress in postwar Europe's leisure paradise. In 1963, tourism officials identified domestic tourism as 'a means to demonstrate upward mobility keeping with the trajectory of Spanish standards of living.' Spanish clientele also helped to correct sharp seasonal imbalances at many resorts and brought tourism development to interior regions untouched by foreigners.[53] In general, co-mingling between Spanish and foreign tourists was most frequent at posh destinations, while one or the other group predominated at popular resorts.[54] In the more famous resorts, Spaniards might have felt the most foreign of anybody. They comprised slightly over one-tenth of hotel guests in the Balearics and Costa Brava, while tending to predominate at the newer resorts of Murcia and Almería.[55] One can identify an emerging nexus in this period between leisure, upward mobility, and xenophile attitudes: An advertisement in interior Castile from the mid-1960s proclaimed, 'Spaniards are taking their summer vacations on the Costa Brava just like everybody else.'[56]

Images of modern leisure and its infrastructure did not alone imply any kind of political opening. The appearance in Spain of the human and architectural accoutrements of democratic Europe's leisure civilization dovetailed with the post-ideological, politically demobilized Spanish future endorsed by the regime's technocratic elements. Indeed, after Fraga's departure from the cabinet in 1969, a prominent technocrat proudly took credit for several coastal tourist highways between 1970 and 1973.[57] The symbolic value of economic and infrastructural development added considerable strength to Fraga's ministry and the interests it represented, but it was the debates surrounding moral tolerance and plural identity that would stir more genuinely political debate. The official contempt for foreign influence of the earlier period disappeared completely in the 1960s. The state newsreel service issued the new 'social catechism' of the era in a 1964 segment: 'Spain is a country open to all and where foreigners feel at home.'[58] In numerous features on tourism throughout the 1960s, the newsreel revealed current feminine swimwear fashions, including particularly daring examples worn by identifiably Spanish women.[59] The *sueca* – literally, Swedish woman – became an icon of contemporary popular culture. Scantily clad and blonde, she appeared in numerous films in the role of temptress of virtuous Spanish family men. To many, the *sueca* represented the ultimate threat to Spanish values, though one Nationalist veteran turned tourism promoter proudly declared, 'These 'suecas' in Spain are not always foreigners.'[60] Another Franco loyalist, Ricardo de la Cierva, addressed the issue of moral degradation in a 1963 manual on tourism, considering it a 'false problem' and maintained that the 'limits on morality are relative and changing.'[61]

Attitudes among the clergy varied. The majority stance resembled a generic postwar internationalism, emphasizing the role of tourism in economic development and in fostering mutual understanding among peoples while looking past the indecorous behaviours associated with beach tourism. A few individual clergy voiced opposition to what they saw as a passive endorsement of moral relativism. The Bishop of the Canary Islands attacked 'the use of the bikini, which has become the symbol of the delinquency and degeneration of today's woman.'[62] The Minorcan archbishop worked tirelessly throughout the 1960s to prevent the construction of an airport on his island for the same reason, though he eventually lost the struggle.[63] Fraga's office received numerous letters from incensed social conservatives. In response to one such protest, he cited the need to 'reconcile the State's responsibility to enforce good customs with the principle of liberty, the natural birthright of the human being.'[64]

In practice, this involved official recognition that the Spanish nation harboured multiple and competing attitudes and identities. Fraga's ministry condoned – even indirectly encouraged – the new European laxity in standards of public behaviour, but it also developed programmes to encourage religious leaders to set up displays for tourists visiting churches and monasteries. Virtually every regional or national conference on tourism, moreover, included at least two panel discussions on its moral implications. To frequent denunciations for its alleged role in undermining moral codes, the ministry responded that its television and radio stations were 'more respectful of the church' than in 'any other country, or in Spain in any other age.'[65] Considerable attention was also given to modernizing, promoting, and commercializing the medieval pilgrimage route to Santiago de Compostela. In a few decades, the route was transformed from a nostalgic relic into a major annual international tourist event highlighting Spain's Catholic heritage and, in the words of one brochure, 'the most fecund spiritual contacts among the Occidental peoples.'[66]

The Ministry of Information and Tourism's project to foster pluralism concerned more than just questions of public decorum and morality. The goal was to accommodate not merely the Two Spains, but the many. The basic economic, geographical, and social fact of Spain's tourism industry was that it remained heavily concentrated in a few coastal and insular regions, dominated by budget beach holidays, and eminently unrepresentative of the finer modes of European cultural exchange. While Northern European travel agents' advertising conveyed this more or less honestly, official Spanish publicity campaigns attempted to improve the Spanish holiday's vulgar reputation. 'The concern now,' a ministry document announced in 1962, 'is to change the face touristic Spain presents to the world. The concern is to present in a massive and digni-fied way attractions of another type.'[67] The favoured genre of advert-isement, the poster series, dramatically reduced allusions to flamenco, bullfighting, and beaches after 1962. The series laid a new emphasis on regional diversity and local festivals, while brochures similarly high-lighted the individual character of each region, including, most strik-ingly, the unique 'ethnic and cultural character [of] ... the Basque race.'[68] Such references were more than tokens: although official posters and brochures did not always reach their nominal target audience abroad, their release made news in Spain and often occasioned the visit of a government official to the specific town or region being featured. The *magnum opus* of the promotions department was the compact and play-fully illustrated *Spain for You*, which was published in 11 European languages. The guide's two central themes could be distilled to 'unity in diversity' and 'Spain is not so different,' the latter contradicting the now famous message inscribed in the book's inside cover. Local customs and cuisine were varied, and the book's 1964 edition even noted the prevalence of the Catalan, Basque, and Galician languages even though they would remain formally outlawed for three more years. The guide described Spain as a monarchy, omitting to mention that no monarch had been designated to succeed Franco, and as an 'organic democracy.'[69]

Vague biopolitical metaphors notwithstanding, Spain of course remained a dictatorship, the more so following the installation in 1969 of a hard-line 'bunker' government resistant to any kind of bureaucratic decentralization or political reform. Yet by this time the postwar tourism boom had exerted irreversible influence on Spanish politics and identity. It had come to represent a broad 'Euro-Spanish' *rapprochement* and a liberal foil to National–Catholic austerity. The sudden appearance of tourism as a major aspect of Spain's economic and political life served to recalibrate the longstanding tension between the xenophile and xenophobe tendencies in Spanish identity. [70] The idea that 'Spain is Different' appeared to defy empirical evidence that tourism had brought Spain closer to the main currents of Europe's economy, society, and culture. One great irony of the final years of the Franco regime was the bunker's appropriation of the erstwhile tourist slogan to justify a post-Franco continuation of the principles of dictatorship. [71]

It is quite imaginable that in a different country, or another age, many groups might have mobilized to expose the tourism industry as the ugly underbelly of modernization, proof of the inherent injustice of globalization. Numerous quaint villages of 1950 had become by 1970 enclaves of hedonism, unsightly congestion, and lowbrow commerce that would have tested the patience of populations anywhere. Many resorts were notorious for ignoring building codes intended to preserve local beauty, and much of the profit went overseas or elsewhere in Spain. Some *marxisant* commentators classified tourism as a form of 'spatial neo-colonialism,' while others on the right identified the negative effects of foreign tourism in terms of moral degradation.

Such positions reflect familiar anxieties about the broad narratives of modernization and globalization, for which Western Europe's burgeoning middle classes were a powerful motor. Spain clearly experienced both of these processes with great intensity during the Franco period. As a result, many of the foundations both of the dictatorship and its opposition were rendered obsolete. Regime leaders attempted to cultivate a new myth of demobilized technocracy to justify their continuation in power, but the dramatic reconfiguration of political interests and social attitudes in this period cast doubt on the viability of such a project. To a younger generation of Spaniards, the touristic metaphor of a xenophile, modern, tolerant, and plural Spain held far more allure.

Notes

1. Amando de Miguel, 'Una revisión de las ideas sobre el turismo,' *Mundo Internacional*, 9 January 1971.

2. Gonzalo Álvarez Chillida, 'Monarquía y cambio democrático: reflexión sobre un debate historiográfico,' *Spagna Contemporanea*, 13 (1998), pp. 147–8. Also see Ángel Viñas, 'Breaking the shackles from the past: Spanish Foreign Policy from Franco to Felipe González,' in Sebastian Balfour and Paul Preston, eds, *Spain and the Great Powers in the Twentieth Century* (New York: Routledge, 1999) and Edward Malefakis, 'Spain and its Francoist heritage,' in J.H. Herz, ed., *From Dictatorship to Democracy* (Westport, CT: Greenwood Press, 1982), p. 218.

3. For example, Pilar Ortuño Anaya, *European Socialists and Spain: The Transition to Democracy, 1959–1977* (London: Palgrave Macmillan, 2002) and Julio Crespo MacLennan, *Spain and the Process of European Integration, 1957–1985* (New York: Palgrave Macmillan, 2000).

4. On 'conservative regenerationism,' see Carlos Seco Serrano, *Historia del conservadurismo español* (Madrid: Temas de Hoy, 2000).

5. The numerous political biographies include John Gilmour, *Manuel Fraga Iribarne and the Rebirth of Spanish Conservatism, 1939–1990* (Lewiston, NY: Edwin Mellen, 1999); Juan Velarde Fuertes, *Fraga, o el intelectual y la política* (Barcelona: Planeta, 2001); Pilar Cernuda, *Ciclón Fraga* (Madrid: Temas de Hoy, 1997). An excellent account of his political style as applied to press reform is Elisa Chuliá, *El poder y la palabra* (Madrid: Biblioteca Nueva, 2001).

6. See José Álvarez Junco, *Mater Dolorosa* (Madrid: Taurus, 2001), pp. 107–16; J.N. Hillgarth, *Mirror of Spain* (Ann Arbor: University of Michigan Press, 2001), passim; Mario Ford Bacigalupo, 'Spain and Europe in eighteenth–century travel literature: an aspect of the "Leyenda Negra",' PhD Dissertation, Brown University, 1973, esp. pp. 112–31.

7. See Pablo Alzola y Minondo, *Las obras públicas en España* (1899; reprint, Madrid: Turner, 1979); David Ringrose, *Transportation and Economic Stagnation in Spain, 1750–1850* (Durham: Duke University Press, 1970); and José Ignacio Uriol Salcedo, *Historia de los Caminos de España*, Vol. 1 (Madrid: Colegio de Ingenieros de Caminos, Canales, y Puertos, 1990).

8. Lina Lenček and Gideon Bosker, *The Beach: The History of Paradise on Earth* (New York: Viking, 1998); and Ian Littlewood, *Sultry Climates* (Cambridge, MA: Da Capo Press, 2001).

9. See Carlos Larrinaga Rodríguez, 'El turismo en la España del Siglo XIX,' *Historia Contemporánea*, 2 (2002), pp. 157–79; M. Barke and J. Towner, 'Exploring the history of leisure and tourism in Spain'; and John K. Walton and J. Smith, 'The first century of beach tourism in Spain: San Sebastián and the Playas del Norte from the 1830s to the 1930s,' in M. Barke, J. Towner, and M.T. Newton, eds, *Tourism in Spain: Critical Issues* (Wallingford, UK: CAB International, 1996); John Pemble, *The Mediterranean Passion: Victorians and Edwardians in the South* (Oxford: Clarendon Press, 1987), pp. 48–9, p. 87; Enrique Obregón, 'El turismo rancio en España,' *Historia y Vida*, 21 (1988) p. 245; Luis Lavaur, *Albores del turismo moderno (1850–1870)* (Madrid: Instituto de Estudios Turísticos, 1976); Alet Valero, 'Oriente, playas y castillos: Pratiques, images et politiques touristiques en Espagne, 1830–1928,' PhD Dissertation, Université de Provence, 1993.

10. Ana Moreno Garrido, 'Turismo y Nación. La definición de la identidad nacional a través de los símbolos turísticos: España, 1908–1929,' PhD Dissertation, Universidad Complutense de Madrid, 2005; and Hervé Poutet, *Images touristiques de l'Espagne* (Paris: Éditions L'Hartmann, 1995).

11. Marqués de la Vega Inclán, 'Solicitud y Proyecto para el progresivo desarrollo y organización del Turismo nacional, que el Comisario Regio, Marqués de la Vega Inclán, somete al Gobierno de S. M.' (Madrid: Publicaciones de la Comisaría Regia del Turismo, 1925), p. 140, Archivo Histórico Nacional, FC-PRESID-GOB-PRIMO-DE-RIVERA.
12. *Gaceta de Madrid*, 5 January 1926.
13. Sandie Holguín, '"National Spain invites you": Battlefield Tourism during the Spanish Civil War,' *American Historical Review*, 110:5 (December 2005), pp. 1399–426.
14. John Urry, *The Tourist Gaze* (London: SAGE, 1990), p. 27.
15. Warren Freedman, *The International Right to Travel, Trade and Commerce* (Buffalo: William S. Hein, 1993), p. 315.
16. Alon Confino, 'Dissonance, normality, and the historical method: why did some Germans think of tourism after May 8, 1945?' in Richard Bessel and Dirk Schumann, eds, *Life After Death: Approaches to a Cultural and Social History of Europe During the 1940s and 1950s* (New York: Cambridge University Press, 2003), pp. 323–47.
17. For a more complete description of this process, see Sasha D. Pack, *Tourism and Dictatorship: Europe's Peaceful Invasion of Franco's Spain* (New York: Palgrave Macmillan, 2006), Chapter 2.
18. Juan Pablo Fusi, 'La Cultura', in José Luis García Delgado, ed., *Franquismo: El juicio de la historia* (Madrid: Temas de Hoy, 2000), p. 185. On the demobilization of Falangist activism during World War II, see Stanley G. Payne, *Fascism in Spain, 1923–1977* (Madison: University of Wisconsin Press, 1999), pp. 363–98.
19. Isidro Gomá, *Las modas y el lujo ante la ley cristiana, la sociedad, y el arte* (Barcelona: Librería Tipográfica y Católica, 1913).
20. This is the persuasive thesis developed in Fernando Guirao, *Spain and the Reconstruction of Western Europe, 1945–1957* (New York: St. Martin's Press, 1998).
21. See Roger Bray and Vladimir Raitz, *Flight to the Sun: The Story of the Holiday Revolution* (London: Continuum, 2001).
22. Alba to Subsecretaría de Económica Exterior y Comercio, 12 April 1948, AMAE R-5104, Exp. 6. What Alba called 'socialist tourism' might more accurately be described as 'Fordist tourism,' founded on high volume and low cost.
23. Archivo General de la Administración (hereafter 'AGA'), 10: 26.02/8994, folder PE 3/7; *Cambios de moneda extranjera en España* (Madrid: Banco Exterior de España, 1949).
24. These figures do not include passengers passing through Spain en route elsewhere. Full statistical data can be found, *inter alia*, in Dirección General de Turismo, *Movimiento turístico en España* (Madrid: Ministerio de Información y Turismo, 1956), 8, and Luis Fernández Fuster, *Historia general del turismo de masas* (Madrid: Alianza, 1991), p. 830.
25. Noticiarios-Documentales #452B, 'Turistas en España' (n. d., 1951), Filmoteca de Madrid.
26. Dirección General de Seguridad, 15 June 1953, AGA 10: 77.02/6870.
27. Quoted in *Daily Express* (London), 18 June 1953.
28. *¡Ya!*, 25 June 1953.

29. *Stuttgarter Zeitung*, 11 April 1963.
30. Diputación Provincial de Málaga, 'Normas Municipales de Policía y Buen Gobierno', n. d., July 1964, AGA 8: 23.01/644.
31. See, for example, Juan Plaza Prieto, *Turismo y balanza de Pagos* (Madrid: Ministerio de Información y Turismo, 1954).
32. Carlos Barciela, et al., *La España de Franco (1939–1975)*. *Economía* (Madrid: Síntesis, 2001), p. 199.
33. Sir Ivo Mallet, British Ambassador to Madrid, to British Foreign Office, 16 January 1958, Public Record Office, FO 371/136674.
34. See, for example, Manuel Fraga, *Memoria breve de una vida política* (Barcelona: Planeta, 1980), p. 225.
35. J.A. Martínez Serrano, et al., *La economía española, 1960–1980* (Madrid: H. Blume, 1982), p. 208.
36. Miguel Figuerola Palomo, 'La transformación del turismo en un fenómeno de masas: la planificación indicativa (1950–1974),' in Carmelo Pellejero Martínez, ed., *Historia de la economía del turismo en España* (Madrid: Civitas, 1999), p. 98.
37. Alberto Ullastres, *Discurso del Excmo. Sr. Ministro de Comercio en el Acto Inaugural de la Feria Oficial y Nacional de Muestras de Murcia* (Madrid: Ministerio de Comercio, 1958), p. 21.
38. Mariano Navarro Rubio, quoted in Fraga, *Memoria breve*, p. 111. On the connections between certain cabinet ministers and industrialists, see Carlos Moya, *El poder económico en España (1939–1970)* (Madrid: Ediciones Tucar, 1975), pp. 127–42.
39. Development Plan meeting of 13 September 1963, AGA 3: 49.06/29652.
40. Speech to Cortes, 23 December 1963, published as *El turismo en España, balanza y perspectiva* (Madrid: Ministerio de Información y Turismo, 1963), pp. 8–9.
41. Manuel Fraga, *El turismo en España: balanza y perspectiva* (Madrid: Ministerio de Información y Turismo, 1963), p. 17.
42. Poutet, p. 94.
43. *Resumen del Informe del Banco Mundial* (Madrid: Banco Exterior de España), p. 79.
44. AGA 3: 49.07/31808.
45. Quoted in Francisco Franco Salgado-Araujo, *Mis conversaciones privadas con Franco* (Barcelona: Planeta, 1976), p. 380.
46. Antonio J. Rodríguez Acosta, Undersecretary General of Tourism, Report presented 20 February 1968, AGA 3: 49.22/48975.
47. See David Engerman, et al., eds, *Staging Growth: Modernization, Development, and the Global Cold War* (Amherst: University of Massachusetts Press, 2003).
48. Pedro Suárez Pinillos, *Beneficios económicos derivados de incrementar el turismo* (Madrid: Cámara Oficial de Comercio, 1959), pp. 41–2.
49. Noticiario-Documental #1369 B (31 March 1969), 'España en desarrollo: Palma de Majorca,' Filmoteca de Madrid.
50. Noticiarios-Documentales #1126 B, 'Benidorm: Ciudad internacional turística' (3 August 1964), and #1369 B, 'España en desarrollo: Palma de Majorca' (31 March 1969), Filmoteca de Madrid.
51. Aired on Radio Nacional de España, n. d., 1964. Full text is archived at AGA 3: 49.08/35208.

52. Director of Spanish National Tourism Office, London, to SGT, 17 August 1966, AGA 3: 49.06/28001; J. Miret, director of Madrid branch of Viajes Ultramar Express, to José A. López de Letona, Subdirector General of Tourism, 12 April 1966, AGA 3: 49.09/38833.
53. Tourism Committee, 'Medidas de política económica precisas para el desarrollo de turismo,' 22 July 1963, AGA 3: 49.06/29652.
54. See Pack, *Tourism and Dictatorship*, Chapter 6.
55. Ministerio de Información y Turismo, *El Turismo en 1968* (Madrid: Ministerio de Inforamción y Turismo), p. 105.
56. Yvette Barbaza, *Le paysage humaine de la Costa Brava* (Paris: Armand Colin, 1966), p. 688.
57. Gonzalo Fernández de la Mora, *Río Arriba* (Barcelona: Planeta, 1995), pp. 196–200.
58. Noticiarios-Documentales #1129 B, 'Afluencia turística en España: desde la Costa Brava a la del Sol' (n. d., 1964), Filmoteca de Madrid. On the newsreels, see Saturnino Rodríguez, *El NO-DO, Catecismo social de una época* (Madrid: Editorial Complutense, 1999).
59. Noticiarios-Documentales #1394A, 'La Costa del Sol a dos velocidades' (20 September 1969), Filmoteca de Madrid.
60. Ángel Palomino, *Carta abierta a una sueca* (Barcelona: Ediciones 99, 1974), p. 19.
61. Ricardo de La Cierva, *Turismo: teoría, técnica, ambiente* (Madrid: Editorial River, 1963), pp. 113–14.
62. Antonio Pildain, *El turismo y las playas, las divisas, y los escándolos* (San Sebastián: M. Torres, 1964).
63. Juan Victory Manella, president of Fomento Turismo de Menorca, to SGT, n. d., 1964, AGA 3: 49.06/27270; Jean Bisson, *La terre et l'homme aux Îles Baléares* (Aix-en-Provence: Edisud, 1977), p. 254.
64. Fraga to Alberto López de Arriba, 28 April 1968, AGA 3: 49.10/40132.
65. 'Consideraciones sobre los "informes" de los secretariados doctrinal y moral de la Comisión Episcopal para la Doctrina de la Fé y Costumbres,' AGA 3: 49.10/40132.
66. Brochure filed at AGA 3: 49.05/22599.
67. DGT, 'Ruta de Santiago: Estudio Turístico Preliminar,' n. d., 1962, AGA 3: 49.05/22599.
68. On the poster series, see Centro de Documentación Turística de España, *Catálogo de Carteles Oficiales de Turismo del Centro de Documentación Turística de España*, Vols. 1–2 (Madrid: Instituto de Estudios Turísticos, 2000). Brochures are catalogued at AGA 3: 49.05/22601.
69. Máximo, *Spain for You* (Madrid: Ministerio de Inforamción y Turismo, 1964), passim.
70. See Claudio Sánchez Albornoz, 'Spain and Europe,' in *Spain: A Historical Enigma*, Vol. 2, trans. Colette Joly Dees and David Sven Reher (Madrid: Fundación Universitaria Española, 1975), pp. 1137–210.
71. See Mary Kate Barker, 'The European Economic Community, the Catholic Church, and the Transition to Democracy in Spain,' PhD Dissertation, Columbia University, 2004, pp. 130–31.

4
The Change in Mentalities during the Late Franco Regime

Walter L. Bernecker (Translated by Jacqueline Cook)

The development boom and mental attitudes

Taking the rapid socio-economic change experienced by Spain and the Spanish in the 1960s as a starting point, the question arises as to what degree the new society – urban, industrialized and service-orientated, in contrast to the previous, mainly rural and agricultural society – was going to preserve the traditional attitudes and mentalities of a society that in a very few years would disappear definitively. Another question also arises: were the profound changes in society and mentalities of the late Franco regime an exclusive result of the *desarrollo* or development boom? The change in economic orientation, introduced in 1957 with the technocrats and in 1959 with the Stabilization Plan was, to some degree, a response to the serious social riots of 1956 arising from workers and students on strike.[1] There are, therefore, indicators that Spanish society had overcome stagnation, was moving in advance of the economic changes introduced at the end of the 1950s. To consider the social and mental changes exclusively as a consequence of the economic changes would be an inadequate simplification of a complex and inter-related process.[2]

The *desarrollo* was not only an economic phenomenon. It was also the consequence of a change in attitudes and mentalities. This change became evident, for example, in the disposition to emigrate, to leave the *pueblo* or village where a family had lived for generations, to look for work and well-being in a different environment, be it national or international. The fact that the status quo which had characterized their forebears was no longer passively accepted is already a clear sign that a big part of the Spanish population – measured in the millions – was submerged in this change of mentalities before the economic boom or parallel to it.[3] A condition and, at the same time, a consequence of the rapid changes of the 1960s was the soaring rise in school attendance. Illiteracy thereby descended from 19 per cent in 1940 to 9 per cent in 1970. Between 1960 and 1975, the number of students in secondary education grew sevenfold: this spectacular increase ran parallel to the process of urban concentration, at the same time reinforcing it. The increase also reflects the aspiration of many lower-class families to ensure that their children had better educational opportunities. Recognition of the importance of education for a professional future is symptomatic of a change in mentality that must have preceded the decision to send the children on to secondary education.[4] The same can be said of the universities: in 1961 there were fewer than 65,000 students in the state universities; by 1976, the number had risen to 400,000. While the Spanish population grew, between 1960 and 1970, at a rate of 0.97 per cent a year, the number of registered students rose in the same period by 9.65 per cent each year. Thus, the student boom far exceeded the average for economic growth in the years of development. The underlying reason for this unusual growth stems from the expectations that parents had for their children in terms of achieving a higher social standing by way of education.[5] The mental readiness to change one's life in order to improve material conditions forms part of the development boom of the 1960s. This was, therefore, an economic event and, at the same time, a mental attitude. As such, it cannot be separated from the social and cultural developments of the time.

Social anthropologists have emphasized the enormous importance that the Civil War (1936–39) and the post-war period (1940s) had in explaining the mental changes which occurred in the traditional Spanish agrarian society.[6] These studies insist that the war transformed people's life-styles completely, that people no longer found the usual ways of behaviour from before the war to be adequate. The change in life-style was, according to the opinion of many people polled, due to the fact that during the war connections between their 'village' and 'the exterior' had been established which had not existed before. The empirical data allows one to see that the change in mentality preceded the change in the production system. Changes in vital attitudes are not short-term processes but rather long-term ones. And the dominant attitudes in a social group are immersed in a socio-cultural framework.[7] As long as a traditional system of values and norms prevails, only with great difficulty will new dispositions and conducts be developed. Only once the traditional culture and the control mechanisms that are inherent to it are fractured can a new mentality emerge.[8] The Civil War seems to have been an event of this type.[9] In the opinion of the great majority of people polled in relation to this topic, what changed most in their 'village' was 'the way of life'. By 'way of life' they referred to eating habits, the way of dressing, the style of houses (building, furniture, decoration), the purchase of a car, going to bars, the type of work, how money was spent, and 'living better'. All were convinced that their way of life had changed substantially after the war, just like the level of consumption. In response to the question 'When did "the change in the way of thinking" start?', almost 60 per cent of those polled said 'during the Civil War.' It does not seem too far-fetched to state that in the war years a decisive change in people's system of values and norms took place. And this change of mentality is not only described as symptomatic of a new life-style, but also as one of its determining factors. The effective process of change had already begun, in this appraisal, before the 1950s, accelerating noticeably in the 1960s.

The conflict of 1936–39 broke the taboo of pre-war 'class' behaviours, inducing a deterioration in the order of values that had characterized life in the villages for generations. The first fissures in traditional convictions appeared and the social controls of village life were no longer operable due to the 'opening up' of the community and the influence of social groups originating from other communities.

Migrations also indicate change: two-thirds of those polled said that migration to the cities had begun immediately after the Civil War or in 'the years of hunger'. In other words, the migratory factor – so characteristic of the social changes of the 1960s – allows one to see that attitudinal changes started before the changes in the economic sector. The first wave of emigration was due to the post-war poverty and generalized unemployment of the 1940s and not to the (still non-existent) perspectives of a substantial material improvement as a result of new industries. The impetus of the Civil War was focused, after 1939, on the 'design' of a particular way of life: some changed their habits within the framework of the village, others decided to emigrate. Whatever the case, a type of autonomous process of change, what Arthur Marwick would call unguided change, took place.[10] The process of industrialization and development in the 1960s, therefore, encountered a society that mentally and physically was already in movement.

About the concept of 'mentalities'

If one wants to analyse the change of mentalities in the late Franco regime, it is as well to clarify – albeit briefly – what is understood by mentalities. There is a whole sub-discipline of historiography that deals with this topic. The history of mentalities emerged in France in the 1970s, ending a cycle of socio-economic predominance in the historical discourse. From studying secular tendencies in their socio-economic contexts or the reconstruction of economic cycles, there was a shift towards the study of material culture and mentalities. As on so many previous occasions, there was talk of a 'new history', which in this case vindicated the richness of, and the ambiguity inherent in, the idea of mentality.[11] At the end of the 1980s, the history of mentalities went into decline, having produced advocates and adversaries like no other historiographical trend. Before then, it seems, everything was usable as a source, 'from great classic texts revisited to testaments that reveal to us the gestures of death, from pious images to the ancient civil registry which discloses the secrets of couples, from processes to confessional handbooks', as Delumeau puts it.[12] Anything could be converted into an object of investigation for the historian. Perhaps the essence of the history of mentalities was the sanctity of objects and methods and a tenacious rejection of the socio-economic.

Looking to sociology or anthropology, drawing on versatile concepts such as 'structure' and 'context', historians of mentalities began working almost exactly like socio-economic historians, although varying the questions that they asked of the sources. To a certain extent, therefore, historians of mentalities partook in the boom of quantitative methods and trusted in the 'scientific' nature of history. They subjected the object of study to quantifiable analysis with techniques used in economic history. It would not be until later that their qualitative and anthro-pological orientation would be reinforced. According to Philippe Ariès, the great socio-economic changes (in the Spanish case, those of the 1960s) are explained by preceding changes in mentality: 'Variations in birth rate, longevity, density distribution [demographics], movements of population, just as they have occurred throughout time, emerge for us as innumerable manifestations of more profound and more secret changes of human *mentality*, of the idea that man makes of himself. Demographic statistics shed light on the way man lives, the concept he has of himself, of his own body, of his familial existence: *his attitude towards life.*'[13] In this (static) type of history of mentalities, change still needed to be included. For Michel Vovelle, the history of mentalities can accommodate a greater movement in history by creating space for the mechanisms of 'change'. This is arrived at by way of the concept of collective imagination. Seeing how the collective imaginations shift is a relevant project for the historian.[14] In the case of development under the Franco regime, this included dechristianization, subversive mentalities, opposition to rigid political and cultural centralism, and attitudes regarding traditional family values, religion and consumption, as well as attitudes towards Europe. Robert Mandrou defines the history of mentalities as a way of interpreting the visions of the world. It has as its objective 'the restructuring of forms of behaviour, of expressions and silences which translate the conceptions of the world and collective sensibilities; representations and images, myths and values recognized by groups or by society as a whole, and which constitute the content of collective psychologies.'[15] The collective or group character converts mentalities into a form of social history. For Ernest Labrousse, the history of mentalities was, in its deepest sense, a history of resistances. Fernand Braudel even spoke, metaphorically, of a history of prisons in the long term. If they wanted to insinuate with these metaphors that they were dealing with the investigation of a mental structure and a collective world-vision that was imposed on their contemporaries without them knowing it, it is, on the other hand, necessary to highlight the fact that the history of mentalities also concerns itself with mental changes, asking when, why, and with what consequences, these take place. As a result, structure and change alike characterize the objects of investigation in the history of mentalities.

Social mobilization and change of mentalities

The years of the late Franco regime were, undoubtedly, a period of intense social mobilization: students, workers, regionalists, nationalists, as well as far from negligible sectors of the Catholic Church, formed their collective identities during this time. It was then that forms of joint action emerged which characterized these movements. Rafael Cruz and Manuel Pérez Ledesma highlight, in a collective study published a number of years ago, the idea that all social reality is one constructed by its subjects, who begin with the cultural tools on which they rely at all times.[16] The analysis of objective reality should therefore go hand in hand with the perceptions, visions and interpretations that these individuals have of it and that, together, form their mentality. Only in this way is it possible to understand the historical subjects' behaviour given that neither social discontent nor the existence of conflict leads necessarily and mechanically to collective action. Collective action, rather, is the result of a series of cultural codes by which social agents experience, define, and interpret social relations and mould their behaviour. Naturally, this is not about celebrating culture as the only motor of history, via mental representations or mentalities, but rather to give it the role that it is due in social history.

In speaking of a change in mentalities in the late Franco regime, it should be stressed that, independently of the speed with which change is undertaken, 'the new' never emerges alone: there is always a mixture or combination of new and old values or mentalities. The English anthropologist Peter Marris even speaks of the 'conservative impulse' in man and society.[17] Both rely on steady guidelines to interpret social events. The new is only admitted if it is not perceived as a threat and can be integrated into what is already familiar. In the transition from the old to the new – independently of how this process occurs – feelings of tension, anxiety, and insecurity emerge, almost automatically, to accompany the processes of change. A process of rapid change, such as that which took place in the late Franco regime, can be seen not only as a challenge, but also as a challenge with risks and threats. The most characteristic aspect tends to be a mixture of ambivalent feelings that result in ambiguous mentalities.

In an attempt to systematize the range of reactions in the face of social change and modernization, four basic reactions have been identified.[18] The first is a gradual adaptation to the new situation in which new symbols and elements of value are incorporated into the existing way of thinking. 'Continuity and change' or 'reform' are the terms used to reflect this form of change. For example, the gradual change of taste and the incorporation of new features in relation to consumption.

The second is a fundamental change of structure. What is crucial in this form of change is that certain elements are not only incorporated but that the whole value system, including mentality, is restructured. This is the case when, in the realm of politics, we speak of 'revolutions' or – in the mental – when an entire society is obliged to change ideologies (at least, seemingly), for example after a civil war.

The third form of reaction consists in offering a more or less open resistance to the pressures of change, defending traditional mentalities, which, almost unnoticed, grow in strength when questioned and threatened. To a certain degree, traditional attitudes and forms of behaviour are defended and stressed; what had been common practice and belief almost imperceptibly gains renewed presence and strength once questioned and threatened. For example, the autochthonous culture, the vernacular language, age-old customs and religious beliefs are emphasized if called into question. The fourth type of reaction – quite likely when dealing with an accelerated change – entails the dissolution of old networks of values and norms without any new way of thinking emerging as a substitute. Frequently, value vacuums emerge in which the lack of guidance can cause anomie-type reactions, such as withdrawal from the family circle, or even criminality, drug addiction and, in certain circumstances, protest. According to the classical thinking of Emile Durkheim, anomie is defined as a consequence of the breakdown of norms and the destruction of values, something very frequent in the case of dictatorships that violate the norms and values that reign in a society, thereby destroying the acceptance, on the part of the citizen, of the norms imposed by the dictatorship and thus undermining the latter's own stability. Spain in the later years of the Franco regime, and during the first phase of the Transition, is a good example of this type of behaviour. It is clear that this typology is not exhaustive and that, furthermore, none of the different forms of reaction cancels out the others. The world of mentalities and of the processes of change is characterized by an extraordinary complexity. In contrast to the traditional approach, based on an assumed bipolarity and linearity of these processes, there is an ever greater insistence today on their pluridimensional character, their ambivalence, and their reversibility.

Changes of structure and mentality in the late Franco regime

Social change in the second half of the Franco regime surpassed in speed, depth and extent what happened in any other European society: from demographic to economic and social change.[19] All of these structural mutations formed a close and dialectical relationship with cultural or mental changes, whereby the process of secularization would culminate in an 'outbreak of plurality' in the post-Franco era.[20] In only a decade and a half, Spain joined – at least in a number of ways – modernity. The process was, therefore, different from that in other Western industrial societies of the 1960s and 1970s. Within the Western world it was a question of attitudinal readjustments to permanent, deep-seated mentalities, whereas in Spain a true exchange of basic values took place. A good example is the extremely rapid secularization of Spanish society, which formally remained Catholic with its rites of baptism and marriage, but which in fact was no longer, to a great extent, what is called a 'practising Catholic' society. To a degree, during the late Franco regime a new historical era erupted – in the world of mentalities – which would reach its most decisive point during the post-Franco years. A striking aspect of the Spanish case is the level of acceptance with which a considerable part of the population received change. The 'other' Spain to a certain extent seemed to stop existing, and within some groups no efforts were spared to present Spain in a way that fitted in with the model of a 'modern' nation. Traditional opinion was not represented by a part of society, but rather by the Franco regime. The gap between the State and society widened more and more. And in the course of the struggle between the traditionalist regime and the opposing movements of innovation, any prejudice against, or resistance to, the modernization of the country was to a large extent worn down. Upon the death of the dictator, therefore, traditionalism was already substantially exhausted as a serious option.

The change in mentality, first minor and then more extended, emerged within society before the structural changes. This early evolution in mentalities explains the speed that characterized the whole process of modernization as this converged with structural, socio-economic, and, later, political changes. In this way, a spiral of interde-pendencies or structural and mental simultaneities emerged which in little less than a generation led to, in many aspects, 'another' society.

In one sector the change in mentalities seems to have emerged late. The resistance to change, and the need for a decisive impulse, charac-terized one of the areas that, historically speaking, is most associated with the onset of modernity: the area of business practices, which continued suffering – according to research done by Santiago García Echevarría – from deficient 'economic rationality', a lack of innova-tion, and a lack of long-term planning.[21] Despite the deep structural changes from the 1960s onwards and the renovation of its technical skills, the Spanish productive system continued suffering from low levels of competitiveness. García Echevarría compared it in international terms and concluded that due to an inadequate use of manpower, which in itself was cheaper, the Spanish economy lost one of its competitive advantages. The main cause stemmed from the Spanish businessman's system of values which did not allow for the process of formation that was necessary in order for pioneering companies to take off. The results of this comparative study showed that the Spanish businessman worried above all else about the administrative and technical adjustments that were necessary in order to reduce labour costs while displaying an excessive orientation towards the national market, a limited future outlook, little perception of opportunities, a low acceptance of risk, a lack of strategic and logistic capacity, and, in general, little capacity to integrate with 'the other' as a point of reference in order to see if his company was competitive in an open context.[22]

Where a collective conduct can most easily be identified in the 1960s is in the new consumerism, the Spanish having just emerged from a situation of extreme poverty. The absolute penury of the 1940s and the somewhat improved economy of the 1950s began to give rise to a ferocious materialism, the aim of which was to enjoy what had until then been unattainable for the majority of Spaniards. Not only did material consumption change but so did customs, the result of social mobility and the ever greater presence of elements from foreign cultures, especially the Anglo-Saxon. The accelerated change in the economic sector of the 1960s necessarily had repercussions for the structure of society. Although the relative differences in income of the different groups of the social pyramid did not diminish – they actually grew – it must be stressed that all the social layers registered a clear gain in their incomes, and that the change from agricultural work to industrial work or work in the service sector meant for millions of people a significant improvement in working conditions: regularized working hours, the right to annual holidays, protection against accidents and illness. Above all, the middle layers experienced a rapid expansion, due as much to the boom in the tertiary sector of the state (administration, education) as to the private bureaucracies (banks, insurance, the mass media). The acquisition of a flat or a vehicle of one's own – the Seat 600 became a symbol of the relative prosperity of a whole generation – as well as family holidays at the beach or in the country, are characteristic symptoms of the growing 'consumerism' of a society that no longer had to struggle for material survival.

Society, so different from that of the past, nevertheless continued to be fraught with contradictions within a political regime that was trying to make itself compatible with economic liberalization. One of these contradictions was between a relative 'modernity', which was quickly achieved in the economic sector, and the lack of basic liberties (freedom of association or organization, freedom of demonstration, of trade unions, elections, etc.). And it was exactly contradictions of this type, derived from 'partial' modernization (in one sector alone, and not as an overall process), which led to the political and social tensions that characterized the late Franco regime.[23] The modifications in the standard of living of the middle classes, the result of an extraordinary expansion, led them to appreciate much more clearly than before the gap between their material status and their cultural and political situation.

The economic transformation of the *desarrollo* was interconnected with the social and politico-cultural spheres. Massive emigration,[24] the growing numbers of consumer durables that changed the nature of housekeeping in Spanish homes, the capacity of consumption to change fundamental expectations, the flood of tourists with new customs,[25] and the arrival of means of mass communication, altered the social and cultural perspectives of the greater part of the Spanish population.

The enormous change in the macro economy was linked to a greater social mobility and to a collective change of mentality. Important sectors of society mobilized politically and socially, defying the regime, aiming to establish new rules for the working of trade unions, and fomenting political cultures from outside the regime that sought to supersede the cultural and social limits of the dictatorship. The consumer society was emerging. At the same time, there was a great, progressive emptying of the regime as far as ideas were concerned, which further increased the gap between society and the regime.

The evolution of dissident and subversive mentalities

In order to analyse the dissident and subversive mentalities of the late Franco regime, one must go back at least to the 1950s, or even earlier, to the 1940s. During these two decades, one can study the early evolution of the beliefs and behaviour of certain university and labour sectors which were to become extremely important later on. One ideological tendency within these groups was Christianity. The first post-Civil War generation, which was constituted mainly by the children of the victors, moved to an extent over to the losers' side partly out of religious conviction and partly because they became aware of the social injustice within Spain, which contradicted the moral exigencies of a faith committed to human freedom, equality, and fraternity. In an impressive study titled *Cristianos y marxistas contra Franco* (Christians and Marxists against Franco), Daniel F. Álvarez Espinosa describes how this youth became reconciled with the children of the defeated in the university and were shocked by the working and living conditions in the labour camps, the outlying city areas, and in the shanty towns where many rural immigrants lived.[26] This led them to commit themselves politically to the working class and to acquire a subversive conscience, which tended to embrace Marxism as the method of social analysis, and to collaborate with the labour movement. All of which posed a series of religious, philosophical, and ethical problems (such as how to reconcile their Christian faith with an atheist ideology), in dealing with their comrades-in-struggle in the fight against a repressive regime.[27]

One of the guiding influences in the theoretical debate that advanced this new Christian critique of the Church's identification with the dominant classes and their ideology was the Christian communist Alfonso Comín. It was the identification of the majority of the Catholic hierarchy with Franco's repressive regime that contributed decisively to the distancing of swathes of Spanish society from the Church, which was perceived as an ally of the dictatorship. One consequence of this alienation was the rapid secularization of Spanish society in the 1960s. A single fact illustrates the change in mentalities: in 1960, 91 per cent of Spanish youth declared themselves to be 'very Catholic' or 'practising', a percentage that fell by 30 points by 1975 and which would plunge even further afterwards. [28]

The change, by which university students from well-to-do backgrounds would join the ranks of the intellectual opposition, marked Spanish youth more deeply than their European contemporaries, and this can be seen as a product of the conditions imposed by the Franco dictatorship. To publicly ask for 'a greater participation from the people in the national task' – a demand contained in what is called *Testimonio de las generaciones ajenas a la guerra civil* (The Testimony of the post-Civil War Generations), from April 1957 – was, in the Spain of the time, an act of immeasurable consequences. The young student or professional did not only break the ties that united them with their family and social circles but also ran the risk of a sudden, and at times prolonged, interruption of his university studies as a result of time spent in prison or even in exile. [29] It was, therefore, not merely a 'clash of generations' that was taking place in the university from that point on, but rather a complete change in mentality. [30]

From February 1956, when the university students in Madrid confronted the government, the Franco regime began to lose control of the university. In the same way, some years later, the *Comisiones Obreras* (CC.OO.) (Workers' Commissions) trades unions would organize the workers in such a way as to undermine Falangist syndicalism from within. [31] Amongst university students and workers, who were joined by intellectuals and a far from negligible number of clergy, dissident groups were formed which in the late Franco regime can be characterized as movements of opposition. [32] The struggle of these groups for civil liberties and a *de jure* state has been impressively described in its different facets by Pere Ysàs in *Disidencia y subversión*. [33] It was these dissident and subversive mentalities which undermined, during the years of the economic boom, the foundations of the dictatorship, and which forced the Franco regime to react in a repressive manner. Pere Ysàs describes in detail the government's perception of subversive dissidence, thereby revealing the full scope and weight of anti-Francoism during the second half of the regime, in contrast to the widespread view of the opposition as ineffective and irrelevant.

What began in 1956 and 1957 in the Spanish universities as an isolated phenomenon spread rapidly throughout the 1960s: that is to say, the emergence of Marxism in all its variants, of existentialism, and of other ideological tendencies, all of which were from the left. Analytical philosophy, the teachings of Karl Marx, modern sociology, linguistics, symbolic logic, and socialist economics were some of the tendencies that made their way into the universities. Publications such as *Teorema*, *Argumentos*, *Sistema*, *Papers* or *Recerques*, amongst many others, illustrate this affirmation.[34] The influence of Marxism on students must be stressed. Progressive Christianity, which in the 1960s still played a very prominent role, gave way to a growing interest in psychoanalysis and Marxist thinking. Although this Marxism was not always very profound or analytical, it did represent the dominant culture of the left-wing democratic opposition. The mentality of many students can be characterized at this point as secularized and hedonistic. Although differences in class and region continued to exist, the generalized tendency was directed towards forms of 'modern' behaviour in all aspects of life, religion, sexual conduct, reproductive behaviour, and with regards to social inequality, professional success, and in relation to each individual's own basic goals. Modernization was also reflected in the evolution of degrees: law degrees declined notably whereas those in business administration and economics increased. Furthermore, in 1966, 30 per cent of the students were already women.[35] These new generations did not accept uncritically rules laid down by the regime, the Catholic church, or parents. University strikes and demonstrations were the order of the day and little by little the fear of State repression disappeared. In a sense, it can be argued that the Francoist victory of 1939 was, from an ideological point of view, rather ephemeral. In the 1960s Spanish society was already more politicized, urbanized, and secularized than ever before, in stark contrast to the aspirations of the victorious coalition in the Civil War. This was the result of the majority of the changes of the authoritarian–conservative modernization of the 1960s and an unintentional consequence. Massive industrialization, for example, led to an enormous growth in the number of industrial workers and an increase in the number of clandestine organizations of opposition, whose methods (due to the system of labour repression) were much more radical, direct, and violent than the moderate strategies of trade unions in the industrialized democracies of the West. The fundamental aim of the *desarrollista* (development) model, to ensure the social and political stability of the regime, was not achieved. On the contrary, in the 1960s, protests increased to such a degree that repression of labour had to be intensified.

As for the political behaviour of the students, what united them from the mid-1960s onwards – regardless of their many differences, including ideological ones – was the distinction between 'us' (the students, the people) and 'them' (the authorities, the regime). This dichotomy would continue to be a cause for relative student unity as long as the regime existed, although the student movement naturally also diversified, developing different strategies and interests.

Still, it was not the students alone who, in their outlook and behaviour, were moving farther and farther away from the regime. Even in the Falangist youth movement, the *Frente de Juventudes* (The Youth Front), the younger members did not fit the out-moded and ideological profile of the organization very well. Reports about the youth movement in 1958 already revealed a rather worrying situation for the regime and for the youth organization itself as they spoke of a crisis of moral values, of apathy, of desertion, of a lack of austerity and of adherence to the 'principles', of a very low assessment of the Falange itself, which was seen as not having any influence whatsoever, including a general mistrust of its high-ranking members. In other words, at the heart of the *Frente de Juventudes* there was great deal of concern about the future.[36]

Without a doubt, therefore, towards the end of the Franco regime much of Spanish society had adopted a critical attitude towards the regime. Within certain social sectors, this critical conscience had emerged over the previous decades. Jordi Gracia highlights, in his study on the *Silent Resistance* that, in the case of intellectuals, the opposition to the Franco regime began as a result of an exercise in linguistic re-education which was tentatively pursued in a number of cultural magazines.[37] He writes about the unsung heroes within Spain, the non-exiles, about the subsistence of a liberal tradition in dark times. He reveals the subtlety of certain intellectuals in their fight against the Francoist mindset and the gradual change of mentalities in intellectual circles. Gracias's doctoral thesis dealt with *El despertar de una conciencia crítica bajo el franquismo* (The Awakening of a Critical Conscience under the Franco Regime), in which he discovered the first openings in literary magazines, especially in *Escorial*, edited by Pedro Laín Entralgo, who was interested in recovering the Generation of 1898 and in this way maintaining contact with the liberal tradition while the dictatorship was in full swing. Despite the difficulties in evaluating and especially in quantifying this critical culture, it is possible to say – based on the FOESSA reports which were extremely limited because they were not permitted to ask people directly about political issues[38] – that in Spanish society in general conservative values continued to dominate and that there was concern especially when circumstances seemed to alter the existing situation. According to Sevillano Calero, conformity was especially widespread amongst the 'lower classes, the small provincial bourgeoisie'.[39] It is a striking fact that in 1966, when the German Minister of Foreign Affairs Gerhard Schröder visited Spain, his Spanish counterpart José María Castiella remarked in relation to the behaviour of Spanish workers: 'They only want work, security and peace.'[40]

On the other hand, in the reports prepared by the German ambassador in Madrid, Helmut Allardt, the change that was taking place in Spain in the mid-1960s was very evident. In one report sent to Bonn in October 1966, he pointed out that 'the freedom of assembly and of association, the freedom of press and of conscience remain today, despite advances that are impossible to ignore, highly problematic concepts, but every day it becomes more and more difficult to impose restrictions on rights and freedoms.'[41] In his report, he spoke of the strikes which had become an everyday socio-economic reality, of the space available to intellectuals to express non-conformist ideas, of the illegal union organizations, of the time of change that the country was living through:

> The winds of freedom coming from Europe have crossed the Pyrenees some time ago, the image of the 'proud Spaniard' is dissolving, and the Spanish are learning now about the pride of being European. The Spain of today can no longer be painted in black and white; it is neither a petrified dictatorship of a pauperised people, nor is it a prosperous nation sustained by ideas of liberty. It is a country in transition, a country that is fighting against the weight of its past, but which at the same time has recognized its aim, Europe. The evolution of Spain is advancing step by step. It is to be expected that in this process, deficiencies, inconveniences, and injustices cannot always be avoided. The establishment of a democracy also encounters resistance in the human factor.[42]

According to the German ambassador, four phenomena had conditioned the evolution of the regime: a process of de-ideologization of the dictatorship, with military officers and veterans of the regime being replaced by European-inclined technocrats; the economic liberalization that was launched at the end of the 1950s; the coming of age of a new generation of Spaniards who for the most part had not (consciously) lived through the Civil War; and finally, the impact of the Second Vatican Council, which had an evident influence on priests, on young believers and on lay organizations that championed social progress and political accountability, while rejecting the identification of Church and State. To a certain degree, Allardt summarized in his report the structural conditions of politics, economy, society, the Church and international relations which shaped the change in mentalities during the late Franco regime.

Despite the regime, in the 1960s and 1970s a culture in defence of the basic values of democracy would emerge from among people that organized trade unions and neighbourhood movements, that studied at the university, or who mobilized in their place of work: this constituted a great collective experience for growing sectors of the population. The opposition groups – from within Spain and abroad – were varied and their aims were not always the same. But the anti-Francoist struggles forged something like a minimal democratic consensus which was achieved by 1962 in the meeting at Munich, where exiled parties met with those of the interior in the heart of the European Movement – with the exception, that is, of the Communists. The different organizations quickly agreed on certain principles of democratic political coexistence, demanding representative institutions for Spain, guarantees for individual rights, the recognition of the personalities of the different regional communities, the exercise of the freedom of association and the right to organize political parties. They also demanded the 'setting up of authentically representative and democratic institutions that guarantee that the Government be based on the consent of the governed', a clever formula that avoided speaking of a republic or monarchy.[43] Although transferring this political programme to the totality of the opposition groups in Spain could not be achieved immediately, it was a programme whose democratic principles made inroads into the different opposition groups, including the Communists. It is also worth mentioning the anti-Francoist mobilization of Spanish emigrants in different European countries. In the German case, Carlos Sanz Díaz has stressed that, far from the image of a demobilized and passive emigrant community, the initiatives undertaken by the workers reveal an unquestionable activism on the part of a significant sector of the emigrant community.[44] Spanish political mobilizations – as much amongst the emigrant community as within Spain – should not be measured merely in numerical terms, but should also be seen in terms of the extent to which they undermined the pretension of the Franco regime to maintain complete political control over Spanish workers. Finally, the varied experience of mobilization and associationism also offered a means of political and democratic apprenticeship during the latter years of the Franco dictatorship.

In the 1960s, widespread rejection of the dictatorship was under way. Although it was probably limited to a minority, and fear of repression was ever-present, it none the less laid the foundation for political change, forcing regime reformists to pact with the opposition after 1975. This is an issue which has already been the object of research, but it is still worthy of scrutiny as it may well shed new light on the relationship between the changes in attitude of the late Franco regime and the advent of a democratic culture during the Transition.

Notes

1. See J.M. Maravall, *Dictatorship and Political Dissent: Workers and Students in Franco's Spain* (London, 1978); R. Mesa Garrido, *Jaraneros y alborotadores. Documentos sobre los sucesos estudiantiles de febrero de 1956 en la Universidad Complutense de Madrid* (Madrid, 1982); P. Lizcano, *La Generación del 56. La Universidad Contra Franco* (Barcelona, 1989).
2. A. Longhurst, 'Culture and development: the impact of 1960s "desarrollismo" ', in B. Jordan and R. Morgan-Tamosaunas, eds, *Contemporary Spanish Cultural Studies* (London, 2000), pp. 17–28.
3. F. López-Castro, 'La redefinición del pueblo. Entorno sociológico del desarrollo local en la España meridional', in F. López-Casero, W.L. Bernecker, and P. Waldmann, eds, *El precio de la modernización. Formas y retos del cambio de valores en la España de hoy* (Frankfurt am Main, 1994), pp. 327–56; J. Maestre Alfonso, *Modernización y cambio en la España rural* (Madrid, 1975).
4. J.L. Abellán, *La industria cultural en España* (Barcelona, 1973); J. Fontana, ed., *España bajo el franquismo* (Barcelona, 1986); R. Navarro Sandalinas, *La enseñanza primaria durante el franquismo, 1936–1975* (Barcelona, 1990); A. Mayordomo Pérez, ed., *Estudios sobre la política educativa durante el franquismo* (Valencia, 1999).
5. J.J. Carreras Ares, M.A. Ruiz Carnicer, eds, *La Universidad española bajo el régimen de Franco (1935–1975)* (Zaragoza, 1991); R. Montoro Romero, *La Universidad en la España de Franco (1939–1970). (Un análisis sociológico)* (Madrid, 1981).
6. See in this regard, C. Lisón Tolosana, *Belmonte de los Caballeros. A Sociological Study of a Spanish Town* (Oxford, 1966); E. Luque Baena, *Estudio antropológico de un pueblo del Sur* (Madrid, 1974); V. Pérez Díaz, *Estructura social del Campo y éxodo rural. Estudio de un pueblo de Castilla* (Madrid, 1972); J.B. Aceves, *Cambio social en un pueblo de España* (Barcelona, 1973); R.A. Barret, *Benaberre. The Modernization of a Spanish Village* (New York, 1974).
7. See *Fundación FOESSA: Estudios sociológicos sobre la situación social de España 1975* (Madrid, 1976), p. 969.
8. E.M. Rogers, *Diffusion of Innovations* (New York, 1962).
9. This is the main thesis of an empirical study in social anthropology by F. López-Casero, 'Die Generation des Umbruchs. Veränderung der Lebens – und Produktionsformen in einer spanischen "Agrarstadt" ', in P. Waldmann et al., *Die geheime Dynamik autoritärer Diktaturen, Vier Studien über sozialen Wandel in der Franco-Ära* (München, 1982), pp. 287–401. What follows is based on this study.

10. See A. Marwick, *War and Social Change in the Twentieth Century* (London, 1974).
11. See E. Hernández Sandoica, *Tendencias historiográficas actuales. Escribir historia hoy* (Madrid, 2004), pp. 289–322.
12. Quoted in E. Hernández Sandoica, *Tendencias*, p. 291.
13. P. Ariès, *Histoire des populations françaises et de leurs attitudes devant la vie depuis le XVIII siècle* (Paris, 1948), p. 15, quoted in E. Hernández Sandoica, *Tendencias*, p. 295.
14. See E. Hernández Sandoica, *Tendencias*, p. 300.
15. R. Mandrou, 'L'histoire des mentalités', in *Encyclopedia Universalis*, Vol. VIII (Paris, 1968), pp. 436–8.
16. R. Cruz, M. Pérez Ledesma, eds, *Cultura y movilización en la España contemporánea* (Madrid, 1997).
17. P. Marris, *Loss and Change* (London, 1974).
18. F. López-Casero and P. Waldmann, 'Introducción: reflexiones comparativas sobre el proceso de modernización en España', in F. López-Casero, W.L. Bernecker, and P. Waldmann, eds, *El precio de la modernización*, pp. 15–8.
19. See F. López-Casero and P. Waldmann, 'Introducción: reflexiones comparativas', in F. López-Casero, W.L. Bernecker, and P. Waldmann, eds, *El precio de la modernización*, pp. 29–40.
20. R. López Pintor and R. Buceta, *Los españoles de los años 70: Una versión sociológica* (Madrid, 1975); R. López Pintor, *La opinión pública española del franquismo a la democracia* (Madrid, 1982).
21. S. García Echevarría, *El reto empresarial español* (Madrid, 1990).
22. S. García Echevarría, 'Actitudes y comportamientos empresariales', in F. López-Casero, W.L. Bernecker, and P. Waldmann, eds, *El precio de la modernización*, pp. 207–42.
23. For more detail on this question, see W.L. Bernecker, 'El debate sobre el régimen franquista. ¿Fascismo, autoritarismo, dictadura de modernización?' in M. Albert, ed., *Vencer no es convencer. Literatura e ideología del fascismo español* (Frankfurt am Main, 1998), pp. 29–49.
24. As a case study, see C. Sanz Díaz, *España y la República Federal de Alemania (1949–1966). Política, economía y emigración, Entre la Guerra Fría y la distensión*. Unpublished Doctoral Thesis (Complutense University of Madrid, 2004–2005), especially pp. 895–1069.
25. M. Marchena Gómez, *Territorio y turismo en Andalucía* (Sevilla, 1987).
26. D.F. Alvarez Espinosa, *Cristianos y marxistas contra Franco* (Cádiz, 2003).
27. See R. Díaz Salazar, *Nuevo socialismo y cristianos de izquierda* (Madrid, 2001); F. Montero, 'Los intelectuales católicos, del colaboracionismo al antifranquismo, 1951–1969', in *Historia del Presente* 5 (2005), pp. 41–68.
28. J.J. Tamayo, *Adiós a la cristiandad. La iglesia católica española en la democracia* (Barcelona, 2003).
29. J.M. Colomer i Calsina, *Els estudiants de Barcelona sota el franquisme* (Barcelona, 1978); J. Gracia, *Estado y Cultura. El despertar de una conciencia crítica bajo el franquismo (1940–1962)* (Toulouse, 1996); J. Alvarez Cobelas, *Envenenados de cuerpo y alma. La oposición universitaria al franquismo en Madrid (1939–1979)* (Madrid, 2004).
30. H. Heine, 'La contribución de la "Nueva Izquierda" al resurgir de la democracia española, 1957–1976', in J. Fontana, ed., *España bajo el franquismo*, p. 144.

31. S. Balfour, *Dictatorship, Workers, and the City: Labour in Greater Barcelona since 1939* (Oxford, 1989); C. Molinero and P. Ysàs, *Productores disciplinados y minorías subversivas. Clase obrera y conflictividad laboral en la España franquista* (Madrid, 1998); J.A. Gómez Roda, *Comisiones obreras y represión franquista* (Valencia, 2004).

32. S. Mangini, *Rojos y rebeldes. La cultura de la disidencia durante el franquismo* (Barcelona, 1987); R. Pereda, *Contra Franco 1968–1978* (Barcelona, 2003); J. Alfaya, *Crónica de los años perdidos. La España del tardofranquismo* (Madrid, 2003); N. Sartorious and J. Alfaya, *La memoria insumisa. Sobre la dictadura de Franco* (Madrid, 1999).

33. P. Ysàs, *Disidencia y subversión. La lucha del franquismo por su supervivencia (1960–1975)* (Madrid, 2004).

34. S. Giner, 'Libertad y poder político en la Universidad española: El movimiento democrático bajo el franquismo', in *Sistema* 24/25 (1978), pp. 19–58.

35. See D. Goetze and C. Solé, *El dificultoso camino de la emancipación femenina en España*, in F. López-Casero et al., eds, *El precio de la modernización. Formas y retos del cambio de valores en la España de hoy* (Frankfurt am Main, 1994), pp. 113–48.

36. J. Sáez Marín, *El Frente de juventudes. Política de juventud en la España de la posguerra (1937–1960)* (Madrid, 1988). See also the summary in J. Gracia and M.A. Ruiz Carnicer, *La España de Franco (1939–1975). Cultura y vida cotidiana* (Madrid, 2001), p. 286 ff.

37. J. Gracia, *La resistencia silenciosa. Fascismo y cultura en España* (Barcelona, 2004).

38. Fundación FOESSA, *Informe sociológico sobre la situación social de España 1966* (Madrid, 1966); FOESSA, *Informe sociológico sobre la situación social de España 1970* (Madrid, 1970); FOESSA, *Informe sociológico sobre la situación social de España 1975* (Madrid, 1977). On the same theme, see G. Hermet, 'Espagne: Changement de la Société, Modernisation autoritaire et Démocratie octroyée', in *Revue française de science politique*, Vol. 27, no. 4/5 (1977), p. 582 ff.

39. F. Sevillano Calero, *Ecos de papel. La opinión de los españoles en la época de Franco* (Madrid, 2000), p. 206.

40. Quoted in C. Sanz Díaz, *España y la República Federal de Alemania (1949–1966)*, p. 426.

41. Quoted in C. Sanz Díaz, *España y la República Federal de Alemania (1949–1966)*, p. 426.

42. Quoted in C. Sanz Díaz, *España y la República Federal de Alemania (1949–1966)*, p. 427.

43. See S. Juliá, 'Proyectos de transición en la oposición antifranquista', in W.L. Bernecker, ed., *De la Guerra Civil a la Transición: Memoria histórica, cambio de valores y conciencia colectiva* (Augsburg s.a., 1997), pp. 9–37.

44. C. Sanz Díaz, *emigración española y movilización antifranquista en Alemania en los años sesenta* (Madrid, 2005) (Work Document 4/2005 from the Fundación Primero de Mayo).

5
How 'Different' Was Spain?
The Later Franco Regime in
International Context

Tom Buchanan

In April 1970 Amnesty International launched a campaign aimed directly at holidaymakers departing for Spain. Posters were displayed near airports in Britain that showed an imprisoned face behind bars against a background of sand and blue skies. The slogan read: 'Have a good time – but remember, Amnesty for Spain's political prisoners'.[1] Amnesty's interest in Spain at this time is understandable given that it currently recognised some 250 Spanish 'prisoners of conscience': more prisoners than in any other country in the Western world and a caseload equivalent in size to that for the Soviet Union.[2] While it is unlikely that Amnesty's intervention had any significant impact on the increasing numbers of foreign tourists flocking to Spanish beaches and resorts (34 million by 1973), this episode does capture the interconnection between, on the one hand, Spain's increasing prosperity and economic development and, on the other, the new opportunities that were thereby created for mobilising international criticism of the Franco regime. This was but one of many examples of the tarnished modernity which characterised the regime's international standing in its latter years.

Although the current chapter is not specifically concerned with international opposition, it is essential to start with this point as the problem of the regime cannot be separated out from any comparative analysis of Spain's development during the period between 1960 and 1975. Some of the more positive recent interpretations of the later Franco regime tend to ignore this. For instance, John Gillingham, a leading historian of European integration has recently written: 'Psst! Franco was not all that bad... [he] set his nation on a long, looping course of accommodation with the West after 1945'. The economic liberalisation of the later 1950s, he adds, turned Spain into a 'growth dynamo during the last fifteen years of Franco's reign'.[3] Spain's economic performance was, indeed, impressive during these years. The rate of growth (6.9 per cent of GDP per annum in 1960–1975) was one of the highest in the world and even stronger in certain sectors of industry, as well as in services and tourism. Even so, Gillingham's 'looping' accommodation with Western Europe represented an abandonment of the regime's autarkic dreams of the 1940s and 1950s in exchange for an unfulfilled quest for European integration – a quest that was unattainable so long as Franco remained in power. Political and economic reform cannot therefore be disarticulated, as they were two sides of the same coin. Moreover, Gillingham's use of the term 'reign' reminds us that this period was, inevitably, overshadowed by the question of whether – and in what form – the regime could survive the death of its increasingly frail founder.

Political perspectives

Relations between Franco's Spain and the rest of Western Europe were 'normalised' relatively quickly after the initial frost of the later 1940s. Full diplomatic relations had been re-established at a bi-lateral level by the early 1950s, and Spain was progressively admitted into a range of international organisations such as the United Nations (1955), the International Monetary Fund, and the Organisation for European Economic Cooperation (both in 1958). Although Spain was excluded from NATO, the 1953 Pact of Madrid, which allowed the United States to establish military bases within Span, meant that it played a de facto role in the defence of 'the West'. Such normalisation did not mean, however, that relations could ever be wholly normal, as the regime not only failed to escape from its own history, but also retained the power to shock and scandalise international opinion. Although the blanket repression of the Civil War and its immediate aftermath was long gone, the regime's image continued to be sullied by episodes such as the execution of the underground Communist leader Julián Grimau in 1963, the Burgos trials of Basque separatists (including two priests) in 1970, the imposition of 'states of emergency' in 1968–70, and the trial of the 'Carabanchel Ten' trade union leaders in 1973. As late as September 1975 the execution of five terrorists sparked Europe-wide protests. Indeed, hundreds of EEC officials and two Commissioners demonstrated outside the Berlaymont building in Brussels, calling for the suspension of trade talks with Spain. [4] The regime's behaviour made it impossible, therefore, for sympathetic European politicians of the centre-right to integrate Spain more closely with 'the West', and served to replenish and sustain an international opposition that was otherwise flagging. (Radicals in the 1960s tended to be far more interested in Vietnam and Latin America than Spain, a cause which had come to seem rather passé.)

The essential 'abnormality' of the Franco regime aside, however, to what extent was there political, social, and economic convergence between Spain and Western Europe during this period? Clearly, one must be wary of drawing simplistic parallels. For instance, just because Franco's Spain and de Gaulle's Fifth Republic both witnessed student unrest, heavy-handed policing and state control of broadcast media does not mean that there was no difference between them. The Fifth Republic might be derided by its opponents as a 'permanent coup d'état', but there were regular elections, free trade unions, a free press, a vibrant intellectual life, and the tangible presence of a legal Communist Party. None of these applied to Spain, which despite the evolution of the regime and the steady marginalisation of its Falangist element, was still at heart a dictatorship which derived its legitimacy from the military rebellion of 18 July 1936. At the same time, however, during the first half of the 1960s the regime did appear to set a political course towards greater democracy. During this period the dictatorship's image was softened, a rhetoric of modernisation and even of 'democratisation' was adopted, and limited political reforms introduced. While many of these reforms were subsequently reversed in the later 1960s, it is important not to draw too sharp a division between Spain and a 'democratic' Western Europe which, as we shall see, often left much to be desired.

Between 1960 and 1974, Franco's Spain sat comfortably within a southern Europe that consisted of Salazar's Portugal and the Greek Colonels' Junta (1967–74): conversely, the collapse of both of these authoritarian regimes in 1974 greatly reduced the Spanish dictatorship's own prospects of survival. However, some wider political comparisons can also be drawn. It is easy to forget that throughout this period 'democratic' Europe was still small, constricted and in many respects under threat. In effect, it did not extend beyond Scandinavia, the original EEC 'Six', the UK, Ireland, Austria and Switzerland. The nature of Europe's post-war 'democratic age' has been reassessed in some important recent articles by Martin Conway[5] in which he has argued that until the early 1970s West European democracy was far more concerned with balancing social and economic interests than with extending rights and political participation (be it by women, young people or the working class). Moreover, the position of democratic government remained perilous in many West European countries. France, for instance, experienced profound domestic instability in 1958, during the latter stages of the Algerian conflict (1960–62), and again during the strikes and street protests of 1968. Likewise, Italian democracy was threatened from both the extreme Left and Right, and its future was regularly in question as late as the mid-1970s. (Indeed, the first edition of Paul Preston's *The Coming of the Spanish Civil War* in 1978 drew overt parallels between the overthrow of Allende's government in Chile in 1973, contemporary Italy and the Spanish Second Republic.) West German democracy also experienced a prolonged – and ultimately beneficial – examination of its political values in the decade after 1966. Therefore, while it would be fatuous to argue that there was no distinction between Franco's Spain and 'democratic' Europe, it should be noted that for much of the later Franco period the benefits and resilience of West European democracy were far less evident than hindsight might allow.

However, these strictures apply less forcefully for the 1970s. Indeed, it was precisely in the early 1970s that, in political terms, the gulf between Franco's Spain and democratic Western Europe became unbridgeable. For, just as the short-lived and largely cosmetic reforms of the mid-1960s were being abandoned in Spain, elsewhere in Western Europe the student and working class unrest of the later 1960s precipitated a very significant tranche of political and social reforms. For instance, following de Gaulle's resignation in 1969, Jacques Chaban-Delmas (Prime Minister, 1969–72) called for a 'New Society' that would be 'prosperous, young, generous and liberated'. Both he and Valéry Giscard d'Estaing during the early stages of his presidency (1974–81) appreciated the need for a limited reform and liberalisation of the French state. In Italy, during the same period, governments of the centre-right conceded a Labour Charter, the devolution of power to the regions, and a new right for citizens to call a referendum. In West Germany Willy Brandt took office as Chancellor in 1969 pledging that his new government was not 'the end of our democracy: we are only just beginning'.[6] Although his period in office was dominated by his *Ostpolitik*, it was also marked by domestic reform and a political opening to the young. Across Western Europe, moreover, in the early 1970s there was a spate of social reforms in the realm of divorce, birth control and abortion, akin to those already introduced in Britain in the later 1960s.

In addition to the widespread extension of political and social rights, there was also a greater sense of cohesion and common identity within 'democratic' Europe. In particular, the emergence of an internationally recognised language of human rights provided a means of regulating Western Europe's relations with non-democratic regimes and set standards of behaviour for those states which sought closer economic integration. Institutions such as the Council of Europe, the European

Court of Justice and the European Parliament all played a significant role in this regard, but one should also note the rise of trans-national pressure groups such as Amnesty International. The case of Amnesty, which was founded in 1961, is particularly significant as its development owed much to long-term concern over the human rights abuses of the Franco regime.[7] Therefore, the period between 1960 and 1975 was one in which the Franco regime was groping, albeit in an indecisive and half-hearted way, towards modernity. However, this was also a crucial period in the modern history of Western Europe, in which the norms of West European democracy were being defined and consolidated. By 1974–75 a Western Europe hard hit by economic recession but still far more confident in its political and social structures confronted the crisis of the south European dictatorships. If there was to be a process of 'transition' to democracy in Spain, Portugal and Greece, which was by no means apparent to many contemporaries, the benchmarks for democratic government had been set during the late 1960s and early 1970s.

Social, economic, and cultural perspectives

Spain should also be considered in relation to pan-European social, economic, and cultural trends. The central question is this: in what ways did Spain experience 'the 1960s'? As with the concept of democracy, the '1960s' is also one that historians have stretched and debated. Indeed, recent work has increasingly tended to detach the '1960s' from their temporal moorings altogether. Arthur Marwick, for instance, has defined the 1960s as a period of 'cultural revolution' that lasted from 1958 to 1974, while Martin Conway (referring to social legislation) has pointed out that 'much of that which we think happened in the 1960s in fact occurred in the 1970s'.[8] While there were significant differences between states (for instance, in terms of attitudes to censorship and permissive legislation) there is now broad agreement on the central importance of 'the 1960s' (however, we choose to define them chronologically) as the watershed in the social and cultural development of post-war Europe. Spain could not be immune from the forces at work in 'the 1960s', although the Franco regime was incapable of responding to them with the 'measured judgement' that Marwick has attributed to the governments of Britain, France, and Italy. As Rees and Grugel have argued, the Franco regime perceived the challenges of the 1960s through the prism of the 1930s and responded accordingly. As a result, these challenges intensified into a 'cycle of protest and repression'.[9]

In many respects, therefore, the Spanish experience between 1960 and 1975 was not atypical. The argument developed below will be that during this period Spain was experiencing (albeit in an idiosyncratic manner) trends which were common across contemporary Europe. For instance, many of the symptoms of the breakthrough to modern industrial capitalism that were evident in France and Italy from a slightly earlier date were also discernible in Spain (such as rural depopulation, rapid and often unplanned urbanisation, and the emergence of a consumer society). Likewise, Spain also experienced the upsurge of new forms of protest and social movement amongst workers, students, and other groups that was so characteristic of Europe in the late 1960s and early 1970s. In August 1968 the veteran journalist William Forrest commented *apropos* the revival of Basque separatism that 'In a year that has seen demonstrations of rampant nationalism by Welsh and Scots, Czechs and Slovaks, Ukrainians, Flemings and Bretons, it would have been too much to expect the Basques to lie doggo...'[10] In many respects, therefore, Eric Hobsbawm's comment that Franco's victory in the Civil War 'merely kept Spain...isolated from the rest of world history for another thirty years'[11] does not accord with the experience of the latter years of the regime.

I will begin with a brief comparative review of Spain's social and economic development, and then examine five specific areas; student unrest, working class unrest, religion, gender relations, and freedom of expression.

The regime's model for economic development between 1959 and 1975 was crude but effective.[12] The introduction of substantial, if hardly comprehensive, trade liberalisation in 1959 began to reintegrate Spain into the world economy. However, the Spanish state remained interventionist, and a series of economic Development Plans were put into effect after 1964. To a considerable degree, Spain's economic success rested on three significant factors largely beyond the government's control. First, there was a plentiful supply of cheap labour as many rural workers abandoned the countryside in search of a better life in the industrial cities. Secondly, there were increasing levels of foreign investment, principally from the United States. Finally, there was the unanticipated bonanza of mass tourism, which the state did its best to encourage. Like the rest of Western Europe, Spain also benefited from cheap energy, although Spain was becoming dangerously – if not abnormally – reliant on imported oil. By 1974, 67.8 per cent of Spain's energy needs were met by oil, while in Italy and France the figure was 75 and 76 per cent respectively. For all of the rapid growth in industrial sectors such as chemicals, shipbuilding and automobiles, in many respects the Spanish economy trailed behind that of the advanced industrial world. Levels of both productivity and research and development lagged far behind those of Spain's competitors. For instance, a 1971 report found that Spain was spending on average 0.27 per cent of GNP on R&D, compared with between 2 and 4 per cent in other OECD states. [13] By the early 1970s Spain was, in turn, being undercut by the emerging economies of the Far East, and even Spain's pre-eminence as a tourist destination was being challenged by the rise of new resorts in Portugal, Yugoslavia and elsewhere in the Mediterranean. As Spain reeled under the impact of the October 1973 oil shocks and entered a decade-long period of economic gloom, it became pertinent to ask whether the Spanish 'miracle' of the 1960s had come about more by luck than judgement.

Meanwhile, Spanish society was rapidly transformed by the greater prosperity and social mobility of the 1960s. [14] Per capita income doubled in Spain between 1963 and 1971, although other European states experienced similar growth from a higher base line. One of the most obvious expressions of this advance was the great increase in material possessions. Whereas in 1961 there were 60 telephones, 9 TV sets and 12 cars per 1000 Spaniards, by 1971 these figures had risen to 151, 132 and 71, and by 1975 had reached 195, 260 and 111 respectively. Spain was catching up with other European states: for instance, in 1971 the figures for telephone, TV, and car ownership in France were 227, 185 and 245 per 1000, and, in Britain, 298, 289 and 213. Spain was also catching up in ownership of such transformative household amenities as refrigerators and washing machines. In 1960 only 4 per cent of Spanish households owned a fridge and 19 per cent a washing machine: by 1971 this had risen to 66 and 52 per cent. (In 1972, by comparison, 85 per cent of French households owned a refrigerator.) Another sign of Spain's growing prosperity was the declining proportion of the household budget spent on food. This fell from 58 per cent in 1958 to 40 per cent in 1970, compared with 35 per cent in Italy, 25 per cent in France and 23 per cent in the UK. Even more telling within Spain was the significant shift away from expenditure on bread and cereals to meat.

However, Spain's new prosperity was spread unevenly across the country's regions, and substantial poverty remained (especially in rural areas and in urban shanty towns). Nationally 34 per cent of households still did not have running water by 1968, and in some regions this rose to as many as 80 per cent. Unemployment was kept in check by large-scale migration within Europe, which also provided valuable remittances of foreign currency. Officially 2.34 million Spaniards went abroad in search of work between 1960 and 1973, half of them to France.[15] Spanish workers were also forced to work far harder than those in EEC states. In 1969, for example, the average working week in Spanish industry was 55 hours, compared with a European average of 44 (and for half the average European wage). In 1970 it took a German worker 12 minutes to earn enough to buy half a dozen eggs, an Italian worker 22 minutes, and a Spanish worker 31 minutes.[16] By 1974 some 90 per cent of German employees in commerce and industry worked a 40-hour week, fuelling the new leisure industries so evident on the beaches of Spain.

During the 1960s Spanish students, still drawn principally from the social elite, became a significant oppositional force. Parallels with unrest in the campuses of Paris, Berlin and Milan were self-evident, but this was no mere copycat agitation. Although protest within the Spanish universities was inflamed by the events of May 1968 in Paris, students had been confronting the regime intermittently since the 1950s. Even so, the Spanish unrest of the 1960s had similar roots to that elsewhere in Western Europe, notably the rapid expansion of a rather technocratic higher education, and the radicalising impact of events in Vietnam and the Third World. However, the Spanish student movement was inevitably far more focused on the immediate problems posed by the dictatorship – not least the struggle to establish autonomous student organisations. There was less of the anti-materialism, the sheer joy in free expression and the rejection of all conventional hierarchy that one finds in France and Italy. However, the Spanish unrest was, if anything, even more troubling to the authorities as it demonstrated that the regime had lost control over the next generation of the administrative class. The students' demands for basic freedoms were clearly incompatible with the interests of the regime. There is, therefore, only limited similarity between the Spanish student movement and that in some East European states, such as Czechoslovakia and Yugoslavia, which acted as an avant-garde for cautiously reforming regimes. For instance, in Yugoslavia the students were not protesting against Tito, but, rather, demanding more and purer socialism – with slogans such as 'Down with the Princes of Socialism' and 'More schools, fewer automobiles!'[17] This allowed Tito to reach out to the students and call on them to help him in a manner that was impossible for any representative of the Franco regime.

The Spanish labour unrest of this period, likewise, inevitably had a political character. What was at issue was not only the promotion of working class interests, but also the very right of independent organ-isation. A basic framework for collective bargaining had been conceded in 1959, but all workers' organisations apart from the regime's own

Sindicatos were banned. In practice, industrial relations continued to be framed by severe legal restrictions and by the state's ready recourse to violence. A group of British miners who secretly visited Asturias during the coalfield strike of April/May 1962 found themselves in a virtual war zone, facing armed patrols and military tribunals. One commented that 'We had the feeling of being in the midst of a mighty Resistance movement.'[18] If one compares Spanish and Italian industrial relations, however, the starting point in the early 1960s is not too dissimilar. In Italy, unions had been severely weakened during the 1950s and excluded from many factories. Yet this was followed by an upsurge in labour militancy after 1962, culminating in the 'hot autumn' of 1969, which brought not only improved pay and conditions but also rights to trade union recognition under the 1970 Labour Charter. In France, too, the unions recovered from the torpor of the early years of the Fifth Republic, and were able to parlay the largely spontaneous factory occupations of May 1968 into substantial pay increases from a shaken government. By the later 1960s the French unions, notably the Catholic CFDT, were turning with great enthusiasm to ideas of workers' control (autogestion). In Spain, conversely, from 1967 onwards the unofficial 'Workers' Commissions' (CC.OO.) were subjected to heavy repression and driven underground. This was a response to the CC.OO.'s increasing influence within the *Sindicatos* and, in particular, the remarkable success of militant shop stewards in the 1966 union elections. On the surface, at least, by the early 1970s, Spanish industrial relations looked extremely atypical outside of the fellow dictatorships of southern Europe. However, it should be noted that the CC.OO., although still illegal, re-emerged strongly during the intense wave of industrial militancy that marked the final two years of Franco's life.

With regard to religion, it is again evident that the experiences of the Spanish Church cannot be taken in isolation. All branches of the Catholic Church were profoundly influenced by the modernising impact of the Second Vatican Council (1962–65), by the growing engagement with poverty in Catholic circles, and, in the later 1960s, by the radical Theology of Liberation emanating from Latin America and elsewhere in the Third World. There are marked similarities between the politicisation of young Catholic priests and lay activists in, say, Spain and Italy. However, the changes within the Spanish Catholic Church had a particular and unique significance. The Church had acted as a pillar of the Franco regime in the 1940s and 1950s, and nowhere else in Europe, with the possible exception of the Irish Republic, had the Church accrued so much social and political influence. In 1973, however, *On The Church and* the Political Community, issued by the Episcopal Conference, committed the Church to political neutrality and the defence of human rights. Although it had by no means abandoned its claim to leadership in the field of moral and social behaviour, it would no longer do so from within the regime. This retreat from party politics could be observed across Western Europe at this time. However, the fragmentation of political views amongst the Catholic laity in Spain during the 1960s and early 1970s ensured that the Spanish Church was more politically isolated during the transition to democracy than its West European neighbours.

In gender relations Spain remained far adrift from developments elsewhere in Western Europe. For all of the sexual inequalities of post-1945 'democratic' Europe, (for instance, the highly traditional family policy of the 1950s in West Germany), the Franco regime's reversal of the Second Republic's policies for gender equality was without parallel. The position of women within marriage remained highly unequal, while contraception, divorce, and abortion were all illegal. The legal and social rights extended to women in most West European countries (often in the face of political and religious opposition) in the early and mid-1970s were not secured in Spain until the 1980s. One significant difference was the comparative absence of an activist feminist movement in Spain at a time when, from the later 1960s onwards, 'second wave' feminism was gaining potency in Western Europe and the United States. The absence of democracy was also clearly a factor here as in democratic societies women's votes were there to be bid for (hence, Francois Mitterrand's advocacy of birth control in his unsuccessful presidential bid in 1965). However, in some fundamental respects the position of women had begun to undergo steady change in this period. Legal reforms in 1961 encouraged women to enter the workplace, especially in the burgeoning service sector. Over the next 20 years the female proportion of the labour force rose from 14 to 25 per cent.[19]

Although Spain remained a highly controlled society after 1960, it is important to note that the 'permissiveness' of the 1960s was also a novel aspect of West European societies. After all, in Britain in the early 1960s, plays were still subject to censorship by the Lord Chamberlain, and homosexuality was illegal. Thereafter change came very rapidly to urban Western Europe, with the emergence of a new youth culture associated with drugs and rock music, the increasing availability of contraception, the spread of pornography and unprecedented freedom of expression. Despite the ill-fated reforms of Manuel Fraga, as Minister of Information and Transformation, the regime found it impossible to relinquish censorship. It also remained highly puritanical: witness the permissive explosion that accompanied the transition to democracy. In this regard, the Spanish experience was very different from that of Western Europe. Whereas in Western Europe artists were pushing the boundaries of taste during the 1960s, in Spain they were still testing the limits of what was permitted by the State. In particular, Spanish novelists and film-makers continued to explore the boundaries of free expression by the use of allusion and allegory. For instance, the films of Carlos Saura began, very delicately, to explore the legacies of the Civil War. In this and in other respects a more helpful comparison can be drawn between Spain and some of the more open Communist regimes of Eastern Europe, notably Czechoslovakia in 1968 and Yugoslavia. In both cases, the allure of reform clashed with the desire to retain ideological and cultural control (even though by the late 1960s the Franco regime was less ideologically coherent). Moreover, as in Spain, censorship was becoming increasingly porous, allowing intelligent novelists, filmmakers and journalists to explore the contested past or the inadequacies of the present.

Conclusion

Manuel Fraga's slogan writers got it only partially right in the 1960s: instead of 'Spain is different', the true message should have been 'Spain – the same but different'. Indeed, Spain was clearly exposed to many of the same trends as the rest of Europe, from rapid economic growth, increased prosperity and urbanisation, to new social and political movements and pressures for greater freedom and individualism. However, the Franco regime's instincts were inherently conservative, even if there were reformist elements within its younger cadres. The strength of the Francoist die-hard 'bunker' in the early 1970s made it impossible for the regime to adapt to change in the manner of the West European democracies. Economic growth and modernisation alone could never be enough to secure the regime's future and, indeed, compounded its difficulties. The core problem for the regime, however, was that it could never escape from the trap of its own history, no matter how hard it might try to do so. In 1970 the decision was taken to hold the congress of the International Association of Hispanists in Spain for the first time, at Salamanca in 1971. Very soon, however, the regime's latest wave of repression (the Burgos trials) provoked an outburst of concern from foreign academics who feared that the decision to hold the Congress within Spain would be seen to give support to the regime.[20] In the event the Congress went ahead, but the fact remained: like it or not, Franco could never lead a typical European regime. So long as Franco remained in power it was the regime itself which was the prisoner – both of its history and of its more recent repressive conduct – against a background of sand and blue skies.

Notes

1. *The Guardian*, 6 April 1970; *The Times*, 7 April 1970.
2. See Stephen Hopgood, *Keepers of the Flame: Understanding Amnesty International* (Ithaca, NY: Cornell University Press, 2006), p. 232, footnote 13. These figures refer to cases of prisoners adopted or under investigation in April 1971: in this respect, Spain and the USSR led Greece (196), Brazil (150) and Rhodesia (120).
3. John Gillingham, *European Integration, 1950–2003: Superstate or New Market Economy?* (Cambridge: Cambridge University Press, 2003), pp. 211–12.
4. *The Times*, 30 September 1975.
5. See Martin Conway, 'Democracy in post-war Europe: the triumph of a political model', in *European History Quarterly*, 32 (2002), and 'The rise and fall of Western Europe's democratic age', *Contemporary European History*, 13, 1, 2004.
6. Barbara Marshall, *Willy Brandt* (Basingstoke: Palgrave Macmillan, 1997), p. 66.
7. See Tom Buchanan, ' "The Truth Will Set You Free..." The Making of Amnesty International', *Journal of Contemporary History*, 37, 4 October. 2002.
8. Arthur Marwick, *The Sixties: Cultural Revolution in Britain, France, Italy and the United States, c1958–1974* (Oxford: Oxford University Press, 1998); Conway, 'Western Europe's Democratic Age', p. 70.
9. Jean Grugel and Tim Rees, *Franco's Spain* (London: Arnold, 1997), p. 75.
10. *New Statesman*, 16 August 1968, p. 199. Forrest had previously covered the Spanish Civil War.
11. Eric Hobsbawm, *Age of Extremes: The Short Twentieth Century, 1914–1991* (London: Penguin, 1994), p. 157.
12. For a helpful overview see Joseph Harrison, *The Spanish Economy: From the Civil War to the European Community* (Basingstoke: Palgrave Macmillan, 1993).
13. Alison Wright, *The Spanish Economy, 1959–1976* (Basingstoke: Palgrave Macmillan, 1977), p. 47.
14. The statistical information in the following paragraphs is derived primarily from Wright, *Spanish Economy*, Chapter 5.
15. Harrison, *Spanish Economy*, p. 32.
16. Sebastian Balfour, *Dictatorship, Workers and the City: Labour in Greater Barcelona Since 1939* (Oxford: Oxford University Press, 1989), p. 60.
17. Cited in Dennison Rusinow, *The Yugoslav Experiment, 1948–1974* (London: C. Hurst, 1977), p. 234.
18. *Daily Worker*, 3 May 1962.
19. Helen Graham and Jo Labanyi, eds, *Spanish Cultural Studies: An Introduction* (Oxford: Oxford University Press, 1995), p. 386.
20. This episode is documented in the papers of the International Association of Hispanists, Taylorian Institute, Bodleian Library, Oxford, Box 7.

6
Order, Progress, and Syndicalism? How the Francoist Authorities Saw Socio-Economic Change

Antonio Cazorla Sánchez

The Francoist State and social historians

In 1971, Spanish public television (TVE), then the only channel in the country, started to broadcast the series *Crónicas de un Pueblo*. The title means in Spanish something like 'chronicles from a small town', but the world *pueblo* also refers to 'the people', thus implying that these lives reflected the real lives of ordinary Spaniards. Filmed not far from Madrid, and offering a tender but comic view of idealized daily events, the episodes told likely stories of a number of stereotyped characters (the teacher, mayor, doctor, bar owner, local peasants, school children, etc.) who soon became famous all over the country. It was a great success and when the programme was cancelled three years later many people were disappointed.[1] This was perhaps because, for many viewers, these chronicles reminded them of their own rural towns, left behind by millions of people just a few years before during the great waves of emigration to the cities of the 1950s and 1960s. There was probably a second reason, which was perhaps as powerful. In the last years of the dictatorship, as Franco's health was clearly faltering and social unrest was growing, *Crónicas de un Pueblo* gave the public a weekly hour of peace in an ideal Spain with no conflicts, full of gentle adventures, and slow but certain socio-economic progress. The programme certainly reflected many people's fears and expectations, and in this they coincided with what at the time was the dictatorship's self perceived image.

Spanish society changed vastly under Francoism: far more than the regime that ruled it. The mostly agricultural economy of the early 1940s had given way by the early 1970s to one in which the secondary and tertiary sectors were the pillars of the country's booming economy (a boom which was soon to end abruptly with the world recession of the mid-1970s).[2] Economic development brought a deep transformation of the country's social and political values, daily habits, and expectations, which translated into the gradual emergence of a civil society that was constrained by the narrow political margins imposed by the dictatorship.[3] The occasional, chilling political messages offered by the tightly controlled media and by government representatives were quite often received with apprehension by a population that had as its main political priority the preservation of peace. So were the calls by the opposition for radical reform or for the overthrow of the dictatorship.[4] The harrowing experience of the 1936–1939 Civil War was, no doubt, at the root of this widely shared attitude. Francoism was dying with the dictator and change, some sort of change, was on the horizon. The situation created anxieties and hopes but also resurrected the old fears about renewing the fratricidal confrontation that brought about the Civil War. No doubt *Crónicas de un Pueblo* offered a calming dose of nostalgia in times of uncertainty.

The example of the television series is relevant for at least two reasons, which become evident when reviewing the historical bibliography on Franco's Spain. The first is the imbalance in the historical studies on the different periods of the dictatorship. The first, harsh decade is by far the most explored by researchers, while its last 25 years, from 1950 to 1975, are still rather marginalized. The second reason is a direct consequence of the first one. When looking at the works available on the period of the 1960s and 1970s it is striking how most of them are centred on the disciplines of economic and political history. In contrast, there are very few books on the social history of the period, and even fewer on cultural history. This double imbalance is particularly notorious because during the 1960s and 1970s Spain did not only go through an economic boom or 'miracle' but also underwent massive social and cultural change as capital, people, and ideas moved and developed at an unprecedented pace. This phenomenon, of course, did not take place only in Spain but also within the broader Western European context.[5] This has resulted in an intellectual vacuum in most historical narratives on the process of the creation of contemporary Europe which ignores the degree to which change in Spain was substantially similar to the rest of the continent. Perhaps our obsession with political history has prevented us from exploring some of the possibilities that the new cultural history offers.[6]

Many strategies are available in order to move away from this unsatisfactory historiographical state of affairs. Many colleagues are already making admirable forays into many different aspects of the cultural and social history of the last two decades of the dictatorship, such as the use of leisure, the experience of cinema going, the content and messages of television, radio and film, the oral history of migration, the reality of daily life, gender relations, etc. The latter topics connect with other investigations, some of them a couple of decades old, about more traditional themes such as workers' political culture, the changing values of peasant communities, student mobilization, and so on. In tracing the evolution of the different topics and approaches developed by social historians of Spain in recent decades, the outstanding reference source is the superb journal *Historia Social*, published in Valencia since 1988.

There is, however, a significant gap in the historiography: the evolution of the regime's political cultures. We have assumed too often that the relationship of the regime with society remained – albeit hidden behind opportunistic masks – essentially the same throughout the entire dictatorship. No doubt, Francoism was born, and remained until its last day, a harsh, murderous dictatorship. However, arguing that the Francoist regime's relationship with society remained the same for 40 years, in spite of the fundamental transformations that took place in Spanish society, can only be done if we look for historical essences first and then confuse the regime with the State itself, ignoring both the changes in the human personnel of the State and the impact of new ideas and experiences on its personnel and the rest of society.[7] It is difficult to understand how the Francoist State, which was originally created precisely in order to prevent social and political evolution, could have been put so easily and relatively peacefully to the service of a new democratic regime just two or three years after the dictator's death without evolving. Furthermore, the New Francoist State may have penetrated society and shaped many aspects of the daily lives of Spaniards from its inception, but society and its changing values also penetrated the State and laid the ground for the latter's own transformation, while the relationship between State and society, perceived or real, changed. One could also argue that the Francoist State was changed in political terms from the top, and put to the service of a pluralistic system with such ease during the transition to democracy, precisely because it had changed culturally from below, while the pluralistic nature of Spanish society had to some extent permeated all levels of administration and decision-making.

In the last few years, as Spaniards re-think their transition towards democracy, there has been a parallel interest in the roots of the process. This renewed attention (which perhaps is something of a fashion) has produced a growing number of works on the political elites that enabled and led that change. These elites included a wide range of groups, from the reformers within the high ranks of the Francoist State to leaders of the then illegal trade unions. New historical studies on neglected topics are always welcome, but they would be more useful, and enticing to read, if they also went beyond traditional political and institutional history and included more original approaches. It is, for example, somewhat disappointing to note a resurfacing of the most traditional 'workerist-militant versus pseudo-fascist State' explanations of labour conflicts in the Spain of the 1960s.[8] Even more troubling are the celebration of congresses on the assumption that workers and their natural political leadership (the Spanish Communist Party or *Partido Comunista de España*, PCE), were behind, or headed, some of the best known strikes during the dictatorship, which supposedly fell, and was replaced by a democratic regime, because workers had been enlightened by the party. We are not lacking self-proclaimed teachers, pilots, secret masters, and guides of the transition to democracy: what we lack is a knowledge of what was in the mind of those deemed to be the pupils, the majority of ordinary Spaniards.

Order, progress and (single) unions

The following pages have a triple objective. First, and foremost, they explore the political culture of the Francoist State during the crucial years of the economic boom from 1962 to 1972 by explaining how the local authorities saw society – its evolution, conflicts and prior-ities – and what role they expected to play in the changes that were then taking place. Second, they show the regime's lack of preparedness in confronting these changes and the mixture of optimism and barely concealed anxiety with which the authorities viewed their possible continuity after Franco's death. By combining both lines of study, this chapter proves that the Francoist State was not the overconfident, commanding dictatorship of its first two decades but an increasingly confused institution in which a perception, still diffuse in the early 1970s, was growing that it simply could not control society but that new compromises would soon be needed in order to guarantee basic social harmony. A third, and not necessarily intended, idea present in this work is that it undermines the argument that Francoism was seriously threatened by the organized opposition and that it automatically saw any social mobilization or conflict as the result of subversive activities. On the contrary, it is striking how clearly the authorities distinguished between social unrest and the attempts by the opposition to politicize it, and the extent to which they understood the mechanisms of conflict politicization. If they did not react to these challenges effectively it is because they could not, or did not know how to, something which only further increased the authorities' own confusion about what role they were to play. As for those who protested, they discovered their political answers in the course of the workers' protest, and not the other way around. In this, they were helped as much by self-conscious guides as by the regime's own lack of imagination, which led it to respond either with more promises or with repression. The former having been exhausted, the protestors confronted the latter and drew their own conclusions.

This chapter is as much a tale of political inertia as one about the fears and hopes that socio-political change brought to one particular, key group of servants within the Francoist State, the provincial civil governors (i.e. the supreme representatives of the State in each of the 50 provinces of Spain) and about how their actions, or lack of them, helped to shape the political identities of the people. Most of the data that follows comes from the analysis of about one hundred annual reports (*Memorias de Gestión*) for the years 1962 and 1972 that the governors sent to the Ministry of the Interior (*Ministerio de la Gobernación*). There are also analyses for some intermediate years from reports on the most important provinces, such as Madrid, Asturias, the Basque country, and Barcelona. In the reports, the governors related the political, social and economic events and overall situations of their respective provinces.[9] The general focus on the years 1962 and 1972 is not accidental. The former was, at least on the surface, the critical year of the dictatorship. The negative effects of the 1959 Stabilization Plan were still present (budget reduction, growing unemployment, and price rises) and huge strikes took place, mostly in the mining region of Asturias, but also, to a lesser extent, in the Basque country, Catalonia, Madrid and other areas. Historians of the workers' movement have recently called 1962 'an extraordinary year, obviously one of those rare years in history that mark a before and an afterwards'.[10] Seemingly, 1972 was not as important as 1962, having been chosen for that reason. It was the last year before external factors started to make things difficult for the regime's continuity: Prime Minister, and Franco's appointed watchman for the future, Luis Carrero Blanco was killed by ETA in December 1973, the Portuguese revolution erupted in April 1974, and the oil crisis hit Spain in 1973–1974, while Franco's own health was still holding (if precariously), and the wave of massive strikes and discontent of the last two years of the dictatorship, although looming, had yet to start.[11] In sum, it was for Francoism the last relatively good year, one of economic prosperity, remarkable social peace and political stability, when Spaniards could watch *Crónicas de un Pueblo* and easily identify with the message of material progress and melancholic calm that it transmitted.

By analysing the 1962 provincial governors' reports we can establish that, very broadly speaking, Spain was divided into three distinct areas according to their socio-political problems and the level of social mobilization. These range from those areas that were least problematic for the government to those that were most problematic.

Where nothing (threatening) seemed to happen

The first area includes most provinces in the country. The main traits of this group were economic backwardness, often being a predominantly agrarian society characterized by population loss or at least near negative growth, a lack of industrialization, and a chronic insufficiency of educational and social services. In geographical terms, this includes most of the country, from the Galician North-West to both Castiles, Extremadura, most of Andalusia, parts of Levant, Aragón, and the Canary Islands. This is deepest Spain, which includes provinces such as Lugo, Burgos, Santander, Cuenca, Lérida, Almería, and Las Palmas de Gran Canaria. Within this extended and non-contiguous area, however, there are places, such as medium-size cities, university towns, and industrial districts, which are included in the second and third groups that we will discuss later.

According to the governors' reports, in this extensive area the strikes of 1962 were either ignored by the public or their echoes were minimal. Popular political apathy predominated and the regime felt strong or at least not challenged at all. Moreover, what the regime officials highlighted was the widespread popularity of the dictator who was seen as the guarantor of the prevailing situation of peace and security. Although economic progress was modest, this, combined with the development of the official unions and the health, leisure, and other organizations associated with them, led people to feel that life was getting better. This self-congratulatory vision regarding the development of the unions of the self-proclaimed National-Syndicalist State did not embrace, however, the countryside, where the authorities denounced the lack of activity on the part of the agrarian unions (*hermandades sindicales*).

In all the previous provinces there still existed very small and socially isolated opposition groups, which went from the far left (the Communists usually being the most active among them) to the far right (Carlists), and which included monarchists or *Juanistas* (followers of Don Juan, son of the last King, Alfonso XIII, and father of the future King, Juan Carlos I).

All of them were tightly controlled by the police, who were well aware of the activists' movements. The only unsettling political aspect for the majority of the population was the sense of insecurity regarding Franco's succession. The issue had suddenly become more urgent following the dictator's hunting accident in December 1961, which badly damaged his left hand but could easily have been fatal, or so people suspected as the information about the incident was incomplete and thereby generated rumours. Other than this, the only organization that really caught the attention of the authorities was the Catholic workers' group *Hermandad Obrera de Acción Católica* (HOAC), an organization founded in the mid 1940s, which, by taking a pastoral interest in the workers' situation and by giving them advice and sometimes guidance, had become a real obsession for the Falangist sectors of the regime, and particularly for the official unions, which could not understand the need for a 'competing' organization outside the regime's single union. The HOAC also offered a relatively free and safe environment for the frank debate of sensitive issues, discussions which often drew on the language and images taken from the New Testament in order to convey criticism. As a result, the HOAC, increasingly so since the late 1940s, had become both an object of suspicion and the subject of limited repression in a State that claimed to be nothing less than the world's supreme guardian of Catholicism. It is thus not surprising to discover the satisfaction expressed in some of the governors' reports (Burgos, Ávila, Santander) regarding the recent decline of the organization, this being a product of their own bans and restrictions on its activities. [12]

For the dictatorship, desirable normalcy was equated with deep-seated popular political apathy, and it did not seem particularly worried if this apathy affected the single party, the FET-JONS or *Movimiento* (Movement), including its youth branches. In Segovia, for example, after taking note of the HOAC's activities and the mildly unsettling political behaviour of some members of the clergy, the governor described the political situation as 'calm and normal', as well as noting the 'enormous disorientation among the youth regarding political ideas since only a minority are active within the Youth Organization (*Frente de Juventudes)'*. [13] His colleague from Ávila remarked on the

> general apathy or lack of interest in political matters [...] Every day the lack of interest for the single party [...] grows since the old militants have lost the strength and will to serve and the ranks of the FET-JONS are not renewed and the young people do not find a clear direction that would lead them to join the organization'

For this governor, the future of the regime did not depend on the party but on increasing the standards of living and on Franco's prestige. This last aspect had been recently clouded by the lack of a clear mechanism to succeed him, 'which would ensure continuity within the existing order'.[14] According to the governor of Cádiz, the Movement was composed only of 'a militant minority and a large contingent with no enthusiasm', while the majority of the population lived in 'complete inhibition as regards political matters'.[15]

For the Francoist authorities, the key to the lack of interest in political matters was not repression, which was almost never mentioned. On the contrary, the dictatorship presented the social calm as a product both of the achievements of Franco's Peace[16] – particularly the development of the social institutions of the unions' embryonic welfare programmes – and people's concern with improving their lives. The governor of Salamanca wrote in his 1962 report about the greater 'importance of social matters in relation to political ones' among the public and described how 'workers do not show political interest, being interested only in what helps them to resolve their problems', resorting to the official unions only to obtain 'fair salaries'.[17] In Gerona, it was also noted that political matters were 'secondary' because attention was 'focused on economic matters, so present today'.[18]

Remarks like the previous ones demonstrate that the authorities were aware that for the dreaded workers the regime's labour institutions were only a means of achieving their material objectives, and that they did not identify with them. In this sense, for the governor of Huelva – a province with a large mining population which had suffered a ruthless repression at the outbreak of the Civil War – even if there were no active opposition groups, the regime was still far from attracting workers' active support. For him, the official unions could 'achieve very satisfying results if, with sincerity and courage, we confront social problems'. That the union, after a more than a 20-year monopoly of labour representation, still needed to act with 'sincerity and courage' not only tells us about what it had not achieved, but also where the Francoists were pinning their hopes for the future.

In general, however, the message transmitted by the governors of the provinces included in this first, large group, is of confidence that economic development together with the normal functioning of the unions, even if the latter had to improve, were enough to keep the workers away from politics. These workers were the only ones that seemed to matter, for the countryside, which was continually identified as an area of poverty, emigration, an ageing population, and of neglect by the official unions and the administration in general, does not seem to have caused the regime's representatives deep disquiet. The governor of Las Palmas proudly affirmed that 'today, the working class has faith in the union, because it sees its rights protected and respected', while observing that in the countryside the '*Hermandades* do not enjoy such trust'.[19] His colleague from Palencia, a province with important nuclei of both miners and rail workers, reported some 'minor protest' in the coal producing areas as a result of 'solidarity with the miners in Asturias', but in general the situation was regarded as one of normality 'since, in the industrial sector, the interest of workers is in improving and obtaining fairer salaries in relation to price increases'. The new collective agreements had reinforced 'trust' among workers that this goal would be achieved.[20] The governor of Lugo, after making the usual references to the lack of implantation of the unions in the countryside and complaining about the HOAC's modest activities, displayed his optimism: 'this province's workers do not have a class identity [...] they are conservatives, in spite of their low living standards [...]. Their general aspiration is towards more [sic] independence and the union's autonomy [...] and that their representatives should be directly elected'.[21] In Lérida, while the governor denounced the activities of politically suspicious Catalan cultural associations and the HOAC, he also remarked how workers noted the improvements achieved by the unions in their lives and how they felt 'connected' to them.[22] In Murcia, the year 1962, except for some minor strikes in the chemical and naval construction sector in Cartagena, was of 'real normalcy' because the unions had achieved 'maturity and internal consolidation'. This may have been true, but the same authorities noted how workers were reluctant to denounce to the police the subversive activities of the few opposition activists among them.[23]

According to the reports of 1962, the regime felt quite comfortable with the political situation in deepest Spain. The lack of interest in politics, the towering prestige of the ageing dictator, economic progress and the canalization of social and labour problems through the unions seemed to be the main pillars of this stable situation. The official attitude was essentially passive because, in spite of the rhetoric about the need to strengthen the unions, it was evident that this was not going to happen. Socio-economic matters in Spain were run from 1957 onwards by a group of technocrats who had no time for the pseudo-fascist unionist rhetoric that had had its time in the passionately ideological 1940s, and which had not gone too far. The regime was now backing a dynamic, Western-style consumer economy under tight political control. The pillars of this project were two: Franco and the 'economic miracle'. And while both seemed to be doing well in 1962, both were, for reasons of biology and economics, beyond human control. Peace and progress were the result of circumstances that were necessarily going to change in the future: when, not if, was the question. As for the role of the single union, it was an ideological remnant of a regime that had evolved into an authoritarian, positivist dictatorship, embracing order and progress as its new credo.[24] This would be plain with the launching of the First Plan for Socio-Economic Development in 1964, which, like the two that followed, offered much in terms of the economy, far less in terms of social content, and absolutely nothing in terms of national syndicalist experiments.

The dictatorship's approach towards society was not divorced from its own past. For all its talk and fascist rhetoric, the Francoist regime was, from the beginning, tightly controlled by traditional, conservative forces, mainly the Army and the Church. The single party, moreover, not only played a very secondary role in relation to both the leadership and the construction of the New State, but itself became a recipient of old political traditions and socio-economic interests. The result is that Francoism did not foster political mobilization but limited it to a minimal degree by reducing such mobilization mostly to choreographical roles, which were useful for showing popular enthusiasm for the dictatorship. When, after the Axis' defeat in 1945, the strident fascist front was quietly relegated to a back seat, the shallowness of the New State's fascist–populist rhetoric became clearly evident. From then on, the dictatorship actively encouraged political positivism, even within the single party and unions.[25]

By 1962 the lack of active policies to generate popular political support for the New State had become striking. The dictatorship had managed to create an enormous social and organizational vacuum which it did not seriously intend to fill. All the talk about the need to re-launch the unions has to be understood in this context. The authorities were aware of, and worried about, their lack of political initiative. It was a potentially dangerous situation since other movements and groups hostile to the regime could occupy the social space that the State was neglecting. The rapid process of urbanization, migration, industrialization, and the problems that they generated, were providing the ideal (or nightmarish) breeding ground for the birth and development of such challenges. It is thus surprising not only that these took so long to appear but also that the regime did so little about them. What it did was, in general, rather ineffectual.

The methods used by the authorities to rally political support showed both a lack of imagination and a fear of resorting to popular, radical formulas of mobilization that might go against the dictatorship's grain. The political activities were the same year after year and their powers of mobilization limited to the faithful. In 1962, the governor of Logroño reported that

> perhaps the most important event of the year, from which we will obtain the most substantial political benefits, was the act of renewal of the promise of loyalty to the national flag on the last 18 July. On that occasion practically all the former combatants and their sons older than fourteen were mobilized, offering once again a demonstration of their identification with the ideas that gave birth to our Crusade, and, with their patriotism, arousing the local population[26]

The same governor reported on the other important public activities of the year. They consisted of some public lectures, the inauguration of new buildings, the annual homage to the founder of the Falange, José Antonio Primo de Rivera, and other 'fallen ones' on 20 November, and, finally, a competition for the most improved town in the province. These were hardly exciting activities, and hardly popular, either. This shows how ready the dictatorship was to confront a decade of spectacular economic growth when the GDP increased at an annual average of 7 per cent, doubling in ten years; and when close to two million Spaniards left the countryside for the cities, another two million having done so during the 1950s.[27]

After ten years of socio-economic change in the country, by 1972 the Francoist authorities were still organizing the same kind of activities with limited popular appeal. Either they did not fear the challenge from the emerging new society or they did not know how to respond. The answer probably is both. In Palencia, the report for 1972 states that the 'really important political aspects' of the year were a meeting between the mayors and local chiefs of the Falange in the Cultural Centre, plus a meeting of the Political–Social Union Council (*Consejo Político-Social Sindical*).[28] At the meetings of the councils the local heads of the administration and the party organizations discussed local problems and proposed solutions to the government. Since the government had its own development agenda, which concentrated on investments in just a few designated areas of the country (mostly Madrid, the Basque country, Barcelona and a number of smaller areas), and the resolutions of the councils were mere proposals, they were notoriously ineffectual in making a difference in the provinces' development, particularly in the most backward ones, were such changes were most needed.

In Murcia, also in 1972, the most significant political events were: a mass for the first local Falangist murdered during the Republic (some 3000 people attended), another mass in the Valley of the Fallen (near Madrid) for all the dead local Falangists (200 people), the Youth Week (no attendance provided in the report), some other masses, and a number of small gatherings, plus the usual competition for the most improved town.[29] The same year, the governor of Castellón reported on the 'great support for the *Caudillo*', but then added that the majority of the population 'ignores the political system of the country' and they just ask for 'peace and social justice'.[30] From this, it seems evident that the regime was failing to fill the gap between the prestige of the dictator and those matters which were of concern to the public, or, put another way, that the popular support for the political system was essentially limited to the continuity of the ageing dictator.

In spite of the lack of public initiative and the almost complete political inhibition of the regime, at the onset of the 1970s the dictatorship did not find itself challenged by the majority of Spanish society. Even though illegal political and union activities were increasing, they were still linked to small groups with no steady or extended following. Segovia, for example, exhibited 'an excellent political health' as regards political matters.[31] Cuenca, where in 1962 there were some attempts at strikes, offered, ten years later, 'complete normality'.[32] The report from Almería comments on the 'general political abstention and passivity'. Except for the attempts at mobilization by 'some priests with modern tendencies' and a few minor labour conflicts, there was a general 'support for the *Caudillo*'.[33] In Albacete, there were some very small illegal political groups, the Communist-influenced trade union, the Workers' Commissions (*Comisiones Obreras*, CC.OO.), and some activities by 'progressive priests'.[34] In Lérida, opposition activities had decreased with regard to the previous year, especially those of the Workers' Commissions, which did not organize any public activities, 'not even verbal ones'.[35] In Jaén, except for some minor labour conflicts in the industrial and mining town of Linares, 'absolute normality' reigned.[36] And the same is reported from Huelva, except for the labour tensions generated by the 'crisis of the copper mining sector' (prices were very low and the famous Río Tinto mines were shutting down).[37]

Political passivity did not mean that people lacked political opinions but that they had to adapt them, and their external behaviour, to the circumstances imposed by the dictatorship. It is very difficult today to reconstruct these opinions but it is certainly impossible to categorize them using only, or mostly, categories imported from the disciplines of sociology and political science. If we limit ourselves to these fields it would be quite easy to agree fully with the analysis offered by both the dictatorship and the only sociological study carried out at the time, the 1970 FOESSA report (whose chapter on politics was banned), which pointed to a deep-rooted political conservatism, especially amongst the lower classes. Along with this political conservatism, which basically suggested that Spanish workers identified with the dictatorship, there existed, according to the FOESSA report and to the authorities' perception, a clear, extended desire for both peace and social justice.[38] The FOESSA report failed to extract further conclusions from the relative contradiction between supporting peace and being fully aware, and even angry, at the social inequalities that the regime had generated, and was perceived as seeking to maintain.

A complete reading of the possible political opinions of Spaniards in this period would have to take into account the fact that the ideas of peace and stability were linked to the figure of Franco and that beyond the support for him (which was far more extended than that for his regime) lay historical lessons, possibilities, and hopes that did not necessarily coincide with the interests of the Francoist elites, and even less with those who sought to perpetuate the dictatorship after the dictator's death. In this sense, the reading of the political situation in the 1972 report from Cádiz is very perceptive. The report explained how 'the silent majority clearly tends towards a modern socialism which balances social progress with a fair distribution of wealth [...]. This ideological tendency is easily adaptable to any regime or political system that could implement it'.[39] This interpretation was not very far removed from that of the civil governor of Huesca: 'The mass of the population is mainly concerned with economic development and the consequent improvement of their living standards, an acceleration in the diminution of social inequalities, [...] peace and order in the country, [...] and the desired political evolution of the established order'.[40] This is exactly what would happen after 1976, but certainly not within the narrow political confines that the quoted authorities had in mind. The passing of Franco and the crisis that battered the Spanish economy after 1973, along with the dynamic that both events generated, would help to transform these ideas of social equality and justice by linking them to those of political and personal freedom.

Where (some) threatening things happened

In the remaining provinces of Spain, a clear minority, things were not that easy for the dictatorship, but to say that the regime felt seriously threatened by them or that it had lost its grip on the populace would be an exaggeration. Furthermore, between the deepest Spain that we have analysed and the more urban, better educated, industrialized and conflictive provinces, there was a intermediate group where the vast majority of the population was politically conformist, but where there were also sporadic conflicts and alterations of public order in the early 1970s, some of which had precedents going as far back as the mid 1950s. Behind these incidents there were often university students, a group that by the early 1970s was clearly alienated from the regime. This intermediate group of provinces was mostly composed of middle-sized university towns with a limited industrial presence and often economically backward, including provinces such as Granada, La Coruña, Valladolid, Zaragoza and even larger towns such as Seville and Valencia. In all those cases, student activities met either with open hostility or at least indifference from the bulk of the population, in part because they were perceived as being privileged upper or middle-upper class individuals with views and personal opportunities that set them apart from the rest of society.

This situation was clear, for example, in the 1962 report from La Coruña. While it states that the majority backed the *Caudillo*, it also points out that 'we have to admit that the majority [of students] are not identified with the *Movimiento*', which for them was equated with 'mistakes and injustices'.[41] From Seville, it was also noted in 1962 that the few subversive groups in the university had little influence over workers, even among old republican trade unionists, and how tranquility was the norm in the labour context. Here the main concern was about 'the unjust distribution of wealth', a consequence perhaps, the author of the report states, of the failure to achieve real power for the official unions in economic and social matters. It seemed that the Francoists' own syndicalist rhetoric of justice with a degree of anti-capitalism was being turned against the regime itself.[42] When, in June 1962, Franco visited the province of Valencia, 'it rendered itself completely to him, with a unity of feeling, admiration and respect'. The exception, of course, was the university where there predominated 'scepticism towards the political situation and where the Falangist student organization barely holds on'. This was the province where some promptly resolved strikes, in 'imitation' of Vizcaya, had taken place in the Sagunto steel works. Devotion to the *Caudillo* and social demands were obviously not incompatible; the regime here felt reasonably optimistic.[43]

The Zaragoza students, among whom 'socialism seemed to have many followers', were in 1962 a world apart from the rest of the population. The latter was 'mostly apolitical [and] focussed on improving their living standards [being] in some sense an amorphous mass'.[44] By 1972, the students were even more active and labour relations had deteriorated, but in both cases the governor blamed the university rector and the employers for being intransigent.[45] At the same time, in Seville, his colleague identified the university, the workers, and progressive clerics as the main causes of conflict, 'as in the rest of the country', but the situation was considered 'in general as normal'.[46] Also in 1972, in Granada, the main problem was not the students, often known more for their acts of vandalism than for their political protests, but their non-tenured lecturers, who were on strike. In the meantime, the workers were tranquil. Overall, the political situation was deemed one 'of apathy among the majority of the population', an interesting situation (or opinion) since only two years before the province had suffered a violent strike in the construction sector which was bloodily repressed by the police.[47] In Valladolid, students' protests in 1972 were met with rejection by most citizens because they were considered to be 'members of the most privileged social classes'. And even if there were important conflicts at the Renault factory and amongst the rail workers, the governor seemed less alarmed by them than by escalating inflation.[48]

More problematic for the Franco regime were a third group of provinces that exhibited most, and sometimes all, of the following factors: heavy immigration, strong pre-dictatorial traditions of political and union mobilization, industrial decay, peripheral nationalist movements, and the presence of large universities. The largest, most bitter and internationally best-publicized strike took place in the mining region of Asturias in 1962. It was an area with a deep-rooted leftist tradition that the Francoists had ruthlessly suppressed during the war and afterwards. It was also an area of immigration, mostly from neighbouring Galicia, whose workers had a reputation of working for less and of being used as strike-breakers, but it was also a region in decay since Asturias' coal was too expensive, of relatively low quality, and difficult to mine. This in turn reduced profit margins and the employers' ability to meet workers' demands. Moreover, coal was losing its market share to oil. These structural problems were made worse by the recession caused by the 1959 Stabilization Plan and the steep increase in prices that it had caused, which was not followed by salary increases.[49]

By 1961, the authorities were already aware of the deep discontent among workers in Asturias and how it 'could be used by the Communist Party to infiltrate them'.[50] The following year, once the first great wave of strikes had been subdued, the governor analysed what had happened. For him, the workers' discontent existed 'because they are ill-treated by the companies', which had suppressed bonuses, incentives and overtime pay, resulting 'in a considerable reduction of their income' at a time of high inflation. Furthermore, the official unions not only promised improvements that amounted to nothing but the labour situation actually deteriorated, while companies imposed fines on protesting workers. It was only then that the conflict extended and became a massive strike.[51] After two years of intermittent conflicts, the rapid improvement of the economic situation allowed companies and workers to reach permanent agreements by economic sectors (*Convenios colectivos*) in 1964 within the legal framework of the official unions.[52] The Spanish Communist Party's (*Partido Comunista de España*, PCE) hope of capitalizing on the protest by expanding and consolidating its illegal membership did not materialize, but it did manage to infiltrate an area that not only had a militant tradition but an industry in decline along with tens of thousands of workers at risk of losing their identity – and salaries – as the aristocracy of the Spanish working class.

The 1962 strikes spread to several provinces of northern–eastern Spain, Barcelona and Madrid, as well as isolated enclaves in the centre and south of the country. Except for Madrid, these brought together three distinct types of protest which were among the most dreaded and demonized by the dictatorship: those of the militant students, workers, and regional nationalists (Basque and Catalan). The latter, which had an inter-class appeal, would be very difficult for the ultra-nationalist Spanish dictatorship to identify. In Navarre, regional nationalism had a double identity, being on the one hand the heart of conservative Carlism and, on the other, claimed by the Basque nationalists as part of their future independent homeland. Many Carlists, or rather their children, would move over to Basque nationalism in the 1960s. Being more conservative than Vizcaya or Guipúzcoa, the Navarrese authorities, in the critical year of 1962, were confident that the 'main concern is the economy' and that the region was not affected by the strikes.[53] But by 1965 they were aware of the growing activities of the Basque Nationalist Party (*Partido Nacionalista Vasco*, PNV), the HOAC, and the student movement. Workers were also more restive, progressively ignoring the official unions because of 'the rising prices' and 'political influences'.[54] By 1972, the situation had deteriorated still further as both the PNV and the terrorist organization ETA had increased their activities, while the mounting difficulties of local companies were causing 'an enormous proliferation in conflictive situations'. Most of these conflicts were waged in a peaceful way, but there were clear signs of a departure from the regime's boundaries in symbolic challenges, such as when workers started to celebrate the banned Labour Day holiday, the first of May.[55]

In nearby Álava in 1962, also a conservative Basque province and part of the Carlist heartland, the civil governor reported on 'the deepening political neutrality, with total scepticism towards high-sounding slogans, which people consider devoid of meaning. This conformism translates into positive support for Franco, but also in apathy towards political problems and participation in public affairs'. There was, nevertheless, a timid nationalist feeling, which was encouraged by sectors of the clergy, the HOAC and its youth section (JOC), and sometimes galvanized by the still very scarce actions of ETA.[56] By 1968 public order had deteriorated because of ETA and the governor asked for police reinforcements to deal with the problem.[57] By 1972 economic difficulties had mounted for many companies and the workers' protest had increased, sometimes bringing new levels of violence (e.g. during the long strike at the Michelin factory). The governor, once again, asked for reinforcements, but now for anti-riot police too. It was, no doubt, a qualitative change as the Franco regime felt, for the first time since its inception, permanently challenged in the street.[58]

The most threatening challenges for the dictatorship came from the two neighbouring Basque provinces, Vizcaya and Guipúzcoa. In 1962, there were several strikes in both provinces but the authorities were convinced that they were caused, as the civil governor of Vizcaya explained, by 'high prices, insufficient salaries, and lack of attention by the companies [...] plus the disillusion of workers with the official unions'.[59] Taking advantage of this situation, the governor of Guipúzcoa reported that the Basque nationalist union (STV) controlled 'the vast majority of workers' and was behind most of the conflicts. ETA was very active in Guipúzcoa, mainly attaching explosives to electricity pylons. By 1968 the situation had deteriorated to the point that ETA killed for the first time and the regime had to impose martial law in Guipúzcoa. Once again, Basque nationalist clerics were identified as a source of spreading discontent.[60] When in 1972 workers started striking en masse, the Guipúzcoa authorities were confident that the workers, although encouraged by the banned unions, were mobilizing for economic reasons and, curiously, felt that, 'at least as regards the immediate future, the impressions [were] not unfavourable' for the regime.[61]

The two most important provinces of Spain, Barcelona and Madrid, were not as conflictive as Vizcaya and Guipúzcoa. The regime was aware that Catalan national identity remained strong, to the point of remarking in 1961 that 'it had changed little in the last forty years'. None the less, people were wary of politics, leaving the opposition political parties devoid of any significant mass of militants.[62] Three years later, the report from Madrid was basically stating the same as regards people's aloofness from organized politics.[63] In 1972 the situation had changed little, except for the fact that the growing problems of the economy had created in both provinces numerous conflicts in the workplace. Even if the authorities were concerned by the increasing role played by the Workers' Commissions in directing protest, they were also very much aware that behind these conflicts were mainly economic demands as inflation was running out of control. As the report from Barcelona for 1972 stated, the action of the illegal parties and unions 'although they have not managed to politicize workers they have made them more sensitive to the spirit of [workers'] solidarity'. Real political protest was not coming so much from the workplace as from the university.[64] Protests by workers over salaries arose in 1972 in different ways: in Barcelona, there were mostly strikes for better salaries, but in Madrid, in the absence of significant conflicts, workers protested by not turning up to work.[65] Both were aiming to achieve the same thing: to obtain as many advantages as possible from the situation.

Social and labour unrest under a dictatorship is bound to become political. Not so much because this is the intention of the protesters, but because a dictatorship eventually finds itself with no arguments to respond to new challenges. In the Spain of the 1970s, the dictator was clearly senile, the economic boom was almost over, and the syndicalist illusion had proved to be precisely that, a pipe dream for a regime which did not seem to have a clear future role. The regime was looking at a society still unsure about the future but fairly sure about what it rejected from the past. Above all, it rejected the use of violence. There was no widespread support for violence either inside Spain or outside, or within Europe. The era of dictatorships, of strong men, or of middle classes terrorized by Bolshevism was long gone. On the contrary, the very same values of social peace and stability that had helped the Franco regime to win social support since the 1940s were now turning against it. Spaniards wanted peace, and that could only come through dialogue. The most intelligent or flexible among the Francoists could see that, and also that the regime did not know how to resolve the dilemma. Others confused the desire for peace and stability above and beyond liberty with the existence of a conservative society, while the same could be said about the still-feeble political and social activism in the country.

One of the two main problems with the interpretation given above about the process of political transition in Spain is that it is incapable of inserting the citizen in its narrative. Moreover, when this is done, the citizen simply follows, protests, resists or moves according to the rhythm and interests defined by the elites. The same happens with the State, which is merely reduced to the role of an object, a machine. Yet this ignores the fact that the State was also made-up of forces, ideas, and perceptions emanating from the society that it ruled over. Until we understand the relationship between State and society we will continue to ignore the social and cultural roots of the transition to democracy. We will be obliged to repeat the patronizing interpretations that ignore the question as to why the dictatorship was able to secure for itself the future of Spain in the 1940s and why it was unable to retain the prize in the 1970s. During the former decade the dichotomy was one of dictatorship or war, while during the latter it was dictatorship or peace. Negotiations between elites – between regime reformers and the leadership of the opposition – made the choice possible, but people knew what they wanted or, rather, what they did not want. Even the reports of the Francoist authorities reveal that the complex, relatively affluent, cultured, and basically egalitarian Spanish society of the 1970s was not going to repeat the mistakes of the very different Spain of the 1930s.

Notes

1. A proof of its popularity is that as this chapter was being written, the complete series, more than 30 years after its last transmission, is being bought by nostalgic people on the Internet for about 60 euros.
2. An overview of the economic transformations can be found in Keith Salmon, *The Modern Spanish Economy* (London–New York: Pinter, 1995).
3. Víctor Pérez-Díaz, *The Return of Civil Society* (Cambridge: Cambridge University Press, 1993).
4. The political aspects of the 1970 FOESSA report have been recently published in Amando de Miguel, *El final del franquismo* (Madrid: Marcial Pons, 2003), pp. 223–361.
5. The best account is in Tony Judt, *Post-War. A History of Europe Since 1945* (New York: Penguin, 2005).
6. Lynn Hunt, ed., *The New Cultural History* (Berkeley: University of California Press, 1989), pp. 1–22.
7. For this opinión see the introduction in Joseph Fontana, ed., *España bajo el Franquismo* (Barcelona: Crítica, 1986).

8. Teresa Ortega López, 'Algunas causas de la conflictividad laboral bajo la dictadura franquista en la provincia de Granada', *Ayer*, 50 (2003), pp. 235–54.

9. These documents are in the Archivo General de la Administración, sección Gobernación (AGA-G).

10. Xavier Doménech Sanpedro, 'El cambio político (1962–1976). Materiales para una perspectiva desde abajo', *Historia del Presente*, 5 (2005), pp. 46–7.

11. An overall view of conflict during the dictatorship can be found in Carme Molinero and Pere Ysàs, *Productores disciplinados y minorias subversivas* (Madrid: Siglo XXI, 1988).

12. For Burgos, AGA-G 11323; for Santander, AGA-G 11330; for Ávila, AGA-G 11324.

13. AGA-G 11330.

14. AGA-G 11324.

15. AGA-G 11326.

16. Antonio Cazorla Sánchez, 'Beyond they shall not pass: how the experience of violence reshaped political values in Franco's Spain', *Journal of Contemporary History*, 40 (July 2005), pp. 503–20.

17. AGA-G 11330.

18. AGA-G 11326.

19. AGA-G 11329.

20. AGA-G 11329.

21. AGA-G 11328.

22. AGA-G 11328.

23. AGA-G 11328.

24. Juan José Linz, *Totalitarian and Authoritarian Regimes* (Boulder: Lynne Riener, 2000).

25. Antonio Cazorla Sánchez, *Las políticas de la Victoria: La consolidación del Nuevo Estado Franquista (1938–1953)* (Madrid: Marcial Pons, 2000).

26. AGA-G 11328.

27. Salmon, *Modern*, p. 5; Eduardo Sevilla Guzmán, *La evolución del campesinado en España* (Barcelona: Península, 1979), p. 217.

28. AGA-G 447.

29. AGA-G 476.

30. AGA-G 474.

31. AGA-G 478.

32. AGA-G 475.

33. AGA-G 473.

34. AGA-G 473.

35. AGA-G 476.

36. AGA-G 476.

37. AGA-G 475.

38. De Miguel, *El final*, pp. 358–9.

39. AGA-G 474.

40. AGA-G 475.

41. AGA-G 11.325.

42. AGA-G 11.325.

43. AGA-G 11.331.

44. AGA-G 11.325.

45. AGA-G 11.320.

46. AGA-G 478.
47. AGA-G 475.
48. AGA-G 479.
49. Ramón García Piñeiro, *Los mineros asturianos bajo el franquismo, 1937–1962* (*Madrid: Fundación Primero de Mayo, 1990*).
50. AGA-G 479.
51. AGA-G 11.329.
52. AGA-G 11.693.
53. AGA-G 11.329.
54. AGA-G 11.639.
55. AGA-G 476. Molinero and Ysàs, *Productores*, pp. 202–58.
56. AGA-G 11.324.
57. AGA-G 480.
58. AGA-G 473.
59. AGA-G 11.331.
60. AGA-G 483.
61. AGA-G 475.
62. AGA-G 11.323.
63. AGA-G 11.962.
64. AGA-G 473.
65. AGA-G 476.

7
New Political Mentalities in the *Tardofranquismo*

Cristina Palomares

The period known in Spanish as the *tardofranquismo* (a term that means the last stage of Francoism) are years of change and evolution inside as well as outside the regime. Change inside the regime, with the emergence of new political mentalities, started to unfold during the 1960s. The emergence and evolution of a reformist sector within the regime and its consolidation during the *tardofranquismo* are fundamental to understanding the contribution and positioning of the Francoist reformists during the crucial period of the transition to democracy. These reformists understood that their political future might well depend on a pact with the moderate opposition and it was therefore amongst these Francoists that the democratic opposition encountered regime interlocutors who were approachable and open to cooperation.

Regime moderates were especially useful in passing the 1976 Reform Law, which was the crucial measure in dismantling the Francoist regime by legal means. In brief, the purpose of the Reform Law was to (i) hold elections for a bicameral Cortes through a universal, direct, and secret ballot; (ii) draw up electoral procedures; and (iii) grant the freedom to form political parties. The historian José Casanova argues that 'while one should not minimize the role which the pressure of the opposition may have played in forcing this option [the Reform Law] upon those in power [. . .], it is clear that the opposition had nothing to do with this project, nor was it an option available to them'.[1]

From this perspective, the widespread idea that the regime constituted an homogeneous block that aspired to the continuation of Franco's regime after the death of the *Caudillo* and, therefore, that the democratic opposition was the main factor behind the transition to democracy in Spain is simply wrong. The pressure and moderation of the democratic opposition were, undoubtedly, important factors which contributed to the establishment of democracy. Still, the existence of a reformist sector within the regime was also, without any doubt, essential for the success of the process, but, despite the reformists' importance, a thorough study of their emergence and evolution during the *tardofranquismo* has hitherto been neglected.

As I shall argue in this chapter, the fundamental role played by regime moderates (especially the reformists) during the transition process was, in my view, largely the result of their early awareness and advocacy (either genuinely or as a mere strategy for political survival) of the need for political reform, especially in the area of political representation. Indeed, it is precisely over this issue that the differences between reformists and *inmovilistas* (hardliners) became most evident during the *tardofranquismo*.

Franco's regime underwent important changes throughout its existence. The international isolation of the economy and Franco's sympathy towards the Axis during the Second World War meant that the Spanish regime was excluded from the major international institutions. After the War, Franco was obliged to transform the image of his regime from the dominant fascist one to a more Christian-coloured State. By the early 1950s and the onset of the Cold War, the change in image had paid off for the Spanish regime. For the Western democracies, the threat of Communism taking over Spain was minimal under Franco.

The gradual incorporation of the regime into the international community in the 1950s was followed, despite Franco's initial refusal, by the controlled opening-up of the economy. The application of the Stabilization Plan in 1959 and the three Development Plans (1964–67, 1968–71, 1972–75) by a new wave of ministers – sympathetic to the conservative Catholic organization Opus Dei – resulted in the outstanding performance of the economy during the 1960s. The implementation of liberal measures yielded unparalleled results. During the 1960s, European countries, namely France, Germany and Switzerland, welcomed an important number of Spanish workers. Workers' remittances to their families and the inflow of foreign currency, largely from the expanding tourist industry, as well as foreign investment, also contributed to Spain's economic growth.

By the second half of the 1960s, the rustic, traditional Spanish way of life was being overturned by the spectacular influx of tourists. The tourists brought other lifestyles to the public's awareness for the first time, further transforming a rapidly changing society. This socio-economic transformation changed the face of Spain from a basically rural to an industrial country in less than two decades. The rural population went from 4.8 million in 1960 to just half, 2.4 million, in 1978.[2] Economic recovery led to the emergence of a large middle class and brought unprecedented prosperity to many Spaniards. The student population grew from 64,000 in 1962–63 to 93,000 in 1966.[3] This period was also marked by countless student protests, similar to those seen in France and around Europe. This transformation also touched the Spanish bureaucracy with the arrival of a new generation of civil servants, thereby lending a new air to obsolete institutions. These young professionals, more or less linked to the regime, sought a career in public administration, some joining with new ideas that had been acquired in visits or study periods abroad. This new breed of civil servants was to play an important role during the years of the transition to democracy.

The economic boom was not accompanied by a parallel programme of political reforms. The economic and social transformation brought to the surface the contradictions between Franco's institutions and the economic capitalist system that had been developed in Spain, accentuating the existing tension between the so-called 'real Spain' and 'official Spain'. The 'real Spain' was enjoying better standards of living but was also starting to be conscious of the political limitations to Franco's regime. The access to foreign and hitherto forbidden political literature as well as the more critical tone gradually adopted by the press from 1966 (following the passing of the Press Law) helped to raise the political awareness of the person in the street. As the sociologist Víctor Pérez-Díaz observes, this decade witnessed 'the return of Civil Society'. By contrast, the 'official Spain' (that is to say, Franco's entourage and the most orthodox regime members) refused to accept the need for modernization, driven by a fear of provoking the weakening of the system: the system that, after all, kept them in power.[4]

The socio-economic transformation inevitably affected the regime itself, which became broadly divided into *inmovilistas* or intransigent conservatives,[5] and the more moderate elements of the regime.[6] The *inmovilistas* resisted change and wished to extend the regime after Franco's death. By contrast, new political mentalities represented by the regime moderates emerged within the regime during the 1960s around the idea of introducing reform into the political system. The political scientist Alfred Stepan explains the emergence of a moderate sector within an authoritarian regime in the following terms:

Some major institutional power-holders within the ruling authoritarian coalition perceive that because of changing conditions their long-term interests are best pursued in a context in which authoritarian institutions give way to democratic institutions.[7]

Some historians have observed a division among the regime moderates between *aperturistas* and *reformistas*. Broadly speaking, we can say that *aperturistas* occupied important positions in the Francoist institutions in the late 1950s and 1960s and gradually came to favour a tightly controlled liberalization of the regime in order to meet popular demands for political modernization and as the best means of guaranteeing their political survival in the future. On the other hand, the *reformistas* belonged to Prince Juan Carlos's generation. They were university students during the mid-1950s and started to occupy important positions in the Francoist institutions at the end of the 1960s and early 1970s. In short, they belonged to a younger generation.[8] Still, it is important to emphasize that, given their common loyalty to the Francoist Fundamental Laws,[9] both *aperturistas* and *reformistas* were only prepared to reform the political system by means of procedures sanctioned by that system. By the early 1970s, in the midst of a serious socio-economic crisis, most of the moderates had clearly understood that it was necessary to come up with a political alternative to the complete rupture proposed by the democratic opposition, which they believed would be disastrous for the populace as a whole. Their political survival was at stake, but so was the stability of the country.

The programme of reforms of both *aperturistas* and reformists had evolved over time. From the early 1960s, the *aperturistas* had advocated reform of the political system particularly in the area of political representation. They defended the legalization of a series of political associations. Yet the Francoist system, defined by a curious form of popular participation, known as 'Organic Democracy', only allowed participation in political affairs through well-defined channels: 'the natural representative institutions: family, municipality, and syndicate', giving no opportunity to other forms of participation.[10] Thus, although the right of association was theoretically guaranteed under the Franco regime by various laws,[11] this was not the case for political associations. Political associations that could become political parties, and therefore threaten the stability of the Francoist model, were never to be accepted. That issue was reinforced by Point 6 of the 26 Points of the Programmatic Norms of the Francoist regime, which read as follows: 'Our State is a totalitarian instrument in the service of the integrity of the fatherland. All Spaniards will participate in it through its familial, municipal and trade union functions. No one will participate in it by means of political parties. All political parties are implacably abolished'.[12]

It was not until 1964 that the regime approved a long-awaited Law of Associations. It is not difficult to imagine the disappointment felt by the *aperturistas* when they realized that the Law completely ignored political associations, or those with 'political aims', even within the framework of the Movement. The Law gave the populace the opportunity merely to create entities that had cultural purposes – in the widest sense – and not political ones. As in the previous laws and decrees, the Law of 1964 excluded from its jurisdiction those associations that were part of the Registry of Commercial Societies; religious, worker (trade union), and military organizations, along with student societies and any other type of association regulated by special laws.

From the beginning of Francoism, freedom of association and assembly had been basically restricted to Christian circles (obviously on the understanding that the purpose of meetings was religious). The 1964 Law did not change this practice but it emphasized that these associations would be considered to be under its jurisdiction when they exercised activities of a non-religious character.[13] Some of the most important Spanish political groups – formed by *aperturistas* and reformists – created between the 1950s and 1970s had their origins in large Catholic organizations such as the *Asociación Católica Nacional de Propagandistas* (ACNP) and *Acción Católica* (AC). Still, it cannot be said that these Catholic organizations were in opposition to the regime – on the contrary, they were collaborators [*colaboracionistas*] – but many of their members raised their voices in defence of a more pluralistic society.

Given that freedom to assemble was restricted mainly to Catholic organizations, the need to obtain official permission for gatherings of 20 or more people (even if it was for a family event) led to the use of alternative channels for the discussion of political issues. These channels included private gatherings, publications (newspapers and magazines), study groups or clubs (which were normally formed around a publication), trading or commercial societies, and cultural associations. The arrival of the 1964 Law of Associations did not change this pattern. The new Law was still restrictive and cramped the freedom of Spanish citizens. For those who did not want to form proper political parties and therefore be recognized as part of the democratic opposition, the practice of meeting through alternative channels to discuss politics continued after 1964.

There is obviously no record of all the private gatherings – of friends or family – in which participants discussed politics. Nevertheless, some cases have been recorded of meetings taking place even before the economic boom of the 1960s. This was the case of the *Cafés de Rodríguez Soler* (of the monarchist José Rodríguez Soler) and the *Cenas de los nueve* organized by young men of Christian Democrat background such as Alfonso Osorio, Federico Silva, José María Ruiz Gallardón, Florentino Pérez Embid, and Leopoldo Calvo-Sotelo, among others. These people, mainly young people linked to various degrees to the regime, became aware of the political problems of the country in the mid-1950s. Their main concern was to discuss such problems and, to some extent, the potential problems of post-Francoist Spain. Years later, some of the participants to these meetings became identified with the reformist sector of the regime while others – the most progressive – became part of the democratic opposition.

Another way of discussing politics was through study groups and publications. A large number of study groups were organized as informal meetings and as a result there is no official documentation of them. But we know of study groups created around publications as early as the late 1940s. A few examples are the *Cuadernos Hispanoamericanos*, *Árbor*, and the *Revista de Estudios Políticos*. The *Revista de Estudios Políticos* was the journal of the Institute of Political Studies; *Cuadernos Hispanoamericanos* was linked to the Institute of Hispanic Culture, which was presided over by Joaquín Ruiz-Giménez; and finally *Árbor*, a platform of intellectuals of Opus Dei led by Rafael Calvo Serer, used the *Consejo Superior de Investigaciones Científicas* (CSIC) of Madrid as its base.

Generally, neither study groups nor publications exercised much influence on the regimen, but this pattern changed after the approval of the Press Law in 1966. This controversial Law, elaborated by the *aperturista* Manuel Fraga in his capacity as Minister of Information and Tourism, was criticized by many at the time for being very restrictive, which it was. But many also agreed that this Law constituted an irreversible step towards modernization, which undoubtedly contributed to the weakening of the foundations of Francoism.[14] From 1966, Spanish newspapers acquired a different complexion. The Law opened up new channels of opinion through dailies and magazines where people expressed their opinions, though obviously with some degree of self-censorship. For instance, journals like *Cuadernos para el Diálogo*, which appeared in 1963 and was created by the Christian democrat Joaquín Ruiz-Giménez, became, after 1966, in the words of the journalist Tom Burns Marañón, 'a microcosm of the opposition to the regimen where there were those who were to have a political career on the Right and future leaders of the Left'. Years later, in the early 1970s, a new publication appeared on the scene: *Cambio-16*. This weekly journal became a point of reference for those who favoured a democratic system in Spain after Franco.

Apart from publications, towards the end of the 1960s there emerged various study groups formed generally by young progressives – linked to differing degrees to the regime – with a political vocation who wrote collective articles on social or political issues for influential journals. A couple of illustrative examples are the groups *Juan Ruiz* and *Equipo XXI*. Another channel was the one used by those who 'challenged' the restrictive Law of Associations of 1964 by creating cultural associations with the sole purpose of discussing politics. But this practice happened even before the approval of the law. This was the case of the *Spanish Society of European Co-operation* that appeared in 1954. Concerned with the problems they foresaw in post-Francoist Spain and the rigidity of the regime, its members came to the conclusion that the only way to modernize the country was by becoming close to Europe. Among its members were Alfonso Osorio, Joaquín Ruiz-Giménez, José María Ruiz Gallardón, and Fernando Álvarez de Miranda (all of them names that will appear later at the time of the Transition). Around the same time, in the mid-1950s, the *Friends of UNESCO Club* was created using the curtain of legality to organize activities to promote democracy. Its members were clearly of a leftist tendency, which provoked 'not a few problems for them in order to continue with their activities'.[15] But the regime would not close it down as Spain had been a member of UNESCO since 1952.

Following the passing of the 1964 Law, some Spaniards used the cloak of legality of the cultural and commercial associations in order to meet in a quasi-legal way and discuss politics. In the period 1965–74, none of these associations were suspended. Thus, even if an association was carrying out illegal activities (which was the case for some associations, as we shall see later), they were not discovered by the authorities. There is, however, a record of a commercial company – not an association – whose underground activities were discovered. The entity was registered as a Limited Liability Company – for profit – under the name of *Centro de Enseñanza e Investigación, S.A.* (CEISA) on 4 October 1965. CEISA 'has been intellectually fruitful' in 'linking students, particularly in the social sciences, to professors of different shades of opinion, from moderate to radical, younger staff members'. Yet, '[it] has not achieved some of its political goals. Some of the intellectual mentors of academic protest have had second thoughts about the course which it has taken'.[16] In 1974, the society was fined by the Francoist authorities on the grounds of promoting partisan proselytism within the Complutense University of Madrid in opposition to the Spanish regime.

Among the cultural associations, it is worth mentioning two very different ones: the Centre for the Study of Contemporary Problems and the National Association for the Study of Current Problems (ANEPA). One the one hand, ANEPA was created by members of the regime with the purpose of debating issues of interest, though from a strictly cultural point of view. These issues included the future of the monarchy in Spain, relations between the Church and the State, political participation and regionalism. ANEPA also promoted dialogue between *aperturistas* and *inmovilistas*. On the other hand, the Centre for the Study of Contemporary Problems, which was more critical of the regime, promoted dialogue between reformist members of the regime and members of the moderate democratic opposition as well as journalists, members of the foreign diplomatic service, etc. It also dealt with similar issues but from a more divergent point of view. Although these associations were fundamentally different, they both worked to promote political dialogue through the organization of conferences, seminars, and other activities. The Centre for the Study of Contemporary Problems even organized massive conferences for up to 500 people.

In the short term, all these initiatives – private meetings, study groups and publications, and commercial or cultural associations – did not represent a threat to the regime. However, in the medium term, they helped to create spaces where politics could be discussed and, through the press, to form public opinion. Moreover, in the long term, they helped to channel the demands for change that came from ample sectors of the populace by the mid-1970s.[17] The emergence of these initiatives also demonstrated the lack of a voice for the general public in Spanish politics. As mentioned earlier, Francoist authorities had defined the Spanish political system as 'an organic democracy'.[18] Through this peculiar system, Spanish heads of households [family representatives] chose one-third of the *procuradores*, or national deputies, from each of three institutions. In practice, however, this system of representation did not mean that the Spanish public had a voice in the politics of the country.

The year 1967 was of great importance for the *aperturistas*. The regime approved the Organic Law of the State or the Francoist Constitution (LOE), the Law of Family Representation, and the Organic Law of the National Movement (or Franco's single party). The LOE opened the door to the possibility of introducing reforms with regard to public particip-ation. Yet, despite the expectation that the new law raised among the *aperturistas*, it did not provide any real openness in that area. Still, it introduced the figure of the President of the government (although Franco did not in effect appoint a President until 1973). The *aperturistas* also had hopes of the Law of Family Representation. The approval of this Law brought to the Cortes a large number of deputies of the family sector, or *procuradores familiares*, of the 'generation of Prince Juan Carlos'.[19] This new breed of moderate Francoists, although fully integrated into the regime, was to play a decisive role in the success of the transition to a democratic system (among them Alfonso Osorio, Marcelino Oreja, and Adolfo Suárez).[20] A group of around 60 *familiares* decided to organize their meetings outside Madrid, earning the nickname of 'the wandering Cortes'.[21] However, following several meetings, the Spanish political authorities stopped them. As a group, the *familiares* may not have exerted much influence upon the regime, but they achieved something of lasting importance. The press wrote about them, and it was through this publicity that people became aware of the existence of a progressive current within the regime, one willing to modernize the political system.

The *aperturistas* also saw potential for reform in the area of political representation in the Organic Law of the Movement. According to this Law, the Movement had the function of 'channelling the contrast of opinions within its Principles'. But the National Council still had to approve a statute and an additional law in order to legalize political associations. In the end, it took the Council two years to approve the ambiguous 'associations of public opinion'. The growing impatience of some members of the regime was such that, while still waiting for Franco's ratification of the Law, they began the formation of associations.[22] In total, five associations were created. Ironically, however, after all this trouble, the *Caudillo* did not ratify the law.

The summer of 1969 witnessed two incidents that momentarily diverted the attention of the political class from the issue of associations. The first one was the appointment of Prince Juan Carlos as Franco's successor to the position of Head of State with the title of King. The second one was the exposure of a financial scandal by the company Matesa, in which various ministers – linked with the Catholic organization Opus Dei – were tainted. The scandal, which led to a cabinet crisis, reflected the acute divisions within the regime. As a result of the crisis Manuel Fraga was dismissed from the Ministry of Tourism and Information.

In the autumn of 1969, the Minister Secretary-General of the Movement, Torcuato Fernández-Miranda, took up the issue of the associations again by proposing to replace the old 'Delegation of Associations' with one for the 'Family, Political Action and Participation'. The proposal would be presented to Congress on 15 December 1969. That day, four national councillors made speeches in reply to Fernández-Miranda's proposal. One of them was Manuel Fraga, who, although he was already out of the government, remained as a *procurador* in the Cortes. His speech clearly reflected the concerns of the reformist sector formed by many young people who supported his idea of modernizing the regime. However, Fraga upset the *Caudillo*, who regarded his speech as disloyal. Once again, however, discrepancies between Admiral Luis Carrero Blanco (Franco's right-hand man) and Fernández-Miranda, as well as the *Caudillo*'s reluctance to accept any reform, led to a complete halt in the development of political associations. It seemed unbelievable that the government had managed to freeze the issue before such an expectant, and already restless, public. Articles and interviews with political personalities could not avoid the issue, and even Prince Juan Carlos was said to believe that the introduction of a network of associations would ease the transition to a post-Francoist Spain. Also, at the time, an important number of the Spanish clergy were becoming more and more critical of the regime and demanded, among other things, freedom of expression and political association. They were seconded by students and other sectors of civil society. The number of members of the regime aware of the divorce between the regime and the general public was also increasing considerably. The political evolution of the regime was clearly being outpaced by the socio-economic evolution of society, and this imbalance was destined to become a serious problem. By the early 1970s, people started to organize 'political dinners' as temporary substitutes for political associations, where people could meet informally to discuss political issues. These 'political dinners' attracted personalities from both the clandestine democratic opposition and regime reformists, becoming very fashionable, at least in Madrid.

Meanwhile, the Prince had privately shown interest in the possibility of reforming the Francoist Fundamental Laws, despite having sworn loyalty to the Laws in 1969. Moreover, since his appointment as Franco's successor, the Prince had been widening his circle of visitors to the Zarzuela Palace in an attempt to prise himself out of his political isolation. Among his new visitors, Juan Carlos included a range of figures from the regime as well as a number of independents, some foreign journalists, and even some members of the moderate opposition. Gradually, he was gaining the support of the reformists. But the Prince had no support from the orthodox supporters of the regime and even less from the democratic opposition, who regarded him as a mere puppet of the *Caudillo*. However, he enjoyed the support of Admiral Carrero Blanco. The idea of an authoritarian monarchy after Franco, as advocated by Admiral Carrero Blanco, was not shared by the future monarch. But the relations between them were good. Juan Carlos had even proposed Carrero's name for the presidency of the government. This was for two main reasons. First, because he knew that Carrero was Franco's favourite candidate, and, second, because he was convinced of Carrero's loyalty to the Crown.[23] In June 1973, Admiral Carrero Blanco was appointed president of the government. However, only six months later, the Admiral was assassinated by ETA. With the disappearance of the most promising candidate for securing the continuation of Francoism after the death of its *Caudillo*, the regime suffered a major setback. Indeed, many members of the regime understood 'that their survival depended on giving change before it was taken by force'.[24]

Also in 1973, two major reformist groups had emerged onto the political scene. First, there was Manuel Fraga and his study group and, second, a group of young Christian Democrats who gathered around the *Tácito* group. Generally, members of these groups were linked in varying degrees to the regime, were university-educated, enjoyed elite positions in either the public administration or the private sector, and the majority belonged to a financially comfortable social class.

Since his dismissal in 1969, Manuel Fraga had pursued the idea of elaborating a centrist political programme that could serve as the basis for the creation of a political association in the event of associations being approved by the regime. Before his departure to London as ambassador in the autumn of 1973, Fraga had already set up a study group, the *Gabinete de Orientación y Documentación, S.A.* (GODSA) (Advice and Documentation Office). Fraga created GODSA with young people linked to the *Equipo XXI* like Carlos Argos, Gabriel Cisneros, and Jesús Aparicio Bernal, among others, as a commercial society. From his embassy in London, Fraga controlled his study group and, through it, kept in contact with the Spanish political scene. The embassy also gave Fraga the possibility of meeting of a great variety of Spaniards from different tendencies, many of whom came to regard him as the 'white hope', the 'Fragamanlis' who would bring democracy to Spain. On the other hand, *Tácito* was formed by a group of young Christian Democrats (Alfonso Osorio, Marcelino Oreja, Leopoldo Calvo-Sotelo, Rafael Arias-Salgado, etc). Initially, the *Tácito* group did not intend to become a political party. Its members wrote articles in national and regional newspapers. *Tácito's* public relations activities attracted a wide and influential section of the economic, social, and political establishments. By the mid-1970s, it had become so influential as a pressure group that the new President, Carlos Arias Navarro, could not ignore it (Arias had even appointed various *Tácito* members at the secondary level of his government as undersecretaries). Both GODSA and *Tácito* members played leading roles in attempting to bring about political liberalization, reform, and, eventually, the introduction of a democratic system in 1977.

While these reformist groups were developing their political positions, a divided democratic opposition made an attempt to combine forces. In mid-1974, in Paris, some groups – which included the Communist Party (*Partido Comunista de España*) (PCE) – announced the creation of the *Junta Democrática*. The *Junta* demanded a 'democratic break'[25] with the regime, which included the formation of a provisional government, the legalization of all political parties, and the calling of elections.[26] For the regime, a united opposition represented a threat, but even worse was Franco's advanced age and fragile health. In July 1974, Franco fell ill and was taken to hospital. The uncertainty over the future of the country exacerbated the division between *continuistas* and *aperturistas/reformistas*. The precedent had been set: Franco was mortal. Spaniards, especially the prince, had to prepare themselves for a future without the General. Indeed, the president of the government, Carlos Arias Navarro, found himself trapped between the diehard Francoists – who blamed Arias for the problems with the democratic opposition and condemned his high degree of tolerance – and the reformists, who were pressing for change.

In February 1974, Arias promised an unprecedented programme of reforms which included a 'Statute of Political Associations'. Once again, his offer was very restrictive and unacceptable even for some of the reformists. The Statute allowed the creation of political associations but strictly within the framework of the Movement and, even worse, it defended the obsolete system of 'organic democracy'. In an attempt to defend the Statute, Arias tried to create a macro-association made up of representatives of several currents of thought within the regime. The so-called 'Triple Alliance' would be led by Manuel Fraga, José María de Areilza, and Federico Silva, but they refused to join. The Alliance did not work but neither did the Statute, though the latter split the *Tácito* group between those, like Alfonso Osorio, who accepted it despite the restrictions, and those, like Marcelino Oreja, who rejected it altogether.

In fact, Marcelino Oreja together with 75 other personalities of the so-called 'civilised Right' – including Areilza, some *Tácito* members (Gabriel Cañadas) and some members of GODSA (Manuel Fraga and Rafael Pérez

Escolar) – created *the Federación de Estudios Independientes* (FEDISA) (Federation of Independent Studies) in July 1975. FEDISA was registered as a commercial society in response to the Statute. The government seemed eager to avoid any potential backlash and tried – without success – to make FEDISA a centre-right association similar to the failed 'Triple Alliance'. In the end, FEDISA failed to succeed as an association, but that did not matter. FEDISA represented perhaps the most significant challenge the regime had received from the many people that had collaborated with, and even constituted a part of, it. Moreover, FEDISA revealed the deep differences between those members of the regime that defended the urgent need for reforming the political system and those who were still holding onto the idea of continuing the regime after Franco's death.

As had happened before, the restrictions of the Statute did not stop some enthusiasts from registering their political formations. By the spring of 1975, a total of ten political associations had been formed. By contrast, in the opposition camp, some left-wing groups that had not joined the *Junta* a year before – including the Socialist Party (*Partido Socialista Obrero Español* or PSOE) of Felipe González – formed the *Plataforma de Convergencia* in July 1975.[27] They felt that the end of Francoism was getting closer. Yet, in a defiant move, the *Caudillo* confirmed death sentences for five terrorists in September 1975. Their executions provoked a wave of national and international protest against the Spanish regime, which the *Caudillo* ignored. By then, the level of uncertainty about post-Francoist Spain was feverish.

In the autumn, Franco fell seriously ill, and some politicians attempted to guarantee themselves a place in the new cabinet. Franco died in the early hours of 20 November 1975 in the conviction that, as far as the law was concerned, 'all was tied down, and well tied down'.[28] However, his successor had different plans. Two days later, the Prince was crowned King Juan Carlos I. The Transition had begun, although not in the way that Spaniards expected. The Spanish public was perplexed by the news that Arias was staying on as President.[29] The monarch, however, knew better: though he was planning to carry out political modernization, he could not afford to alienate the hardliners of the regime. As Paul Preston has put it, Arias was a 'necessary evil'.[30] The survival of the monarchy would depend on the success of the transformation of the Spanish political system, but this would require some time. Renowned reformists like Manuel Fraga and José María de Areilza entered the cabinet as the Ministers of the Interior and Foreign Affairs respectively. The new cabinet also contained a promising figure, Adolfo Suárez, who became Minister Secretary-General of the Movement.

Carlos Arias Navarro's second presidency was greeted by an unprecedented social crisis. In the first three months of 1976 alone, a total of 17,731 strikes were recorded nationwide. The government promised reforms while replicating the repression used during Franco's time. Fraga's reputation in particular was deteriorating rapidly. In no time, the reformist minister went from being the 'Fragamanlis' to being the most hardline member of the regime. The unrest of the public was manifested in a national press that adopted a critical, even oppositional, tone, while reflecting the concerns of many ordinary Spaniards.

Meanwhile, Fraga's group continue to grow. On 25 February 1976 members of GODSA presented their new political platform, *Reforma Democrática* (RD) (Democratic Reform). The group wanted to attract that part of the Spanish middle class which desired 'a peaceful and orderly transition and which desired to reform the regime while keeping the best of it'.[31] Fraga supported his group from a prudent distance, but he was gradually destroying the reformist image that had guided him ever since his dismissal from the Ministry of Information and Tourism in 1969.

After months of ignoring the clamorous demands for reform, the government presented the bill for the Right of Political Association. The project was strongly defended by Adolfo Suárez in his capacity as Minister Secretary-General of the Movement. Suárez acknowledged that '[there was] a minimum tacit agreement, even at a popular level, with regard to change without risk, to a deep and ordered reform, to political pluralism, to a chamber chosen by universal suffrage, to the existence of political groups which channel ideological participation, to the popular freedoms of expression, assembly and demonstration', etc. He uttered before the *procuradores* the famous phrase: 'Let us, sirs, simply remove [the] drama from our political [life]. Let us raise to the normal level of politics what is common in the street'.[32] Young, charismatic, and a good connoisseur of the ins and outs of the Movement, Suárez was soon regarded as potentially *presidenciable*. It was clear that Arias could not provide the required changes. Even worse, Arias could not even see the need for change. He had to be replaced. Suárez was finally appointed President of the government in early July 1976, after the King – unable to stand the pressure – dismissed Arias. The situation had changed, but, from the democratic opposition to many *aperturistas* and much of the general public, many regarded Suárez as a mere Francoist. People wondered why the King had chosen him. Many thought the monarch was taking too many risks. In September 2005, Suárez's son, Adolfo Suárez Illana, revealed something unknown to many until now.

According to him, between 1968 and 1969, Juan Carlos (still Prince) and Adolfo Suárez (father) designed the whole process of the Transition detail by detail. It was therefore clear to the king that, in choosing Suárez, he was not taking a risk.[33]

Suárez's cabinet was formed of young politicians (with an average age of 44), who were politically well prepared (seven of them were members of the *Tácito* group),[34] and – in its majority – were identified with the reformist sector. Fraga and Areilza had refused to form part of the cabinet despite a personal appeal by the King. Still, Suárez had two aces in the cabinet: the two Vice Presidents, Alfonso Osorio and General Manuel Gutiérrez Mellado.[35] They had the difficult task of generating support for the Reform Law among the *procuradores* and the military, a task which both performed extremely well. Soon after the presentation of the new cabinet, Suárez announced the government's plans for the immediate future. These included a series of talks with representatives of all political ideologies, including ETA,[36] an amnesty for political prisoners, and the holding of a general election before 30 June 1977 (which had to be preceded by a referendum on the proposal for constitutional reform).[37] In addition to the difficulty of 'selling' the Reform Law, the government had to deal with an acute socio-economic crisis which translated into an increase in strikes and demonstrations.[38] A few months before, on 17 March 1976, those who had formed the *Junta Democrática* and the *Plataforma de Convergencia* reached an historic agreement. The Socialist, Communist and various Christian Democrat parties joined forces with other smaller left-wing parties and formed the 'Democratic Co-ordination' – popularly known as *Platajunta*. In the end, the *Platajunta* failed to reconcile Socialists and Communists, but it served as a warning to the government that the left might become united.

The reformists were also in full associative effervescence. Fraga was convinced that the alliance of several associations of the Movement would attract both financial backing and a large share of the electorate (according to contemporary surveys around 66 per cent of Spaniards would give their vote to such a conservative alliance[39]). The National Administrative Council of *Reforma Democrática* gave Fraga a vote of confidence to form a political alliance, but many disagreed with Fraga's choice of partners. Fraga's dream was realized at last when, on 9 October 1976, seven prominent Francoist political figures united their groups to form the *Alianza Popular* (AP) (the Popular Alliance). Fraga's *Reforma Democrática* provided the political programme for the Alliance although wrapped in Francoist nostalgia. The King considered AP to be 'an explosive mixture' and reproached its members for not having supported Suárez.[40] Fraga had always complained that Suárez stole his idea of the centre, and he could be right. Fraga may not have invented the term 'centre', but in the early 1970s he became its main promoter. However, his centrist programme – considered to be far too liberal by the orthodox elements of the regime – had become obsolete after Franco's death. Fraga had gradually moved to a conservative position. That was confirmed with the creation of AP (before Suárez's party was formed). Maybe he realized (too late) that Suárez was playing the centrist card and that the President's reform programme was more advanced than his. To make things worse, the majority of Fraga's followers left him to join the centrist party that Suárez was to lead a few months later.

After intense negotiations, on 18 November the Francoist Cortes overwhelmingly approved the reform bill. Of the 531 members of the Francoist Cortes, 425 voted in favour and 59 against (mainly the ultra-rightist sector) with 13 abstentions.[41] By voting in favour of the reform, the Francoist Cortes accepted its own dissolution and the prospective implementation of a democratic system. On 15 December the Spanish people ratified the decision of the Cortes in a referendum. Of the 77.4 per cent of the electorate that voted, 94.4 per cent voted in favour of the reform proposal.[42] It was the end of Franco's dictatorship.

In anticipation of the upcoming elections, on 8 February 1977 the government passed the Decree of Political Associations. The doors were finally open to all political parties except those subjected to international restrictions and whose objectives or political manifestos included the introduction of a totalitarian system. Attention was thereby focused on the PCE.[43] Suárez did not plan to include the PCE in the first general elections, but a chain reaction altered the President's own stance.[44] To everyone's surprise, the PCE was legalized on 9 April 1977. The date was key: it was the Easter holidays and the majority of the general public was on holiday, and that included the military elite. The reaction to the legalization of the Communist Party in Francoist circles was turbulent, especially among the military.[45] Manuel Fraga judged the early legalization of the Communists as 'a grave political error and judicial farce' and as 'a true coup d'état that has transformed reform into rupture'.[46] But, Suárez would not have legalized the PCE without the acquiescence of the King. In fact, Alfonso Osorio, like many others, although he disagreed with Suárez's decision, accepted it purely out of loyalty to the King. The truth is that the PCE was a renovated party: among other things, the party's leader, Santiago Carrillo, had modified the party statutes to make them compatible with Spanish requirements.[47] That was difficult to ignore. With the legalization of the PCE and the creation of Fraga's *Alianza Popular*, the political left and right were now covered. That left only the centre as the space without a leader and President Suárez as a leader without a political space. The opportunity for a political marriage proved to be ideal. Suárez saw the *Centro Democrático* (CD) (Democratic Centre) as his best option. The CD had a centrist political ideology rooted in Christian Democracy which had its origins in FEDISA and the *Tácito* group. The party, however, was led by José María de Areilza, but, in a successful political manoeuvre, the President 'got rid of him'. On 3 May 1977, Adolfo Suárez became leader of the *Unión de Centro Democrático* (UCD) (Union of the Democratic Centre), the result of the fusion of the CD with 42 other small political groups.[48] UCD was an enterprise whose aim was to pass from an authoritarian system to a democratic one peacefully and with the collaboration of all.[49] Indeed, UCD represented a fusion of Francoist reformists and members of the moderate opposition.

On 15 June 1977, Spain finally went back to the polls after a slow march that had lasted 40 years. The UCD won the first democratic elections since the 1930s with 35 per cent of the votes confirming Adolfo Suárez as President. The electorate had chosen the centre option rather than risk the unpredictable nature of the more extreme parties. The Socialists of Felipe González finished in second place behind Suárez's UCD with nearly 30 per cent of the votes, thereby becoming the main opposition party. The third place was for the Communist Party of Santiago Carrillo with 9.4 per cent of the votes and the fourth for Fraga's AP with a humiliating 8.3 per cent.[50] For the first time, the political proclivities of the country converged in a single parliament, the Spanish Cortes. Some members of the Francoist Cortes maintained their seats in the parliament as elected members of AP and UCD. In total, 16 per cent of UCD and 80 per cent of AP parliamentarians were previously members of the old Cortes. However, the majority of the Francoist elite had been replaced by a wide range of professionals from across the social classes. There was also a massive decline in the number of military seats.[51]

For years, the insistent refusal of the regime to reform its system of representation by creating a network of political associations increased the discontent of certain sectors that gradually came to regard this refusal as an obstacle to their political survival after Franco. Following Franco's death, although institutionally nothing had changed, especially in the area of political representation, it was clear that the regime had changed profoundly. There was a clear distinction between those who favoured the reform of the system and those who favoured its continuation after Franco's death. After the failure of President Arias Navarro to introduce the long-demanded reforms, and a year of unprecedented socio-economic crisis, King Juan Carlos appointed Adolfo Suárez as the new President of the government. Suárez and his reformist team became a bridge between the democratic opposition and the most conservative members of the regime. Indeed, the consensus achieved between the reformists and the moderate opposition was a fundamental factor in the success of this process.

The new democratic Cortes was the successful result of the '*reforma pactada-ruptura pactada*' formula.[52] In accordance with this formula, the authoritarian regime was peacefully transformed into a democracy by strictly legal means: from 'the law to the law'. The Reform Law of 1976 had the blessing of the King and been put forward by Suárez and his reformist team. The positioning of the reformists at the time of the Transition in favour of a democratic system was largely the result of their earlier advocacy of political reform, especially in the area of political representation, which was initiated in the early 1960s by the *aperturistas* and evolved over time until embracing the establishment of democracy.

Notes

1. José Casanova, 'Modernization and Democratization: Reflections on Spain's Transition to Democracy', *Social Research*, 50, 4 (winter 1983), p. 940.
2. Víctor Pérez-Díaz, *El retorno de la sociedad civil* (Madrid: Instituto de Estudios Económicos, 1987), p. 100.
3. *Blanco y Negro*, no. 2844 (5 November 1966), pp. 36–9.
4. References to the official and real Spain can be found in Miguel Herrero de Miñón, *Memorias de estío* (Madrid: Temas de Hoy, 1993), p. 57. See also José María Maravall, *Dictadura y disentimiento político. Obreros y estudiantes bajo el franquismo* (Madrid: Alfaguara, 1978), p. 27.
5. Preston identifies within this group of those 'close to the regime' the anodyne technocrats, whom he rightly defines as *continuistas*, and the ultras who were intransigent or *inmovilistas*. Paul Preston, *Juan Carlos. El Rey de un Pueblo* (Barcelona: Plaza y Janés, 2003), p. 284.
6. Tom Burns Marañón also refers to them as *inmovilistas* or 'hawks' and *aperturistas* or 'doves'. See Tom Burns Marañón, *Conversaciones sobre la derecha* (Barcelona: Plaza y Janés, 1997), p. 95.
7. Alfred Stepan, 'Paths Toward Redemocratization: Theoretical and Comparative Considerations', in Guillermo O'Donnell et al., ed., *Transitions from Authoritarian Rule* (Baltimore, MD: The John Hopkins University, 1986), Part III, *Comparative Perspectives*, p. 72.

8. Charles Powell, *Reform Versus 'Ruptura' in Spain's Transition to Democracy*. Unpublished D.Phil. thesis (Oxford: University College, 1989), pp. 10, 16–23; Burns Marañón, *Conversaciones sobre la derecha*, p. 159.

9. As José Amodia explains, during Franco's time the term Fundamental Laws was equivalent to the term Constitution. The Francoist 'Constitution' was, therefore, formed by the following Seven Fundamental Laws: in chronological order: (1) The Labour Charter of 9 March 1938; (2) The Law of the Cortes of 17 July 1942; (3) The Charter of the Spanish People of 17 July 1945; (4) The Law on the Referendum of 22 October 1945; (5) The Law of Succession of 7 July 1947; (6) The Law on the Principles of the Movement of 15 May 1958; (7) The Organic Law of the State (the proper Francoist Constitution) of 10 January 1967 modified Nos 1, 2, 3, and 5. See José Amodia, *Franco's Political Legacy. From Dictatorship to Façade Democracy* (London: Allen Lane, 1977), pp. 36–7.

10. Sixth point of the FET y de las JONS. Lecture given by Víctor Fernández González in the *Círculo de Estudios del Centro de Madrid. ACNP*, Bulletin no. 679 (1 April 1960), pp. 3–6.

11. Until 1964, the right to association was ratified through (i) the Decree of 25 January 1941, which abolished the Law of Associations of 1887 regulating the exercise of the right of association; (ii) the Charter of the Spanish People – or *Fuero de los Españoles* – of 17 July 1945; (iii) the Law of Referendum of 1945; and finally (iv) the Law of Associations of 24 December 1964. See José María Martín Oviedo, 'La representación política en el actual régimen español', *Revista de Estudios Políticos*, no. 198 (November–December 1974), pp. 243–4 and Blanca Olías de Lima Gete, *La libertad de asociación en España (1868–1974)* (Madrid: Instituto de Estudios Administrativos, 1977), pp. 207–8.

12. *Fundamentos del Nuevo Estado* (Madrid: Ediciones de la Secretaria de Educación Popular, 1943), p. 6.

13. BOE, Ley de Asociaciones, 24 December 1964.

14. Juan Luis Cebrián, *La España que bosteza* (Madrid: Taurus, 1980), pp. 105–7.

15. *8º Aniversario del Club UNESCO* (Madrid: Club de Amigos de UNESCO de Madrid, 1968), pp. 19–22, 29.

16. Juan José Linz, 'Opposition in and under an Authoritarian Regime: The Case of Spain', in Robert Dahl, ed., *Regimes and Oppositions* (New Haven, CT: Yale Univesity Press, 1973), p. 213.

17. Charles Powell, *El piloto del cambio. El Rey, la monarquía y la transición a la democracia* (Barcelona: Planeta, 1991), p. 47.

18. Martín Oviedo, 'La representación política', p. 244.

19. Among them were young figures such as Adolfo Suárez, Alfonso Osorio, Fernando Abril Martorell, Tomás Allende, Pío Cabanillas, Rodolfo Martín Villa, Gabriel Cisneros, and Marcelino Oreja.

20. Laureano López Rodó, *Memorias II. Años decisivos* (Barcelona: Plaza y Janés, 1992), p. 118.

21. Some observers also called this group of *familiares* 'Cortes Gastronómicas', since they regularly met in a restaurant in Madrid. See *Don Quijote*, no. 3, Madrid (24 October 1968), p. 5.

22. A special report on the first projects of associations of 'public opinion' was published by the team of Eduardo Álvarez Puga, 'El asociacionismo político español', in *Dossier Mundo*, May–June 1971, pp. 18–20, 28–32.

23. Laureano López Rodó, *Memorias III. El principio del fin* (Barcelona: Plaza y Janés, 1993), pp. 13–14.
24. Paul Preston, 'The Dilemma of Credibility: The Spanish Communist Party, the Franco Regime and After', *Government and Opposition*, no. 11 (winter 1976), p. 80.
25. The idea of *ruptura* with Franco's regime had always been part of the democratic opposition to Francoism. Still, in 1974 the Socialists coined and put into circulation the term 'democratic rupture' or *ruptura democrática* to underline their objectives. *Ruptura democrática* involved the devolution of sovereignty to the people in order to decide the political, economic, social, and syndical system that they preferred (including also the question of republic or monarchy). This also involved the calling of elections, the annulment of extant legislation, and the passing of a political amnesty. Later on, in 1976, the democratic opposition referred to a 'negotiated democratic rupture' as a dialectic process by which the government (or rather the reformist sector of the regime) and the opposition negotiated a programme of reforms. In reality, the 'negotiated democratic rupture' formula chosen by the Adolfo Suárez government made the peaceful transition to a democratic system possible. See *Cambio-16*, 12–18 April 1976, pp. 37–8.
26. Santiago Carrillo, *Dialogues on Spain* (London: Lawrence and Wishart, 1976), pp. 219–20; Paul Preston, 'The Dilemma of Credibility', p. 82; Andrés and Victoria Prego, *La Transición*, Video no. 3, 'La influencia de la revolución de los claveles (abril–Septiembre 1974)'.
27. Raymond Carr and Juan Pablo Fusi, *Spain: Dictatorship to Democracy* (London: George Allen and Unwin, 1979), pp. 195–206.
28. Paul Preston, 'El largo adiós: 1969–1975', in Santos Juliá et al., *Memoria de la Transición* (Madrid: Taurus, 1996), pp. 79–82.
29. Victoria Prego, *Así se hizo la transición* (Madrid: Círculo de Lectores, 1995), pp. 368–9; *Cambio-16*, 15–21 December 1975, pp. 4–8.
30. Paul Preston, *The Triumph of Democracy in Spain* (London: Methuen, 1996), pp. 53–90.
31. Juan de Arespacochaga, *Carta a unos capitanes* (Madrid: INCIPIT Editores, 1984), p. 211.
32. Prego, *Así se hizo la transición*, pp. 474–7. Extracts of Suárez's speech are to be found in the latter, pp. 248–50.
33. *El Mundo*, 18 September 2005.
34. The *Tácito* ministers were: Eduardo Carriles (Treasury), Leopoldo Calvo-Sotelo (Public Works), Landelino Lavilla (Justice), Enrique de la Mata (Syndicates), Marcelino Oreja (Foreign Affairs), Alfonso Osorio (Presidency), and Andrés Reguera (Information and Tourism). See Charles Powell, 'The 'Tácito' Group and the Transition to Democracy, 1973–1977', in Frances Lannon and Paul Preston, eds, *Elites and Power in Twentieth Century Spain* (Oxford: Clarendon, 1990), p. 265.
35. The liberal military General Manuel Gutiérrez Mellado joined the cabinet after another general, Fernando de Santiago y Díaz de Mendivil, resigned in protest at the legalization of the Communist trade unions in October 1976.
36. Preston, *Juan Carlos*, p. 402. According to a recent article, the president of the Basque Nationalist Party, Xavier Arzalluz, recalled that representatives of the politico-military branch of ETA negotiated the surrender of weapons in

exchange for the release of ETA prisoners in May and April 1977 with Adolfo Suárez and Juan José Rosón. Xabier Arzalluz, 'Txiberta', *Gaia*, 2 September 2000.

37. According to *Cuadernos para el Diálogo* Suárez's constitucional reform proyect was elaborated by José Luis Graullera Micó, subsecretary of the presidency. See *Cuadernos para el Diálogo*, no. 178 (25 September–1 October 1976), p. 17.

38. *Cuadernos para el Diálogo*, no. 178 (25 September–1 October 1976), pp. 15–17.

39. *Cambio-16*, 27 September–3 October 1976, p. 15.

40. López Rodó, *Memorias III*, pp. 276–8; Silva Muñoz, *Memorias Políticas* (Barcelona: Planeta, 1993), pp. 347–9; Preston, *Juan Carlos*, p. 407.

41. *El País*, 19 November 1976, pp. 1, 8–9.

42. Prego, *Así se hizo la transición*, p. 596.

43. *B.O.E.*, *Real-Decreto sobre Asociaciones Políticas* del 8 de febrero de 1977 (publicado el 10 de febrero); Diego Martín Merchán, *Partidos Políticos. Regulación legal* (Madrid: Servicio Central de Publicaciones de la Presidencia del Gobierno, 1981), pp. 104–5; Álvarez de Miranda, *Del 'contubernio' al consenso* (Barcelona: Planeta, 1985), pp. 112–13.

44. Alfonso Osorio, *De orilla a orilla* (Barcelona: Plaza y Janés, 2000), pp. 309–23.

45. Admiral Gabriel Pita, Minister of the Navy, resigning from his post to voice his disapproval. The military elite sent a note to Suárez which encapsulated their bitter emotions over the legalization of the PCE. López Rodó records a summary of the note. See López Rodó, *Memoirs III*, pp. 308–9. See also M.A. Bastenier, 'El camino hacia las urnas', in Juliá et al., *Memoria de la Transición*, pp. 201–2.

46. Abel Hernández, *Fue posible la concordia. Adolfo Suárez* (Madrid: Espasa Calpe, 1996), p. 65.

47. Fernando April Martorell, interviewed by Nativel Preciado, in Juliá et al., *Memoria de la Transición*, p. 207; Martín Merchán, *Partidos Políticos*, p. 104.

48. The 13 larger parties were: (i) the *Federación de Partidos Demócratas*, made up of nine smaller parties and led by Joaquín Garrigues Walker and Antonio Fontán, among others; (ii) the *Federación del Partido Popular*, consisting of seven parties and led by Pío Cabanillas, Pedro Pérez-Llorca, and José Luis Ruiz Navarro, among others; (iii) *Federación Social Demócrata*, formed by ten political parties and with politicians like José Ramón Lasuén; (iv) the *Partido Social Demócrata*, formed by six parties and led by Francisco Fernández Ordoñez, Rafael Arias-Salgado, and Luis González Seara; (v) the *Unión Demócrata Murciana*, led by Antonio Pérez Crespo; (vi) the *Unión Canaria*, led by Lorenzo Olarte Cullen; (vii) the *Partido Gallego Independiente*, led by José Luis Meilán; (viii) the *Partido Social Demócrata Independiente*; (ix) the *Partido Social Andaluz*, led by Manuel Clavero Arévalo; (x) the *Acción Regionalista Extremeña*, led by Enrique Sánchez de León Morcillo among others; (xi) the *Partido Demócrata Popular*, led by Ignacio Camuñas; (xii) *Partido Demócrata Cristiano*, led by Fernando Álvarez de Miranda and Iñigo Cavero, among others; and (xiii) the *Federación Social Independiente*, led by Jesús Sáncho Rof. See Martín Merchán, *Partidos Políticos*, pp. 206–10.

49. Hernández, *Fue posible*, p. 76.

50. The results were as follows: *Unión de Centro Democrático* 34.6 per cent – 166 seats; *Partido Socialista Obrero Español* 29.3 per cent – 118 seats; *Partido Comunista de España* 9.4 per cent – 20 seats; *Alianza Popular* 8.3 per cent – 16 seats; *Partido Demócrata de Cataluña* 2.8 per cent – 11 seats; *Partido*

Nacionalista Vasco 1.7 per cent – 8 seats; Others 13.9 per cent – 11 seats. Results taken from Augusto Delkáder, 'Las primeras elecciones libres', in Juliá et al., *Memoria de la Transición*, p. 231.

51. Salustiano del Campo et al., 'La élite política española', *Sistema*, no. 48 (March 1982), pp. 37–8.

52. Preston, *The Triumph of Democracy in Spain*, p. 17.

8
Associations and the Social Origins of the Transition during the Late Franco Regime

Pamela Radcliff

Between 1977 and 1979, the largest and most significant urban social movement in Europe since 1945 exploded in cities across Spain.[1] At the centre of what became known at the time as the 'citizen movement' were several thousand community-based neighbourhood or family associations. Many observers agree that the 'citizen movement' was a major protagonist in the popular mobilization that helped push elites into the formal negotiations that led to Spain's successful democratic transition. While the 'citizen movement' as a democratic pressure group is part of the history of the Transition, the first associations were legally constituted during the Franco regime. As a result, the origins of this new culture of associationism lie in the dictatorship, and more specifically in the latter phase of the regime, when a combination of factors opened up a space for a new generation of voluntary associations. From this longer-term perspective, the revival of associational life forms part of the broader transformation of Spanish society under the Franco regime that helped pave the way for the Transition. Within this framework, this article explores the general scope of the new associational culture and its origins in the changing political and economic environment of the 1960s and early 1970s.

Theorizing the relationship between *desarrollo*, associations and the origins of the Transition

Few people would disagree that the dramatic social and economic transformation of the 1960s and early 1970s contributed in some way to the democratic transition, but there is less agreement on the precise mechanisms or impact. Modernization theorists tried to argue that Spain was proof of the linear connection between economic development, capitalism and democracy, but the numerous counter examples have undermined the popularity of this interpretation. In response to this overly deterministic view, transitologists placed the emphasis on the agency of elite protagonists, whose rational pact making could occur within any social or economic context. In this narrative, the transformation of the 1960s and early 1970s featured at most as a favourable context but was otherwise irrelevant.[2]

While transitology has been dominant in recent decades, critics of the 'rational choice' model complain that this version impoverishes the history of the Transition, both by leaving out the rest of the population and by ignoring long-term factors. In particular, in a now-canonical book, Víctor Pérez-Díaz argued that a broader democratic culture had to be in place before elites could even imagine making certain choices.[3] In this theory, democratic traditions, like mutual tolerance, bargaining and multiple voices, both evolve gradually out of the unconscious actions of many people and are actively invented. In either case, the locus of this 'web of traditions' is civil society, the realm of public independent activity between the State and the family.[4] The civil society framework opens up the study of the Transition both in time and space, pushing the analysis not only deeper into the social fabric but also back before the actual establishment of political institutions. In other words, it brings us back to the transformation of the later Franco period as the site from which to begin a social history of the Transition.

Within this framework, voluntary associations offer an ideal window into collective practices that can flesh out the agency of ordinary Spaniards and analyse them as protagonists vs. simply the products of modernizing forces. Specifically, associations were sites where new practices of citizenship could be explored, practices that reconstructed horizontal relationships between Spaniards who had been atomized by the regime's forced demobilization and developed new vertical relationships with the State, which undermined the passivity on which the authoritarian State relied.[5] But thus far, scholars have paid little attention to associations under the Franco regime beyond quantitative references to the national register of associations maintained by the government.[6] The conclusion drawn from this data, which places Spain on the low end of associational density, has done nothing to encourage deeper research into associational life.[7] And it is true that the number of Spaniards participating in voluntary associations was a minority of the population. Moreover, the density of associationism varied tremendously by region and by type of community, with a concentration in large urban areas like Madrid and Barcelona.

However, the increase in voluntary associations, between the first and the second stages of the Franco regime, was a national phenomenon that marks an important turning point in the relationship between State and civil society in Spain. In other words, while Spain may compare unfavourably in absolute terms with associational membership in other countries, the favourable contrast between the later and earlier decades of the regime is equally significant, both numerically and in the pluralism of associational life.[8] Furthermore, it is equally important to delve beneath the quantitative evidence to explore the practices developed by these associations, which formed the foundation for the later 'citizen movement' discourse. Since there is so little scholarship on grass roots associations during this period, the picture is necessarily spotty and incomplete, but suggestive of a larger trend towards a more pluralist and participatory civil society.

This new era of associationism unfolded in the context of what Juan Pablo Fusi has called 'the reappearance of conflict' among a largely younger generation of those who came of age well after the Civil War. Thus, it was in the 1960s that political opposition to the regime begins to take shape around four points of mobilization, in the universities, the factories, the Church and regional identities.[9] The parallel expansion of political opposition movements and legal associations was not accidental, and many individuals moved between the two realms of collective activity, as conditions allowed. However, the two realms of activity should not be conflated and each contributed to the prehistory of the Transition in a different way. While the political opposition movements elaborated the ideological bases for the future democratic regime and nurtured the core of what would become the first generation of democratic elites in the late 1970s, the legal associations were sites in which democratic practices, such as elections, representation, public campaigns, interest group pressure and even languages of self-representation could be cultivated among much larger groups of people. In the case of the political opposition groups, the shadow of repression that kept them out of the public sphere restricted potential participation as well as the range of collective behaviours that would be relevant to legal and public democratic citizenship. Even if the individual participants were ideologically committed to creating a democratic regime (which by no means applied to all of them), in structural and procedural terms their movements could not operate on a functional democratic terrain as could the neighbourhood associations registered under the 1964 Law of Associations or the family associations of the *Movimiento* (Movement), the State-sanctioned political movement formed in 1937.

The *Movimiento* family associations have never been located within the same functional space as the neighbourhood associations, linked, as they were, to a reactionary political movement on the eve of its dissolution.[10] Since the *Movimiento* of the 1960s had lost much of its political power within the Francoist factions, historians of the regime have ignored the later *Movimiento* initiatives like the family associations as mere acts of desperation, empty of real content. On the other hand, those looking for the origins of the Transition have dismissed the associations as inherently contaminated by their fascist progenitors, without any relevance for a future democratic State. As one contemporary editorial put it, the *Movimiento* associations belonged to the 'official Spain', contrasted with 'the real Spain represented by the independent associations, the citizen associations – of neighbours, housewives, consumers or small businessmen – which were registered under the 1964 Law, the only channel that permits some independence'.[11]

However, beyond the ideological differences in orientation, both family and neighbourhood associations shared a common functional space which can be linked to the democratic transition, despite the former's affiliation with the Francoist regime. This is not to say that each type of association operated in the same way or, equally important, that each local branch had the same sort of impact. On the contrary, it is clear that because the family associations emerged out of a 'top-down' initiative, many of them never materialized as more than a set of statutes written and imposed by the national leadership, while others were so tightly integrated in the political hierarchy that they were mere extensions of the State. On the other extreme, even though the neighbourhood associations emerged out of grass roots pressure, their ability to function legally was limited by police repression. As a result, some of the more 'politicized' neighbourhood associations were forced out of the realm of public practice and into the clandestine world of the illegal political parties. Nevertheless, some family associations took on local lives of their own, despite their origins, and repression was not effective enough to shut down the neighbourhood associations. Within this overlapping space, which applied to individual associations, not to categories, these community-based organizations constituted a major sector of the expanding realm of public and collective engagement that was not directly controlled by the State and, in many cases, was explicitly contrasted with the State.

A point of departure: associational life in the 1940s to 1950s

This expanding associational milieu stands in contrast to the early decades of the Franco regime, when repression and demobilization of the public sphere fostered a return to more traditional forms of sociability, based on the family and the Church.[12] Consistent with the 'totalitarian' discourse of the regime, formal associations were largely limited to those integrated into the vertical hierarchy of the Church or the *Movimiento*. The lay *Acción Católica* (AC) (Catholic Action) organizations had a membership of 442,000 in 1946 and 533,000 in 1956, about two thirds of whom were women.[13] The Church-affiliated *Confederación Católica de Padres de Familia* (CCPF) (Catholic Federation of Heads of Families) claimed 74 provincial federations, 247 associations in individual Catholic schools and a total of 143,500 parent members.[14] The *Movimiento* was the other main channel of legal association, with 932,000 political members and another million in associated organizations like the *Guardia de Franco* (GF) (Franco's Guard) and the *Sección Femenina* (295,000) (SF) (Women's Section), which had to declare fealty to *Movimiento* principles.[15] In addition to these, there were small numbers of other types of business, recreational, cultural and sports associations, whose membership numbers are difficult to estimate, but probably account for most of the 2500 associations on the National Register of Associations in 1965.[16] Juan Linz estimated in 1961 that the total number of voluntary associations, including those registered through the Government, the *Movimiento* and the Church, were 8329.[17]

Although the membership levels of the *Movimiento* associations were higher on paper, the Church was still probably the primary channel of sociability for most communities in the 1940s and 1950s. In some cases, it may have nearly recovered its traditional monopoly over local networks of sociability, as one case study of a Basque *pueblo* concludes.[18] The *Movimiento* institutions did have a presence in municipal life, in the person of the local chief, but its institutions were more directly linked to the State apparatus. It is not until the late 1950s that the *Movimiento* hierarchy became seriously interested in expanding associational life beyond its specialized organizations like the GF, which were more elitist than popular in nature.

While the Church had a more extensive associational network in the 1940s and 1950s, there is still not much information on the local vitality of its lay associations. The major exception is the extensive scholarly attention paid to the new 'specialized' branch of AC dedicated to re-christianizing the working classes, that is, *Hermandad Obrera de*

Acción Católica (HOAC) (Workers' Brotherhood of Catholic Action) and *Juventudes Obreras Católicas* (JOC) (Young Catholic Workers).[19] These associations originated out of the *Cursillos Nacionales de Apostolado Obrero* (National Seminars on Worker Outreach) in 1942 and 1943 and were formally constituted in 1946 and 1947.[20] While the membership levels in these two associations were never high – Adrian Shubert estimates 12,000 for HOAC and 70,000 for JOC[21] – many authors agree that the individuals in these associations made a tremendous impact on early labour organization in the 1950s and early 1960s, which explains their popularity with scholars. These new 'specialized' associations were organized along a quite different model from the traditional Catholic Action, first, in their explicit recognition of different social classes, second, in their overt insertion in social problems and third, in their action-oriented philosophy.[22]

This commitment to social action pushed the HOAC and JOC militants into increasingly critical postures, expressed through their press organs and their attempts to undermine the vertical syndicates of the regime. Many HOAC and JOC members were among the founding militants of the first *Comisiones Obreras* (CC.OO.) (Workers' Commissions) independent syndicates, especially in Barcelona, Bilbao and Madrid. In a story well told by Feliciano Montero, among others, the movement reached its apogee in the early 1960s, with its strong critique of the government's 'Stabilization Plan', its public support of the Asturian miners' strikes in 1962 and an increasingly insistent call for independent unions.[23] It was of course this kind of linkage that turned the government against AC in the late 1960s. By the end of the decade, the combination of government repression and the clampdown of the Church hierarchy decimated the AC associations, which had lost much of their membership by the early 1970s.

The mid-1960s crisis of AC marked a new phase in the relationship between the Church and civil society. If, in the early decades, social organization took place largely inside the institutional framework of the Church, the gutting of AC seriously reduced the presence of Church-affiliated associations in the emerging civil society. Even before the crisis one could argue that the influence of the Workers' Brotherhood (HOAC) and its youth affiliate (JOC) as associations was not as important as the impact of the individual members. In other words, as associations, HOAC and JOC were shackled by the unresolved identity crisis that kept them from establishing a strong autonomous presence in Francoist civil society. Instead, it was the individual members who began making contacts across the Marxism/Catholicism divide and who participated, as individuals, in the formation of the first independent labour unions.[24]

The point is that, even before the mid-1960s, one could argue that the institutional presence of the Church's voluntary associations was perhaps less important than their role in facilitating other forms of social organization. However, this was even more the case after the mid-1960s, when most of the AC militants migrated into the Workers' Commissions or other clandestine unions, as well as into the neighbourhood associations, and by the mid-1970s had abandoned Christian democracy for other non-religious democratic or socialist parties.[25] As William Callahan and Frances Lannon have both argued, once other channels of association opened up, militants no longer needed to pursue labour, political or civic goals through the Church.[26] The irony, as many have pointed out, is that the Catholic activism that contributed so much to the opposition to the dictatorship did not provide the springboard for a Catholic mass political movement during the Transition.

The only possible exception to the Church's inability to sustain a 'Catholic civil society' were the *Asociaciones de Padres de Familia* (APF) or *Padres de Alumnos* (APA) (parents' associations), although it is important to note that these were only affiliated, not fully integrated, lay associations.[27] Originally founded in 1913 to mobilize against the liberal government's anti-clerical education legislation, during the Second Republic they expanded from 34 to 154 local branches and from 9000 to 85,000 members.[28] Even with the dislocation and demobilization of the war, those numbers had almost doubled by the mid-1950s, according to Juan Linz's statistics, and in 1972 the 20th National Assembly of the *Confederación Católica de Padres de Familia y Padres de Alumnos* in 1972 claimed to represent 220,000 members in 758 branch associations, which were grouped into 52 district federations. Of these federations, the one in Madrid had 74 local branches in 1974.[29]

A new era of associations in the 1960s and 1970s: origins

What is more significant than the expansion of the Catholic parent associations in the late 1960s is the parallel growth of multiple associational channels precisely during this period. The result was an increase not only in the number of associations, but in their diverse origin and affiliation. Thus, most new associations created after the mid-1960s registered not with the Church but through either the *Movimiento's Delegado Nacional de Asociaciones* (DNA) (National Commission of Associations) or the new 1964 Law of Associations. While statutes were closely monitored to prevent the formation of 'political' associations or any subversive groups that would undermine the ideological unity of the regime, the new channels legalized a functional pluralism that opened a new era of associational life.

So what explains the expansion of local, voluntary associations after the mid-1960s? The common origins of both forms of association can be located in the dramatic social and economic transformation known as the *'desarrollo'* and the attempts by both the dictatorship and the populace to reduce its chaotic consequences. Without arguing for an automatic link between economic change and political or cultural evolution, it can be asserted that the shift in political culture after the 1950s was a (not the only possible) direct response to the *desarrollo*. From 'above', this shift was reflected in a revival of the idea and practice of popular participation in public affairs. The 1964 Law of Associations provides a convenient marker, but it was only one aspect of a growing sea change within sectors of the regime. Political elites were aware that the economic transformation was creating new tensions in the society at large, within universities absorbing increased numbers of students, in industries adapting to newly liberalized markets and in urban centres attracting massive numbers of rural immigrants. In this increasingly unstable society, they sought to create channels that could give voice to these tensions without opening the door to political reform. From 'below', groups of students, workers and neighbourhood residents, among others, pushed for more channels capable of resolving the new problems in their daily life.

The changing official attitudes towards associationism can be tracked through the *Movimiento* re-organization that began with the creation of the National Commission of Associations. After this point, the *Movimiento* leaders began to formulate a new corporate language of mass participation. Instead of being an ideological vanguard of committed activists, the *Movimiento* was to become a clearinghouse for grass roots public service, bringing in ordinary people who had never been *Movimiento* ideologues and encouraging them to get involved in their communities. Thus, according to José Miguel Ortí Bordás, the fundamental principle of the proposed 1968 Organic Statute of the *Movimiento* was participation or the provision of free and responsible access to public life and the right of all Spaniards to be present where important decisions affecting the community were being made.[30] It is true that the principle of 'participation' itself was not new. In a traditional Falangist universe, participation was linked to a totalitarian vision of enthusiastic national unity, as in Article 6 of the 1937 Charter, which declared that all Spaniards should 'participate' in the State through their roles in family, local and trade union organizations.

What was novel was that participation was to be linked to greater diversity and pluralism in public life. As José Solís Ruiz put it, it was time to 'populate with uncorrupt (*limpias*) voices the national silence' of the previous quarter of a century. Instead of the older model of totalitarian integration, Solís talked about giving voice to different perspectives,[31] and the 1968 Statute recognized the need to promote 'free and spontaneous' associations, whose aims would be 'open according to their own goals like a multi-coloured fan (*un plural abanico*)'.[32] Thus, the new concept of participation envisioned not only the incorporation of the population into the State's project, but the constitution of other collective projects, whose interests needed independent channels. In the words of another *Movimiento* theorist, 'One of the fundamental characteristics of a pluralist organization of society is the fact that people with common problems or identical interests can unite to fight for their interests'.[33]

Nevertheless, pluralism and participation were still meant to be contained within the *Movimiento*'s vision of organic democracy. In ideological terms, this meant the prohibition of any association that promoted 'social division' or opposition rather than unity. In other words, diversity was acceptable only within a broader framework of ideological loyalty to the regime. In structural terms, organic democracy meant that the associations contributed to the vertical organization of society, despite the new acceptance of pluralism. The result was an unstable balancing act between horizontal and vertical social structures and between unity and diversity.

For some within the *Movimiento* as well as other sectors of the regime, this instability was too risky, and internal debates over pluralism and participation continued until the end of the dictatorship. Thus, in competing drafts of the *Movimiento*'s 1968 Statute, proponents disagreed on the crucial distinction of whether affiliated associations had to demonstrate active support for the *Movimiento*'s goals or merely promise not to act against them.[34] But the real sticking point in the debates was over what were called 'political' associations, with the Solís camp arguing for an evolution towards limited ideological and institutional pluralism under the *Movimiento* umbrella. This vision was defeated by conservatives within the regime, partly because enemies of the *Movimiento* did not want to increase its power and partly because of the fear of opening the Pandora's box of political reform.[35] But the high-profile defeat of the *Movimiento*'s project for political associations should not overshadow its more successful promotion of a realm of 'non-political' associations,[36] what became known as the family association movement, whose purpose was to act as the 'main channel between families and State authorities'.[37] Under the family umbrella, the project envisioned both 'general' *Asociaciones de Cabezas de Familia* (ACF), for heads of household, and 'specialized' associations for consumers (*Asociaciones de Consumidores*), domestic servants (*Asociaciones de Empleadas de Hogar*), housewives (*Asociaciones de Amas de Casa*) and for parents of schoolchildren (*Asociaciones de Padres de Alumnos*), of large families (*Asociaciones de Familias Numerosas*) and of children with disabilities (*Asociaciones de Padres de Niños Subnormales*).

The potential independent space opened up even by these 'non-political' associations was realized at the time by opponents of the project. Thus, the government's technical adviser who commented on the draft proposal was disturbed that the new associations were to be encouraged to oversee municipal authorities' management of their responsibilities, which would undermine State authority. He also implicitly criticized the expanding pluralism embodied in the project, since the associations 'overlapped' with existing forms of representation, like the Catholic Federation of Heads of Families. But what most concerned him was the 'open character' of the associations, which were free to elect their own governing boards and were subject to no doctrinal control. He recognized the great paradox of the quintessentially anti-democratic *Movimiento* supporting the creation of what were, in his mind, essentially 'political' organizations, that is, for heads of household to participate in public functions. The result was a 'golden door for sly enemies of the regime'. What appeared to be an insignificant project was in fact an important transformation in the associational life of the country, he concluded.[38] While most of the family associations did not become seed beds of political opposition, as the adviser feared, he was right to see that this new discourse of participation could be taken in unintended directions.

At the same time, as the *Movimiento* was promoting a new generation of associations under its auspices, competing sectors of the regime were pushing for a more general law of association that would spell out the vague rights and qualifications established in the 1941 Law and the 1945 Code of Law (*Fuero*), especially in terms of defining the acceptable goals of association and the mechanics of government approval. The result was the 1964 Law of Associations, under which all associations, other than those regulated by the *Movimiento*, the Church or the other special categories, would have to register. The law was, at least implicitly, a weapon in the internal jockeying for power between regime sectors, in this case aimed at the *Movimiento*'s monopoly control on secular associational life. Thus, the 1964 Law set up an entirely distinct legalization process for associations that was controlled by the Ministry of State, not the *Movimiento*.[39]

But beyond political motives, the Law was a response to a real vacuum of guidelines on associations and to the growing pressure from below to establish clear channels for formulating and making collective demands. While the ideological scrutiny of associations required under the 1964 Law was as great as that claimed by the *Movimiento*, its looser framework created the space for a more diverse range of associations than did the narrower Association of Heads of Household (ACF) blueprint. However pluralist the language of the *Movimiento*, an ACF had to focus on the family, was limited to 'heads' of families and had to claim direct adhesion to the principles of the *Movimiento*. In contrast, the 1964 Law left the goals, scope and membership of associations undefined, except for its primary concern to prevent 'subversive elements' from using associations for illicit purposes.[40] It was this more flexible framework that made the 1964 Law the preferred channel for an emerging generation of local associations that shared certain goals with the family associations, but conceived of their aspirations in terms that went beyond family interests to embrace community or neighbourhood concerns, i.e. the *Asociaciones de Vecinos* (AA.VV.) (neighbourhood associations).

Together, the 1964 Law and the Movimiento's re-organization provided a legal framework that opened a space 'from above' for the revival of non-ideological associationism, but this opening from above was paralleled by the opening 'from below'. Thus, the legal mechanisms were one element of a complex dynamic that included the everyday pressures that pushed people to seek new ways of defending their collective interests. For those who experimented with neighbourhood associations, interests were defined by the economic and social consequences of the regime's abandonment of autarky and its pursuit of economic integration into the liberal world economy. The urban crisis brought on by industrialization, massive urban immigration, spiralling housing costs and lagging public services is too well known to repeat here.[41] It was the enormity of these immediate and everyday challenges that propelled residents to find new ways to resolve them. And it was the fact that the State's responses to these challenges was generally ineffectual that led residents to search for new avenues outside the official bureaucratic channels. The centralized nature of the Francoist State located decision-making in bureaucratic structures far removed from peoples' lives, while the unrepresentative local governments they appealed to had neither the power nor the resources and the political will to act as defenders of their communities.[42] The unaccountability of local government, added to the often labyrinthian chain of command within the regime's bureaucratic structure, created the image of a State that was at best inept and at worst negligent.[43]

One can see the roots of community organization in the gap between urban deficiencies and an unresponsive State, in the growing frustration caused by unfulfilled promises, unanswered petitions and unexplained delays. The various petitions sent by groups of residents to the central government, complaining about their street, their apartment block or their neighbourhood provide a window into the development of new social networks and collective identities. From early on, the regime accepted the legitimacy of mobilizing around shared urban interests, as long as they were not articulated as class warfare. In this context, the neighbourhood association emerged as an alternative form of mobilization that passed under the radar of the regime's censorship, at least at first.

The new era of associations: scope

While the neighbourhood associations emerged out of such local initiatives, often sparked by a particular issue or crisis, the family associations began as a top-down phenomenon, promoted by the National Commission of Associations (DNA) created in 1958 and re-organized in 1970 as the National Family Commission (DNF).[44] The DNA launched its campaign in 1963 to promote the constitution of a family association in every town in Spain. While this goal was never achieved, over the next several years hundreds of local associations and 40 provincial federations were constituted around the country. These Federations in turn constituted the *Unión Nacional de Asociaciones Familiares* (National Union of Family Associations) to 'represent the associational family movement at the national level'.[45] New Associations of Heads of Household (ACF) continued to be created as late as April 1977, but beginning in 1971, the focus turned away from these so-called 'general' family associations towards those dedicated to 'specific' issues.[46] Thus, in June 1971, the 'familiarista' Enrique Villoria reported that there were 2284 ACFs, 43 associations for families with disabled members, 134 parent associations (APAs), 25 housewife associations, 20 consumer associations and 11 domestic worker associations.[47] While the absolute number of ACFs was always greater, after this point, about two-thirds of the new associations

Table 8.1   Associations in Spain

Year of constitution	Total # associations	Associations formed
(Nov–Dec) 1963		6
1964	327	319
1965	498	171
1966	846	348
1967	1672	825
1968	1824	123
1969	2008	185
1970	2200	190
1971	2730	335
1972	3072	371
1973	3486	414
1974	3830	344
1975	4074	244
1976	4300	226
(Jan–April) 1977	4521	221

created were parent associations, with smaller numbers of the other categories. By the time the *Movimiento* was dissolved in April 1977, there were 4521 associations on the national register (see Table 8.1).

Of these 4500, about 50 of them were Housewife (some provincial and some local branches) and 1400 were Parent Associations.[48] While it is difficult to verify the number of individuals who belonged to these associations, the National Family Commissioner in 1972, Carlos Bonet, claimed to have more than a million members in the movement.[49]

However, these million members were distributed unevenly around the country. Using the register of all associations constituted between 1963 and 1977, Zaragoza and Alicante were the only two provinces with over 200 associations, with another 14 provinces registering over 100 (Toledo, Seville, Segovia, Tenerife, Murcia, Málaga, Madrid, Las Palmas, Jaén, Granada, La Coruña, Castellón, Barcelona, Almería). On the other end of the scale were another dozen with fewer than 30 associations (Melilla, Ceuta, Zamora, Soria, Santander, Palencia, Lugo, Huelva, Guipúzcoa, Guadalajara, Gerona, Cádiz, Ávila).[50] There was an even greater gap in the number of Parent Associations constituted, with 26 provinces registering less than a dozen and a handful of provinces, like Segovia, Seville, Alicante and Granada, where up to 150 schools had constituted Parent Associations. Most of the Housewife Associations were provincial in scope, which helps explain the smaller number, but 26 provinces had none at all. On the other extreme, Seville and Madrid were the only provinces with multiple local Housewife Associations – nine and eleven, respectively.

Beyond the bare numbers, there is anecdotal evidence that the initial constitution of the first 'general' family associations (ACFs) in the mid-1960s generated a wave of enthusiasm that was reflected in at least some cases with high levels of participation and great hopes.[51] Even if the associations were initiated 'from above' by provincial or local officials, they were obviously most successful when they resonated with local residents interested in improving what one *Movimiento* report called '*la vida social*' (social life).[52] Thus, the ACF Caspe in Zaragoza was constituted in January 1964 with 45 members, but that number had swelled to 700 by March of 1965.[53] In another Zaragoza district, the ACF of Ejea de los Caballeros was founded by 40 heads of household in March 1964, but had signed up 458 by the end of the year.[54] Likewise, the membership of the ACF Pizarelles (Salamanca) rose from 300 to 500 in the first year[55] and yet another Zaragoza district (Borja) formed an ACF with 80 members, which had grown to 568 by the end of the year, through the strategy of holding small meetings of 15–20 people.[56] In Ventanielles (Oviedo), 750 of the 2300 heads of household of the *barrio* attended the founding assembly of the ACF in June 1964[57] and in Cogeces del Monte (Valladolid), the Provincial Commissioner (DP) (*Delegado Provincial*) reported that 'this association has been born with a lot of energy'.[58] The DP of Lérida related the constitution of four ACFs in early 1964, all in villages of less than 5000 inhabitants, which attracted 72, 98, 150 and 130 heads of families to the founding meetings.[59]

The atmosphere at one of these early assemblies was depicted in a *Diario de Córdoba* article recounting the first assembly of the ACF Cañero, in which every seat was full, many people asked questions and the entire proceeding was marked by 'a climate of intense interest'.[60] A similar undertone of excitement was expressed in the Provincial Commissioner of Madrid's report of the founding of the ACF Ezequiel Peñalver, which he described as very animated and also full of questions from the residents.[61] This grass roots enthusiasm for 'the associational idea that has taken root as a way to resolve their collective needs'[62] can also be glimpsed in some of the initial detailed Provincial Commissioner background reports, before the later crush of applications reduced many of them to repetition of stock phrases. While even the early reports are encrusted in boilerplate language, the variation that emerges reveals something of the specific aspirations invested in the new associations. Thus, a common trope was to describe an association's goals as 'those laid out in the Statutes', followed by, 'with special attention to', which left space for particular goals, both abstract and concrete. In villages the emphasis tended to be on improving social life, although schools were also a pressing problem: 'Education and entertainment', 'education, housing and day care', 'education and entertainment for children', 'improve collective social life', 'inject more life into local meeting spots', 'intensify family life', or, more generally, 'improve the social environment, especially for young people'.

In urban neighbourhoods or larger towns, the goals usually centred on the inadequate infrastructure surrounding newly built housing units, but even in these cases there was specificity to the hierarchy of problems. A selection of reports submitted by the Provincial Commissioner of Madrid provides a good sense of the variety that existed within the basic model[63]:

(1) Ezequiel Peñalver: medical assistance, transport, problems with the construction company
(2) Canillas: transport is the key issue and what gives the ACF its 'popular base'
(3) Avenida Manzanares: education and beautification of the housing project and creating their own administration to replace the one set up by the company
(4) Aravaca: the biggest problem is to find homes for those evicted from shacks
(5) Pozuelo: housing
(6) Campamento: create schools, open spaces and urbanize streets
(7) Carabanchel Alto: scarcity of schools and lack of sufficient running water
(8) El Escorial: to build subsidized housing
(9) Valverde: build secondary school, install a market, bring the metro
(10) San Cristóbal: the main problem is to negotiate the transfer of property titles to individual owners and install a market.

The initial enthusiasm for the family associations that is reflected in these anecdotes appears to have declined in the early 1970s, although more research is necessary to confirm this trend. Given the high expectations with which some of these associations were founded, it is not surprising that disillusionment would have set in when it became apparent that the weakened *Movimiento*'s patronage could not produce all the necessary schools, sewers and cultural centres. The lack of results created what the provincial chief of the *Movimiento* in Guadalajara described in October of 1973 as the 'general if mistaken opinion as to the inactivity (*inoperancia*) of the family association movement'.[64] In practical terms, this meant that many of the family associations simply ceased to function at some point. Thus, just before the dissolution of the *Movimiento*, the National Family Commissioner distributed question-naires to its provincial delegates, asking them to ascertain how many of their registered associations actually functioned. Unfortunately, only 12 of the Provincial Commissioners were able to submit this data, but if their figures are accurate, they were able to verify that 634 of the registered associations in these provinces alone existed only on paper.[65]

Nevertheless, it is important not to equate decline with '*inoperancia*' of the family association movement. Thus, even among the 12 reporting provinces, there were still 1200 functioning associations. Beyond this admittedly limited classification, there are anecdotal glimpses of appar-ently vibrant associations around the country. Thus, the Provincial Commissioner of La Coruña praised the 'magnificent labour' of the ACF Puentes de García Rodríguez in his otherwise dire report of March 1974,[66] and the one functioning ACF of Huelva in Isla Cristina was described elsewhere by the Provincial Commissioner as having 235 members, five years of 'active life', a dozen committees and a series of successful projects.[67] Similarly, in 1973 the Commissioner of San Sebastián singled out the enthusiastic members of the Family Associ-ation of Alza, who 'do a great job',[68] while from Lérida, the Commis-sioner reported that the ACF Tarrega was building a group of 45 homes[69] and the *Movimiento* chief in Castellón enthused that 'it is magnificent to see the spirit that animates the members [of the ACF Alcalá de Chivert] in their centre, in their homes and in their activities'.[70] The Commissioner of Baleares' report mentioned earlier included eight ACFs outside of Palma in 'good condition', four in Mallorca, three in Ibiza and one in Menorca, as well as six in Palma, although two were 'weaker' (*más floja*) than the other four.[71] In Barcelona, where the Commis-sioner admitted in a 1974 report that the *Movimiento* was viewed negat-ively in Catalonia, creating a hostile environment for its associations, a congress held in February 1976 included representatives of 24 associ-ations from the city and another 33 from the province.[72] An interesting window into this apparent paradox was provided by one reporter from Barcelona who felt compelled to publicly disagree with a recent editorial dismissing the ACFs as 'pathetic', 'ineffective' and 'dead', in contrast to other more 'grass roots' and 'representative' associations. According to his own experience of attending many meetings and assemblies of ACFs over the years, he had found often high levels of participation and enthusiasm which were never reported by journalists who had not bothered to come and see for themselves.[73]

The conclusions that can be drawn from this unsystematic analysis are not conclusive, but the material does open the door to a richer and more complex interpretation of the family association milieu. In contrast to the existing presumption which simply ignores or dismisses these associations as 'fascist', non-existent or unrepresentative of the 'true' interests of the people, the reality appears to be much more diverse than such monolithic judgements allow for. Thus, the vitality of these associations depended very much on local conditions, on the actions of *Movimiento* officials, the enthusiasm of groups of residents and the nature of the community's problems. The combination of all these factors determined whether the association was constituted in the first place, whether it remained an invention of a provincial *Movimiento* official or took on the aspirations of residents who were looking for channels to express their collective desires. Beyond this initial enthusiasm, its continued vitality depended on the success of the *Movimiento* model of close collaboration between associations and the State, which in practice meant the effectiveness of collective appeals sent up the *Movimiento* hierarchy. If such appeals did not produce results, as seems likely given the general weakness of the *Movimiento* within a regime that was already overwhelmed by the demands on its resources, the association would lose support and fall into decline or adopt a more confrontative stance that was labelled 'politicization'.[74] If such a hypothesis is generalized, it would support an evolutionary paradigm of the family association movement, which began in the mid-1960s with some (uneven) level of grass roots enthusiasm and then lost steam in the 1970s as the collaborative ideal of State/civil society broke down under the pressures of rapid and uncontrolled development and an unresponsive State.

The decline of the family association movement dovetails nicely with the expansion of the neighbourhood associations. Even though the 1964 Law was passed around the same time as the *Movimiento* created its first family associations, the pace of associations registering through this route was generally slower and later. Although the first neighbourhood associations predated the family associations as well as the 1964 Law, with the exception of Barcelona, they appear to be isolated cases. In Barcelona, according to a remarkably frank Provincial Commissioner report of 1972, the 'great associational current' that had characterized the city since the late nineteenth century had continued with the present generation of neighbourhood associations. He estimated that around 100 of them had already taken advantage of the 1941

Law granting 'freedom of association' and that since the 1964 Law, the number of associations had increased to 140 or 150.[75] Furthermore, these associations appeared to have taken root in a wide variety of local contexts, according to an editorial in *Vanguardia Española*, which commented on the great heterogeneity of a milieu that included business associations, middle-class neighbourhoods, cultural and recreational groups and working-class *barrios*.[76]

At a national level, however, the growth of these and other non-*Movimiento* associations was generally slower and later, with important turning points in 1964 and 1975. According to the National Register of Associations,which was established in 1964 with 2500 mostly pre-existing associations, about 1000 associations of all types were created each year until 1974. Although the increase was gradual, it is important to note that the number of associations created between 1941 and 1964 had essentially doubled only three years after the new law was passed. Between 1975 and 1977 the number of new associations created each year jumped to 2283 and during the final years of the transition, it had reached 5639 a year.[77] By the end of 1979, the number of associations on the register had reached almost 30,000. The majority of these new associations were local in scope and increasingly so from the early 1970s. That is, while in 1972, 56 per cent of the new associations created were local, in 1976 this applied to 65 and 73 per cent in 1978. Of the total number of associations in 1979, about 17 per cent were neighbourhood associations, and another 28 per cent were parent associations, which were often closely linked at the local level. While the 5199 neighbourhood associations represented a small portion of the overall number of associations in 1979, its membership levels were disproportionately higher. Thus, of all people who belonged to an association, 30 per cent had joined a Neighbourhood, and another 15 per cent were members of a Parent Association.

What the intersecting narratives of the *Movimiento* and the 1964 Law suggest is a general trend towards associationism which begins in the mid-to-late 1960s, but is divided into two phases. The first phase in the 1960s was led by the family associations, while the protagonists of the second phase, beginning in the early 1970s and culminating in 1978, were the neighbourhood associations. Even though the ideological orientation of the two types of associations was generally quite different, this chronology suggests that in some sense they operated on the same terrain, among a population searching for ways to reconstitute the collective voice of the public sphere vis a vis an evolving State. From this perspective, the reconstruction of associational life was a more gradual, long-term process than a quick glance at the National Register of Associations might imply. Instead of a quick blip in 1977–78 that one could interpret as a consequence of the political opening created by the Transition, what emerges is a more sustained process that makes Spain's reconstituted civil society look less ephemeral. At the same time, we can see the complex interaction of legal, economic and social changes within the dictatorship that had to come together to create the space for this reconstitution. It was at the juncture between economic development, political reform and social transformation that ordinary people found new ways to solve their everyday problems. And in the process, they became part of the social history of a political transition which most of them could not yet imagine and which still remains largely unwritten.

Notes

1. This is the oft-quoted claim of the classic chronicler of the movement, Manuel Castells. In English, see *The City and the Grassroots: A Cross-Cultural Theory of Urban Social Movements* (Berkeley, CA: UC Press, 1983), Chapter 5, 'The Making of an Urban Social Movement in Madrid', p. 215.
2. For a more extensive review of the interpretive models, see Richard Gunther et al., *Democracy in Modern Spain* (New Haven, CT: Yale University Press, 2004). The authoritative transitology work is the four-volume collection edited by Guillermo O'Donnell, Philippe Schmitter and Laurence Whitehead, *Transitions from Authoritarian Rule: Prospects for Democracy* (Baltimore, MD: Johns Hopkins Press, 1986).
3. Víctor Pérez-Díaz, *The Return of Civil Society: The Emergence of Democratic Spain* (Cambridge: Harvard University Press, 1993), pp. 6–7.
4. Pérez-Díaz differs from Habermas in his definition: 'the autonomous sphere of markets, associations and the public sphere'. *The Return of Civil Society*, p. 56.
5. See Iris Marion Young, *Inclusion and Democracy* (Oxford: Oxford University Press, 2000), Chapter 5, for an elaboration of how voluntary associations contribute to the horizontal and vertical axes of citizenship. See also my article 'Ciudadanía y la Transición', in Manuel Pérez Ledesma, ed., *De súbditos a ciudadanos: Una historia de la ciudadanía en España* (Madrid: Centro de Estudios Políticos y Constitucionales, 2007), for a more detailed analysis of 'citizenship' as a useful concept for exploring popular political agency.
6. There are increasing numbers of local studies, most of which focus on the post-1975 period. Two that begin their analysis in the late-Franco period are: Manuel Domínguez López, 'El movimiento vecinal en el barrio de Bellvitge, 1960s–1980s' and María Isabel Fariñas de Alba, 'Aproximación al estudio del movimiento vecinal en la crisis del franquismo y la transición', both in José Manuel Trujillano Sánchez and Pilar Domínguez Prats, eds, *La crisis del franquismo y la transición: el protagonismo de los movimientos sociales* (Avila: Fundación Cultural Santa Teresa, 2003).

7. Although most of the data comes from membership after the transition, Peter McDonough and his colleagues have situated Spain on the low end of associational participation in comparative studies of transitions. See Peter McDonough, Samuel Barnes and Antonio López Piña, 'Authority and Association: Spanish Democracy in Comparative Perspective', and Peter McDonough, Doh Shin and José Alvaro Moisés, 'Democratization and Participation: Comparing Spain, Brazil and Korea', both in *The Journal of Politics*, 46, 3 (August 1984), pp. 652–88 and 60, 4 (1998).

8. Fabriola Mota, 'La realidad asociativa en España', in Joan Subirats, ed., *Existe sociedad civil en España? Responsabilidades colectivas y valores públicos* (Madrid: Fundación Encuentro, 1999), p. 41, gives some comparative numbers for 1981 for the rate of voluntary association: 31 per cent in Spain vs. 50 per cent in Germany, 52 per cent in the UK and 62 per cent in Holland, but comparable to France and Italy.

9. See Juan Pablo Fusi, 'La reaparicion de la conflictividad en la España de los sesenta', in Josep Fontana, ed., *España bajo el franquismo* (Barcelona: Crítica, 2000).

10. The *Movimiento* was created in 1937 out of the various groups and parties that supported the Nationalists in the Civil War. Modelled after the fascist parties in Germany and Italy, the *Movimiento* was most influential during the initial phase of the regime, but began to decline after 1945 and the defeat of the fascist powers.

11. *Doblón*, 16 August 1975.

12. Rafael Prieto-Lacaci, 'Asociaciones voluntarias', in Salustino del Campo, dir., *Tendencias Sociales en España, 1960–1990* (Bilbao: Fundación BBV, 1993), p. 197.

13. Prieto-Lacaci, 'Asociaciones', p. 199. Feliciano Montero García puts the number in 1955 at 600,000. See *La Acción Católica y el franquismo: auge y crisis de la Acción Católica Especializada* (Madrid: UNED, 2000), p. 248.

14. Juan Linz, 'La realidad asociativa de los Españoles', in *Sociología española de los años setenta* (Madrid: Confederación Española de Cajas de Ahorros, 1971), p. 315.

15. Prieto-Lacaci, 'Asociaciones', p. 199.

16. Fabriola Mota, 'Realidad', p. 48. The associations on the Register would NOT include the special category associations belonging to the Church and the Movimiento.

17. Juan Linz, 'Realidad', p. 313, cites the lack of published statistical data as the obstacle to greater precision. Prieto-Lacaci cites Linz's figure in his 1990 article.

18. Mikel Aizpuru, 'Asociacionismo popular: reverso del modelo de organización social del franquismo? El caso de Barakaldo', in Santiago Castillo and José Maria Ortíz de Orruño, eds, *Estado, protesta y movimientos sociales* (Bilbao: Universidad del País Vasco, 1997), p. 482.

19. Feliciano Montero García, *La Acción Católica*; Basilisa López García, *Aproximación a la historia de la HOAC* (Madrid: Ediciones HOAC, 1995); Javier Domínguez, *Organizaciones obreras cristianas en la oposición al franquismo (1951–1975)* (Bilbao: Ediciones Mensajeros, 1985); Rafael Díaz Salazar, *Iglesia, Dictadura y Democracia* (Madrid: Ediciones HOAC, 1981); José Manuel Cuenca Toribio, *Catolicismo social y político en la España contemporánea (1870–2000)*

(Madrid: Unión Editorial, 2000); José Fernández Segura, 'La presencia de militantes obreros católicos en el movimiento obrero de Barcelona', Enrique Berzal de la Rosa, 'La oposición católica al franquismo en Castilla y León', Mónica Moreno Seco, 'Cristianos y lucha antifranquista en Alicante durante la transición', all in José Manuel Trujillano Sánchez and Pilar Domínguez Prats, eds, *La crisis del franquismo y la transición: el protagonismo de los movimientos sociales* (Avila: Fundación Cultural Santa Teresa, 2003).

20. Jose Manuel Cuenca Toribio, *Catolicismo*, pp. 419–23.
21. Shubert, *A Social History of Spain*, p. 243.
22. See Montero, *La Acción Católica*, Introduction.
23. Montero, *La Acción Católica*.
24. Both Fernández Segura, 'La presencia', and Berzal de la Rosa, 'La oposición católica', make this point, as well as Rafael Díaz, *Iglesia*, 'eran organizaciones apostólicos que creaban militantes obreros, que a nivel personal luchaban en el combate obrero', p. 201.
25. As Víctor Pérez-Díaz puts it, the Catholic organizations of the 1950s and 1960s were sources of apprenticeship for the political organizations of the later period, so that the Church played the same sort of 'prepolitical' function on the left during this period that it had traditionally played on the right. *The Return of Civil Society*, p. 159.
26. Frances Lannon, 'Catholicism and Social Change', in Helen Graham and Jo Labanyi, eds, *Spanish Cultural Studies* (Oxford: Oxford University Press, 1995), p. 282 and William Callahan, *The Catholic Church in Spain, 1875–1998* (Washington, DC: Catholic University of America Press, 2000), pp. 522–3.
27. More research needs to be done to flesh out the activities and scope of these associations, which became an important lobbying group for religious education in the late 1970s and 1980s.
28. Callahan, *Catholic Church*, p. 315.
29. *Boletín* of the *Asociación de Padres de Familia* Colegio Menesiano (Madrid), December 1972. The Madrid federation statistics appeared in the March 1974 edition.
30. 'El Movimiento y su Consejo', in Manuel Fraga et al., eds, *La España de los años 70* (Madrid: Editorial Moneda y Crédito, 1972), p. 1178.
31. Solís was Secretary General of the Movimiento from 1957 to 1969. Cited in Santiago Miguel González, *La preparación de la transición a la democracia en España* (Zaragoza: Universidad de Zaragoza, 1990), pp. 70–1.
32. Ortí Bordás, 'El Movimiento', p. 1180.
33. Enrique Villoria Martínez, *Las asociaciones familiares* (Madrid: Ediciones del Movimiento, 1971), p. 9. See also other Movimiento publications for elaboration of these ideas: *El asociacionismo y el desarrollo político* and *El Movimiento y el asociacionismo*, written by Torcuato Fernández Miranda in 1969 and 1970.
34. Miguel González, *La preparación*, p. 81. The first position was defended by Fernández Miranda and the latter by Solís.
35. This debate is discussed in detail by Miguel González, *La preparación*, pp. 78–81.
36. For example, Miguel González, in *La preparación*, barely mentions these asociaciones in a narrative focused almost entirely on the failure to turn the Movimiento into a framework for a pre-political party system.
37. Enrique Villoria Martínez, *Las asociaciones familiares*, p. 12.

38. The comments are unsigned, but 'Gabinete técnico' is handwritten on the top of the document. Included in the folder with the 'Exposición de Motivos' and the 'Anteproyecto', they were obviously part of a package presented to the appropriate official in the Ministry of the Interior (Gobernación). (Archivo General del Estado (AGE), Ministerio de Gobernación (Gob), caja 388).
39. In structural/institutional terms, this meant that the two worlds of voluntary associations were integrated into different bureaucratic structures, the Interior Ministry, on the one hand, and the Ministry of Culture, where the *Movimiento* was housed, on the other.
40. Associations had to submit their statutes for approval to the Civil Governor, who made a report and passed the petition on to the Ministry of the Interior for final approval. The political police drew up reports on each of the members of the founding committees and rejected anyone with a connection to the defeated side in the Civil War or to 'Marxist' movements.
41. See Manuel Castells, *The City and the Grassroots* for a basic description of the urban crisis in Madrid. For a micro-vision of the crisis from a single neighbourhood, see the book published by the Asociación de Vecinos de Nazaret, *Historia de un barrio: Nazaret* (Madrid: CAVE, 1992). For a more technical analysis of particular issues, see articles written by Francoist officials in Manuel Fraga et al., eds, *La España de los años 70*: Jose Luis Carreras Yañez, 'Construcción y Vivienda: Materiales de construcción', Eduardo Navarro Alvarez, 'La Política de la Vivienda' and José Manuel Romay Beccaria, 'La Política Urbanística'.
42. In one petition to the Ministry of the Interior, 373 residents of a town in Gerona complained that the urban plan proposed by the city government favoured the interests of the property owners and wealthy residents, many of them local officials, at the expense of their poorer district and that there had never been any public consultation on the plan (1 November 1970; AGE, Gob, caja 1089).
43. Many of the petitions sent to the Ministry of the Interior reflect the frustration that more immediate grievance channels had proved unsatisfactory. In one case (10 May 1969), residents of a town outside of Avila complained about the stalled construction of a block of houses begun several years ago but as yet unfinished and no local officials could explain why. Although the Civil Governor had visited several months earlier and was sympathetic to their predicament, his public criticism did not affect the project. The file includes a follow-up letter, sent two months later (8 July 1969) by the Minister to the Mayor of the town, asking for information about the issue (AGE, Gob, caja 1089).
44. The purpose of the reorganization was to separate the family associations from so-called 'political' associations, but this latter project never got the approval of Franco. The documentation of the DNA and DNF can be found in the AGE, in the section of the Ministry of Culture (Cult). I looked closely at all the correspondence and case files for Madrid associations, as well as the correspondence between the National Commissioner and the Provincial Commissioners of other provinces. Thus, the national-level data cited here reflects an incomplete survey of the material.
45. *Boletín de la Asociación de Cabezas de Familia de Getafe*, July 1966 (AGE, Cult, caja 33).

46. The first parent association (APA) was constituted in Barcelona in April 1969.
47. Villoria, *Las Asociaciones familiares* (AGE, Cult, caja 224).
48. Registro, April 1977 (AGE, Cult, caja 316).
49. *Boletín Informativa de la Asociación de Propietarios y Vecinos de Moratalaz,* January 1972.
50. AGE, Cult, caja 316.
51. This analysis is based on a close examination of the *Movimiento* files of the first 75 ACFs which were constituted in late 1963 and 1964 throughout Spain, as well as all of those constituted in Madrid, no matter what the date of constitution. Obviously, a more detailed investigation of the entire archive is necessary before more definitive conclusions can be drawn.
52. General Instructions on Associations Affiliated with the *Movimiento*, January 1976, caja 180.
53. AGE, Cult, caja 26.
54. AGE, Cult, caja 27.
55. *Memoria* (Annual Report) (24 March 1965). AGE, Cult, caja 26.
56. *Memoria* 1964. AGE, Cult, caja 26.
57. DP report, 21 April 1964. AGE, Cult, caja 28.
58. DP report, 2 May 1964. AGE, Cult, caja 27.
59. Reports written 27 April 1964 and 30 April. AGE, Cult, caja 27.
60. AGE, Cult, caja 26.
61. Report, 16 June 1966. AGE, MC, caja 60.
62. In the unusually detailed report of the DP Salamanca on the ACF Pizarrales. 2 December 1963. AGE, Cult, caja 26.
63. AGE, Cult, cajas 42, 44, 48, 55, 63, 65, 66, 68.
64. At the First Provincial Assembly of Family Associations. Manuscript of speech. AGE, Cult, caja 226.
65. AGE, Cult, caja 316. There were undoubtedly non-functioning associations in other provinces, but the numbers are harder to evaluate. In the provinces where the DPs took the trouble to contact each association and determine that some did not function, it seems reasonable to give greater weight to their assertion that others did function.
66. Letter to DN, March 1974. AGE, Cult, caja 228.
67. Letter to DN, 10 June 1972. AGE, Cult, caja 227.
68. Letter to DN, 7 February 1973. AGE, Cult, caja 230.
69. Letter to DN, 1 March 1974. AGE, Cult, caja 227.
70. Letter to DN, 14 October 1975. AGE, Cult, caja 225.
71. Report, 31 December 1971. AGE, Cult, caja 223.
72. Report, 13 February 1974, Letter February 1976. AGE, Cult, caja 224.
73. *Solidaridad Nacional,* 8 October 1970. AGE, Cult, caja 224.
74. One of the earliest instances of such a process may have been in Vizcaya, where the Civil Governor suspended several ACFs in 1972.
75. Report, 24 October 1972. AGE, Cult, caja 224.
76. 29 June 1972. Submitted with the DP report.
77. The analysis in this paragraph comes from Fabriola Mota, 'La realidad asociativa', pp. 44–54.

9
Cultural Diversity and the Development of a Pre-democratic Civil Society in Spain

Elisa Chuliá

Introduction

The Spanish democratic transition has been predominantly interpreted as an arrangement between the reformist elites of the Francoist regime and the opposition elites, both ready to agree on the establishment (according to the former) or re-establishment (according to the latter) of democracy in an ordered way, drawing on the lessons learnt from the traumatic experience of the Civil War (1936–39).[1] Probably this interpretation, in which the prominent role in the transition has been generally attributed to the national elites and their strategic decisions, explains why the society at that time, or more specifically, the way in which people treated and related to each other, their ideas on politics, their values or normative preferences when organizing their lives, setting up their families, receiving information on public issues or enjoying leisure time have attracted only limited attention among historians.

Much greater interest seems to have been aroused by the ideas and views of the opposition elites who were to take up important posts in the different spheres of power in the new democratic regime. Some recent and very influential works have explained how this critical culture of the democratizing elites started early on and was developing from the 1950s. This thesis carries the risk of insinuating that this critical culture was prevalent in the Spanish population or that it was the only one with true significance (i.e. worthy of being called 'culture') in the social context of the time. Yet for many years, this critical culture lived alongside other perceptions and interpretations of the political and social situation and with other priorities and strategies for life, that is to say with other ways of thinking and living life in private and in the community.

My starting point is that this coexistence between cultures which took place during the second half of Franco's regime as the level of well-being of the population rose, as relationships with foreign countries (through emigration and tourism basically) increased and as the informative and leisure offer and the variety of social practices expanded, was crucial for the development of a civil society culture. As a normative concept, civil society fits better with cultural plurality than hegemony, better with diversity than homogeneity. In fact, the supremacy of one culture, valuable though it may appear to be, does not fit in well with the idea of exchanges between citizens with different views and interests, with the search for rational, balanced agreements or with the public debate on options for alternative actions.

Within the framework of cultural diversity which was taking shape during more or less the last 15 years of Franco's regime, the Francoist elites maintained considerable influence over the cultural offer. Even when the regime liberalized the mechanisms for cultural control during the 1960s, it never actually gave them up and knew how to effectively pamper 'cultural producers' widely accepted by the public in order to ensure their complicity. If the dictatorship proved unable to prevent cultural criticism from acquiring a greater public voice and social prestige in the final years it was because the specificity of its own cultural offer was gradually being watered down in the process of enhancing its attraction for broad sectors of the population.

The concept of culture is so extremely difficult to pin down empirically that writing about it is always risky and never more so than when the period in question is a dictatorship which means many cultural manifestations are not easily documented. Aware of the difficulties of tackling this subject, my aim in this article is limited to setting down some reflections on the usual arguments put forward when talking about culture during Franco's dictatorship, highlighting certain facts which are rarely associated with this question and drawing attention to the internal complexity of Spanish society whose behaviour during the transition to democracy has been so highly praised by those who have studied this process.

The development of a pre-democratic Spanish civil society

The historiography on Franco's dictatorship published in recent decades puts forward controversial arguments on numerous aspects of this period in Spanish history. But as research broadens our knowledge of this period, considerable agreement also seems to be developing. Few historians now question that Spanish society progressively experienced significant changes both in its structure and its culture during the second half of Franco's regime from the late 1950s to the dictator's death in 1975. These changes have often been seen as a favourable condition for the transition to democracy. As Víctor Pérez-Díaz has argued, the political elites in the transition operated within the framework of a society which already deserved to be described as 'civil' in the strict sense of the word.[2]

It is definitely possible to talk about a pre-democratic civil society but with two qualifications: first, this civil society did not exclude 'uncivil' behaviour in some private institutions and in the majority of public ones in which arbitrary, abusive interpersonal relationships prevailed, in which there was no respect from the interlocutor or a willingness to share information or other resources to develop relatively symmetrical bonds. Second, the emerging civil society was built more on socio-cultural practices than on solid, private, social institutions (such as associations with free or voluntary participation). These socio-cultural practices had been taking shape slowly and spontaneously from the experiences of social gatherings and conversations between family members, neighbours and friends, breaking the silence arising from the extensive, harsh policy of social control imposed at the start by the dictator and which was later relaxed but not without interruptions. The framework was also being forged in the work environment through contacts between colleagues who might have different attitudes towards public issues but were able to cooperate and get along with each other in order to reach specific objectives. And as the moderate capacity for mobilization of both the regime and the opposition in the face of expected and unexpected issues clearly showed, large sectors of this society had been demonstrating prudent resistance to the idea of being passionately mobilized by political slogans.

According to Pérez-Díaz, all these social–cultural practices and these 'messages' of prudence from Spanish society moulded the perception of the problems and the formulation of preferences for the elites which piloted the process of transition to democracy. The Spanish society at that time not only set the limits but also bestowed legitimacy upon the negotiating strategies and agreements of the politicians by backing their tact and talent in designing the most inclusive political changes possible.

How and why this pre-democratic civil society was developing is far from clear. I argue here that one condition of its emergence was the existence of diverse and concurrent cultures, produced by those who were part of the regime or Francoist sympathizers as well as those who, at one time or another during the dictatorship, were drawing away from it, along with those who were always placed outside it. These cultures found support in different media; in widely read publications strictly controlled by the regime but also in others with a smaller readership and less strictly controlled as well as in those the dictatorship banned from circulation; in the radio and television whose content was submitted to censorship, but also in foreign media which managed to get through the barriers of censorship or interferences (in the case of radio stations); in the cinema and the theatre from directors and script writers who wrote about local customs and supporters of the political and moral principles of the regime but where there were also alternative productions from critical writers.

It is certain that in the mid-1970s the cultures with which dissidents and opponents felt identified (to speak of a culture of the opposition would be to simplify things overly), seemed to have taken over the public voice, edging to one side those who did not form part of it.[3] Important men in Franco's regime admitted so much with frustration.[4] But it seems very likely that below this 'spiral of silence', as Javier Pradera (relying on Elisabeth Noelle-Neumann's coined concept) defined the progressive silencing of the Francoist discourse perceptible in the years prior to the dictator's death,[5] people with different cultural attitudes and identities continued living together, talking and trying to understand one another within families, neighbourhoods, newspaper offices and in many other places of convergence (to a lesser extent in the large companies and universities where the opposition discourse was more pervasive). Even when shot through with tensions and conflicts, this 'culture of cultures' could create a space for learning civic attitudes such as the need to acknowledge and respect the integrity and opinions of those who dissented, or the possibility of living together in peace, and even the articulation of viable compromises with people and groups that did not exactly share preferences on how to organize life together.

The theory of the early failure of the Francoist culture

When it comes to explaining the evolution of Spanish society from the end of the 1950s, probably the most recurrent arguments in the literature on Francoism focus attention on factors related to the modernization and expansion of the Spanish economy arising from the progressive abandonment of autarky from 1950 onwards and the implementation of the 1959 Stabilization Plan. After the first years of recession following the launch of this programme of (partial) economic liberalization, strong economic growth drove the development of the middle classes, progressively reducing social inequalities and softening the serious ideological differences which had been so starkly highlighted in the Civil War. On the other hand, massive emigration to European countries and the growing influx of tourists brought Spaniards into contact with freer styles of life encouraging imitation of types of behaviour which were disapproved of and condemned by the regime.[6] These explanations of a predominately structural nature are consistent with theories of modernization which were formulated in the 1950s and 1960s as well as the famous arguments formulated by Seymour M. Lipset (1959) on how economic development and its likely implications (e.g. the increase in inhabitants in the big cities, the levels of education of the population and the use of mass media and means of transport), while not being either a necessary or sufficient condition for coming out of a dictatorship, may favour the implantation of a democracy.

However, the recent publication of very important works on the cultural resistance to Franco's regime and the evolution of a critical consciousness among significant sectors of intellectuals seem to redirect the explanation for the socio-cultural changes which took place from the end of the 1950s. The interpretation that intellectuals, as protagonists of the cultural world, made a crucial contribution to the development of this pre-democratic civil society is gaining weight more or less explicitly. Furthermore, these works coincide in considering culture as a dimension of change which is relatively independent of socio-economic transformations. If this were not so it would be difficult to maintain that the most outstanding intellectual and artistic culture of the time began to 'agitate', or more specifically distance itself critically from the regime, quite a few years before economic development had a marked impact on society.

In a book which earned the most prestigious prize awarded by Spanish publishers in 2004, Jordi Gracia identified signs of this cultural 'agitation' as early as the 1940s. According to his interpretation, cultural resistance against 'fascist irrationalism' under the auspices of the dictator showed up earlier in terms of form than in terms of the content of cultural production. The use of austere, de-ideologized language lacking the ideological pomposity and hyperbole of the victors demonstrated the willingness of some authors to take up the liberal tradition again. Underlying this reclaimed prose of the liberal tradition there was 'an implicit programme of ethical re-education to produce new civilized, relativist people once again'.[7] So, Franco and his people failed in their attempt to annihilate liberal reason, which was reforming itself slowly and surreptitiously until it pushed the fascist culture into a situation of 'intellectual eviction, and a biological end' towards the mid-1950s.[8]

The idea of fascism as a culture and mentality being superseded and, in short, the cultural failure of Francoism in the face of the reborn liberal tradition had already been noted by other authors. Referring to events which took place at the end of the 1940s and beginning of the 1950s, Juan Pablo Fusi has written that 'Francoism had lost the battle of culture' while the intellectual and artistic elites had recovered the liberal culture which the Franco regime had aimed to liquidate with the Civil War and the cruel repression which followed the military victory.[9] Not even the 'religious culture' which took over from the dismantled 'Falangist culture' after the defeat of the Axis in the Second World War managed to set itself up as a real alternative to the 'liberal culture'.

A conclusion consistent with this argument is Caroline Boyd's book in which she analyses the text books used during these years in the schools, crucial institutions for the social and cultural reproduction of Francoism. According to Boyd, the success of Franco's State in trans-mitting National-Catholic cultural values was very limited. Already in the 1950s the liberal educational tradition and the progressive plans for educational reform which the regime had tried to crush in the Civil War had been recovered to a large extent: from the perspective of cultural transmission 'National-Catholicism was a complete failure'.[10]

Therefore, the arguments of Gracia, Fusi and Boyd, among others, lead to the conclusion that the underlying culture of the Franco regime, either in its most fascist or most National-Catholic aspect, lacked consist-ency from the mid-1950s. From then on what acquired the capacity to appeal to the most dynamic sectors of society and earn the name of 'culture' were the ideas, as well as the intellectual and artistic claims and demonstrations, which were critical of the regime, heirs to the liberal tradition and therefore radically incompatible with the defence of the political order imposed throughout Spain in 1939. In any case, as Fusi argues, the dictatorship offered a 'subculture of mass consumption', made up of football, bullfights, light literature, radio soaps and folkloric films. This offer of escapism and evasion was functional for the regime in as much as 'it masked the failure of the official culture in a certain way'.[11]

If we had to identify a landmark in this cultural failure of Francoism, probably the majority of historians would agree in pointing to the 'rebel-lion' of the students in Madrid at the beginning of 1956. In a book on the public presence of Spanish intellectuals which earned him the

National History Prize in 2005, Santos Juliá has given a detailed account of how the process of critical distancing from the regime undertaken by university students and young writers, children of the victors in the Civil War, laid down new intellectual and moral bases for a discourse on the recent past, present and future of Spain. According to Juliá, 1956 marked the turning point in this process of constructing a cultural project to rival the one represented by the regime's leaders and institutions.[12] It was in February of that year, with the unsuccessful National Students' Congress in the University of Madrid and the repression which followed this initiative, that some of the young people close to the Falangist Movement and the Catholic organizations decided to withdraw their support from Francoism. They had become aware that the regime was stifling any possibility of undertaking the necessary political and social reforms to pull Spain out of the situation of moral and material misery it found itself in. They realized that their social, intellectual and artistic concerns could not find an answer within the current institutional structures and that the founding myth of the regime, the Civil War, had been a 'collective madness' which everyone had been responsible for and which required reconciliation between the victors and the defeated.

The events of 1956 transformed more or less lukewarm loyalties into dissidence and provided a catalyst for very important changes in the composition and strategy of the opposition to Franco's regime. As Pere Ysàs has highlighted, the Francoist leaders were very concerned about these incidents especially as this meant a loss of internal support.[13] The fact that Spaniards belonging to the winning side should produce an alternative discourse to the official one on the history of Spain and the current problems was an important challenge to the legitimacy of the regime. Consequently to think that, when faced with this challenge, the Francoist elites resigned themselves to carrying out the battle for the hearts and minds of Spaniards only by applying repressive measures and promoting an 'escapist, evasive sub-culture' hardly looks convincing and is scarcely consistent with the capacity for survival of the regime.[14] Did they not efficiently control the principal sources of political, economic and cultural information which were circulating among the Spanish population? Did they not dominate, either through the *Movimiento* (the Movement, the sole official political organization during Francoism) or the Church, the social organizations through which many families could gain access to such services as leisure for their children and youngsters, study grants and holidays?[15] After having managed to break their international isolation with such well-known successes as the Concordat with the Vatican and the agreement with the United States in 1953, were the

Francoist leaders really going to accept that this entire web of public-sector organizations of party and Church, as well as the daily press, publications, radio and (from 1959) television, should merely support a minor, defensive culture basically aimed at politically desensitizing the population? Furthermore if, as Fusi has written, Franco and Francoism were the consequences of the history of Spain 'and of ideas, values and beliefs deeply set in many Spaniards',[16] to undervalue these ideas, values and beliefs, which were so widespread and supposedly crucial for the maintenance of the regime, or, in any case, to place them on a secondary level in relation to the culture of the elites, seems hardly justifiable.

Culture and projects for Francoist legitimization

Discourses for the legitimization of a dictatorship make up an essential part of the culture which its leaders represent and hope to disseminate among the governed. If we take this assumption as a starting point, stating that a regime has failed culturally implies that the arguments it uses to justify its government and the values through which it claims to govern are not accepted by society. Franco's regime was probably faced with just such a failure when fascism was defeated in the Second World War. Nevertheless, Franco did not allow this situation of disappointment to become rife because he reacted rapidly by changing his legitimization discourse. One of the main advantages of the Francoist elites being made up of right-wing 'families' lay in the relative ease in making such changes without altering the political principles on which the regime was based: the indissoluble unity of the Spanish nation, respect for the hierarchy and confidence in the capacity of the elites, the commandments of the Catholic religion, the value of the family and the acceptance of gender and income differences as characteristic of a legitimate social order. Strictly speaking, none of the axiomatic ideas of Francoist culture was an innovation of the regime: all of them were deeply rooted in Spanish history.[17] The only novelty introduced by the regime was the fascist discourse expressed in convoluted, bombastic rhetoric and in images which glorified the power arising from the will of well-guided, disciplined groups of people.

As many historians on Francoism have highlighted, from 1945 the regime strengthened the discourse and National-Catholic symbols to the detriment of the Falangist ones of the early days. The cultural project of the Falangists, admirers of fascism, lost weight against the standard borne by the Catholics. It was the representatives of the Catholic elites who, in the summer of 1945, a few days before the end of the Second

World War, took control of the press, books and other cultural products which, up to then, had been dependent on the Vice-Secretariat of Popular Education under the Falangists. These Catholic leaders tried to rid Francoist cultural expressions of the most noticeable signs of fascist identity and above all they adopted the strategy of giving precedence to sources of Catholic culture, particularly to the upper eche lons of the church and Catholic organizations. Nevertheless, the change did not appear as a rupture; there was continuity in the exaltation of the figure of the *Caudillo* (leader), in extolling the capacity of the authorities to resolve any type of problem, in presenting contemporary Spain as a country redeemed from its vices and the Spanish as a people who, under Franco's efficient, principled guidance, was capable of reaching the greatest heights while demonstrating its moral superiority in relation to its neighbours.

In 1956, the regime once again found itself in a similar situation with a weakening of what we could call its 'cultural resources'. From the late 1940s, an 'understanding' stream which advocated greater intellectual opening up in the academic and university fields had gained ground at the heart of the Catholic community and among some former fascist intellectuals. [18] The 'understanding' experiment created expectations among groups of students which were to remain unsatisfied. As I have mentioned earlier, this frustration showed up in public protests, against which the regime applied severe repressive measures: the detention of the main leaders of the protests, the closure of Madrid University and suspension of sections 14 and 18 of the Charter of the Spaniards, a poor imitation of a basic charter of rights, which was passed in 1945.

Even though the initial reaction to the 1956 protests consisted of suppressing the mobilizations of students and intellectuals and dismissing the Minister of National Education, from then onwards Franco was opening up space for a new legitimization project which, far from attempting to approach the critical sectors of the regime, concentrated all its efforts on creating an efficient, modern State capable of satisfying the material needs of ample sectors of the population. The Cabinet crisis of February 1957 marked the unfolding of this project, which was promoted by a group of leaders close to Opus Dei, a Catholic institution founded in the 1920s which only numbered around two hundred members in the mid-1940s. This new legitimization project had two aspects. One consisted of strengthening the power of the State, adapting its structure and operation to a modern State model but without setting this up on the basis of political rights and public freedom. This entailed accepting that the governed had certain rights in relation to the authorities as well as regulating administrative procedures. The other aspect lay in overcoming economic stagnation, substituting the economic policy of import replacement with one of a greater opening up to international markets and a decrease in some State regulations.[19]

Just as the Falangist discourse was not abandoned completely in 1945, neither was the discourse centred on the Catholic religion as the key to a virtuous life, the teachings of the Catholic Church and the spiritual values of the Spanish, eclipsed from 1957. Even so, both in official discourse and in cultural expressions produced with the acquiescence of the regime, values such as peace and economic and social well-being had a much greater presence. Stories of saints, of blessed, pious young people and charitable women gave way to stories of men and women who were moving up the social scale and overcoming the problems they faced through work, the rectitude of their feelings and the decency of their behaviour within and outside the family. Individual progress and happiness could be reached without being involved in politics, but simply by benefiting from the good management of the experts. Economic development in the 1960s helped to put the emphasis of the legitimization discourse on substantive rather than symbolic arguments. In fact, the symbology of the regime which had been so abused in the first two decades of the dictatorship was brought back at specific key dates for celebrations with political and religious origins such as 18 July (day of the National Uprising), 1 April (Victory Day), 1 October (*Caudillo's* day) or the 8 December (the Immaculate Conception). Not even the interpretation of the Civil War, the founding myth of the regime, remained unaltered throughout this period.[20] True, the image of Franco as the '*Caudillo* of Peace' had spread since the mid-1940s since 'it had a greater potential of political cooptation' than the image of the '*Caudillo* of Victory'.[21] But as Paloma Aguilar has argued, since the early 1960s justification of the war turned largely on the exaltation of peace, so the emphasis on the legitimacy of origin (victory in war) was downgraded in favour of an emphasis on the legitimacy of exercise (the achievements of the regime in areas such as public order, material welfare and international recognition).[22]

The culture defended by Franco's regime from the late 1950s fitted perfectly into the new legitimization project which revolved around two core concepts: peace and prosperity. The regime could count on numerous resources to disseminate this culture; some were a monopoly (such as the NO-DO news reports and later television, the only media to broadcast moving pictures of public events) and others were subject to rigorous State controls (for example radio, press, cinema, theatre and books). In the 1960s the political culture of the regime showed a clear predilection for publications, programmes, films and plays which expressed the idea that Spain had modernized unrecognizably and offered a relatively unhampered, entertaining life for anyone who strove for progress, although not without the risk of losing certain human values such as social solidarity.

Even though this constitutes only anecdotal evidence, it is worth mentioning some of the films which were big hits with the public at this time, such as *La ciudad no es para mí* (The city is not for me) or *Sor Citroen* (Sister Citroen), both directed by Pedro Lazaga in 1965 and 1967, respectively. In the first an elderly man from a village travels to Madrid where he comes into contact with the exclusive life-style of his son, a well-known surgeon, and the modern everyday life in the capital. In the second, the nuns in a convent have all sorts of adventures when they buy a car on hire purchase, but this also provides the opportunity of improving the resources for carrying out their work. In the theatre, Alfonso Paso had a huge success with light comedies. Using intrigues and impossible situations, his plays reflected values such as respect for hierarchies, the acceptance of the existence of social classes, the weak morals of women and the 'rationality' of keeping them subordinated. Paso was so successful that at the end of the 1960s up to seven theatres in Madrid were running his plays simultaneously. Echoing this fame, the cartoonist and humorist Antonio Mingote published a cartoon in the Madrid newspaper *ABC* showing a married couple, the husband holding a publicity flier highlighting the works of Paso while asking his wife, 'What do you fancy tonight, the cinema or Alfonso Paso?[23]

Still, radio soaps by authors such as Guillermo Sautier Casaseca had even more far-reaching social implications. His success, which he managed to sustain for the two following decades, started with the 1953 broadcast of *Lo que no muere* (That which does not pass away). This radio soap told the story of two brothers, one of them good, attractive and intrepid while the other was despicable and ignoble, thereby symbolizing the story of National and Red Spain. As Sautier himself stated, what never passed away in the Spanish 'race' were 'the values of religion, tradition, family, home and faith'.[24] This author enjoyed even greater success in 1959 with *Ama Rosa* (Housekeeper Rose), a complicated soap opera in which a poor woman's son was brought up, unaware of his origins, in a well-off family for which his own mother worked in domestic service. Many years later, in the early years of Spanish democracy, Francisco Umbral wrote that this script suffered from 'intellectual poverty' and brought to light the 'replacement of real, historic anxiety with invented, vicarious, cathartic anxieties', but at the same time he acknowledged that the text was more than mere entertainment: 'the implicit content of the text consecrated social differences, the caste system, sexual taboos, the legend of Cain and Abel ...'.[25] Hence it seems clear that the regime promoted these cultural products not only because they were popular and provided harmless 'entertainment' for the people, but because they represented values and messages which were completely in accordance with the discourse and policy of the regime. Incidentally, they also gained the loyalty of the listeners to radio broadcasts by encouraging them to listen to political news which the regime offered every hour, the 'spoken news' from Spanish National Radio which all radio stations were obliged to broadcast.

This evidence suggests the existence of a deeply rooted popular culture and hardly fits in with the view of a culturally helpless regime. Even so, it is true that the type of cultural products defended by the regime was subjected to two contradictory logics: the audience logic and the logic of orthodoxy. Arguably, the plan to achieve larger audiences led cultural producers to push ideological consensus with the regime into the background. Ironically, the strategy of promoting cultural products for the masses in order to widen the regime's bases of legitimacy would lead to the distortion of the messages on which it hoped to build this legitimacy.

The 1966 Press Law and its liberalizing effect on culture

The 1966 Press Law, which is recorded in the history of Franco's regime as the most far-reaching liberalizing measure, gave a strong boost to the audience logic to the detriment of the logic of orthodoxy. It favoured actions focused on winning audiences, either as consumers of information and entertainment or as sympathizers and supporters of the opposition to the Francoist political system. Its erosive effect on the legitimacy of the regime and its impact as a driving force of political and cultural development in Spanish society is beyond question. But the key to these outcomes is not to be found in the letter of the law, which brought freedom of information under fairly restrictive political and moral limits and gave the administration many resources to punish those who transgressed these limits, but rather in the incentives created by its application.

The 1966 Press Law was the final result of a discussion between the Francoist elites of several proposals and drafts, a process which spread over several years and which the sectors most reactionary to change (including Franco himself) tried to slow down, but managed not to block.[26] The 1966 Law repealed a law of 1938 which was inspired by the regulation of the press as organized by the fascist regimes of Mussolini and Hitler and which established measures such as prior censorship of newspapers, governmental appointment of editors and the State organization of a register of journalists. The 1966 Press Law eliminated prior censorship, replacing it with repressive controls (sanctions for the newspaper editors and the news companies which could lead to the former being barred from their position and the seizure and even shutting down of the latter), established the freedom of the company to choose the editors of the newspapers and promoted professionalism as the principal criteria for access to the register of journalists. If we bear in mind that in the mid-1960s prior censorship of the press was no longer applied in many provinces, that the majority of news companies enjoyed the freedom to choose the editors for their newspapers and that the official register of journalists was becoming increasingly like a professional register, the changes in the operation of the control procedures which the new press law established were not so important as the fact that this control became visible and was subject to the possibility of being contested in the law courts.

In fact, when a news publication was the object of a fine, its editor suspended from his job or barred for having being repeatedly fined, or a number of issues were seized, this information, together with the evidence relating to the actions undertaken by the company in rejecting the authorities' intervention, came to the attention of the readers. For those readers most critical of the regime such publicity added to the merit of both the fined publication and the professionals who worked on it. Thus, there were ever greater incentives for the journalists and publishing companies to take risks and lay themselves open to intervention from the authorities, although it is also true that assuming risks entailed disincentives insofar as a fine might make a publication no longer viable. The fact that certain media with a better-educated, more politically-committed readership (such as the magazines *Cuadernos para el Diálogo*, *Triunfo* and *Destino* or the newspaper *Madrid*) took on the role of battering rams, placing themselves in the forefront of the challenge to the regime, allowed other publications with a wider readership to improve their news coverage, not only widening the range of subjects being covered but also contributing a greater number of opinions and furthering the development of a more pluralistic, higher quality journalism, but without displaying the same courage or assuming the same risks.[27]

Even if the Press Law referred solely and exclusively to printed publications and did not make any stipulations about other cultural expressions (such as books, cinema and the theatre), it triggered a causal mechanism which promoted a liberalization process. On the one hand, those responsible for censoring these cultural products, who worked in the same ministry as those responsible for supervising the press, tended to relax the criteria of control not so much as a consequence of a deliberate liberalization policy but more because of a more permissive climate. On the other hand, the cultural producers soon saw the advantages of widening their repertoire of subjects and approaches under the shelter of this relaxation in censorship. So, while the press was liberalizing itself through the strategies of certain journalists and publishing houses, a similar dynamic was being generated in literature, cinema and theatre. The regime's determination to react effectively to the challenges from filmmakers and literary people helped other cultural producers who were less hostile and closer to the public authorities to produce their work with greater freedom. Sautier Casaseca, in an interview given in 1971, put it this way:

> up until now censorship has been limiting us, preventing us from getting away from the story of a completely honest family in which there was no adultery, not even in thought... this restraint which used to result from censorship has loosened up a bit. Now we can deal with other problems which, although they also affect the family and the vast majority of listeners, allow us to capture the interest of certain minorities. Now I receive letters which I would never have received because letters received are always naïve, badly written, from illiterate people. But now I have started to receive letters from colonels, from generals, from university professors, from lawyers, from people who have created a climate of confidence for me which I wouldn't want to lose.

So the cultural producers close to the regime put the logic of audience before that of orthodoxy just as many journalists and publishing companies had done. Their priority was to develop a cultural offer which ensured that they had a wide, interested public. They did not try to branch off from the fundamental values defended by the regime but neither did they seem prepared to sacrifice their popularity to defend them. Their audience did not require a public commitment from them, but rather entertainment which fitted in with their style of life. After all, they were asking for nothing more than audiences in other countries who were increasingly happy with their conditions of life. One critic of Franco's regime might have condemned the 'decadence, escapism and insulation from the realities of the world in which we live', adding phrases such as 'We are currently wealthy, fat, comfortable and complacent, we have a built-in allergy to unpleasant or disturbing information'. But these words were not those of an opponent of the Francoist dictatorship, they were uttered at the end of the 1950s by journalist Edward R. Murrow in a public speech on the recent operation of radio and television in the oldest democracy in the world.[28]

All in all, as a result of its own substantive legitimization project, the content of cultural expressions promoted by the regime was becoming increasingly unspecific and decreasingly incompatible with other forms of government. Meanwhile, the content of cultural products promoted by critics of the regime had clear and specific political connotations and was irreconcilable with the preservation of the regime. Towards the end of the regime there was not one sole dominant culture but rather concurrent sub-cultures, some more focused on public criticism and others on material well-being, life satisfaction and family happiness. But what had practically disappeared was a noteworthy cultural offer in which those who defended the continuity of the dictatorship could find signs of identity and convincing arguments to proclaim that Francoism after Franco was the best political option.

Conclusions

In the historiography on Franco's regime there is probably a tendency to attribute the phenomena, which, from a democratic perspective, could be considered positive or favourable for the transition to democracy, to the initiative of the social sectors critical of the dictatorship while attributing negative phenomena to the deliberate strategies of the Francoist rulers. This tendency also seems to have marked the way in which issues related to culture during the regime were treated. In accordance with this interpretive tendency, the critical culture arose valiantly and heroically from a part of society which was not crushed by the regime and, early on, before economic development began, assumed the costs of being a persecuted, ill-treated, opposition. On the other hand, Franco's regime, overcome by this critical culture of liberal origin and of indisputable quality, devoted its efforts to promoting a popular, escapist, crude, dumb and politically inane sub-culture.

This image simplifies a much more complex reality which cannot be explained without taking into account the fact that, in general, the

Francoist leaders never relinquished governing legitimately: that is to say, they always intended to provide 'just reasons' for doing so. When the Falangist programme ran out of steam in 1945 and the political discourse displayed by the leaders of the main Catholic lay organizations showed its limited persuasive power in the mid-1950s, Franco and his nearest collaborators promoted a legitimization project based on efficient government, the provision of public assets, and a boost to economic development and administrative modernization which affected almost all areas of political life, including that of culture. In line with this legitimization project, as the cultural offer backed by the regime became more attractive for large groups in society it lost focus and ideological specificity. Meanwhile, the cultural offer from the opposition was undergoing an inverse evolution: increasing its ideological load and targeting a specific public, one that was politically committed and eager for institutional changes.

Following the 1966 Press Law, many newspapers and some publishing houses tried to widen the margins of informative freedom and create favourable conditions for the development of a more pluralistic, varied cultural offer which responded to the discourses, outlooks and future aspirations of people with very different values and priorities. A large majority of the elites which led the political transition had joined some of the critical sub-cultures which counted on well-known 'reference points' such as *Cuadernos para el Diálogo* in publications and Luis Buñuel among filmmakers, Alfonso Sastre among playwrights or Raimon among singer-songwriters. Even so, a large part of the society which supported the transition process by voting massively in favour of political reform in December 1977 and in favour of the 1978 Constitution read newspapers and magazines which had not clashed with the Francoist government, had listened eagerly to Sautier Casaseca's soap operas, had watched plays by Paso and enjoyed Lazaga's films, just to give a few examples. The fact that we appreciate some of these cultural products more than others nowadays does not mean that we should strip the latter of the importance which they had in their day for the representation and dissemination of values and social norms.

Finally, the cultural scene in Spain in the 1960s and 1970s displayed the diversity of a complex society enjoying a considerable, hard-won freedom for the private domain while gradually developing a growing plurality of discourse for the public one. Paradoxically, in trying to increase its legitimacy Franco's regime weakened its cultural resources. The undesired consequences of the acts of the dictatorship constitute one of the keys to understanding its evolution, there being no need to attribute to its leaders any intentions other than those of trying to preserve the political regime which allowed them to exercise power free of the periodic control of the populace and without renouncing the use of violence in order to impose their will.

Notes

1. For the large majority of the opposition to Franco's regime, the Second Republic (1931–36) was a valuable democratic precedent. On the learning process furthered by the collective memory of the Civil War see P. Aguilar, *Memory and Amnesia. The Role of the Spanish Civil War in the Transition to Democracy* (Oxford: Berghahn Books, 2002). One of the best-known examples of the interpretation of the Spanish Transition in terms of the elites' strategic behaviour is J.M. Maravall and J. Santamaría, 'Political Change in Spain and the Prospects for Democracy', in G. O'Donnell, P. Schmitter and L. Whitehead, eds, *Transitions from Authoritarian Rule. Southern Europe* (Baltimore, MD: The Johns Hopkins University Press, 1986).

2. V. Pérez-Díaz, *The Return of Civil Society* (Cambridge, MA: Harvard University Press, 1993) differentiates between 'civil society' in the strict sense and 'civil society' in the broad sense of the word. Only the former can emerge in the context of a dictatorship, while the latter requires the existence of a democracy respecting individual freedoms and the rule of law.

3. It seems to me that the differences between the 'anti-Francoist opposition cultures' have often not been sufficiently underlined. J. Muñoz Soro, *Cuadernos para el Diálogo (1963–1976). Una historia cultural del segundo franquismo* (Madrid: Marcial Pons, 2006), gives a compelling hint of this internal diversity when he analyses the various ideological streams which coexisted within the influential magazine *Cuadernos para el Diálogo*.

4. For example, one ex-minister of the Franco regime wrote '...neglected by the principal centres of public and private cultural power, we lost the battle of thought'. G. Fernández de la Mora, *Río Arriba. Memorias* (Barcelona: Planeta, 1995), p. 120. According to a high-ranking military officer, 'the public mass media did not manage to direct opinion. As for the rest, the opposition wrote with names and surnames, while elements sympathetic to the regime were hidden behind pseudonyms'. J.I. San Martín, *Servicio Especial. A las órdenes de Carrero Blanco (De Castellana a El Aaiún)* (Barcelona: Planeta, 1983), p. 67.

5. J. Pradera, 'Jeringas, agendas y silencios', *Claves de Razón Práctica*, 32 (1993), pp. 48–55.

6. Giuliana di Febo gives a recent example of this line of argument: '...industrial growth and the changes arising from this in the economic and administrative spheres, the increase in tourism, the greater enjoyment of consumer goods, growing cultural exchanges and contacts with Europe, encouraged new social norms, both work and behavioural'. In G. di Febo and S. Julia, *El Franquismo* (Barcelona: Paidós, 2005), p. 109. More than 1,300,000 Spaniards, about one-tenth of the Spanish active population, migrated between 1960 and 1970 to Europe, especially to France and Germany. See J.P. Fusi and J. Palafox, *España: 1808–1996. El desafío de la modernidad* (Madrid: Espasa, 1997), p. 355.

7. J. Gracia, *La resistencia silenciosa. Fascismo y cultura en España* (Barcelona: Anagrama, 2004), p. 25.
8. Gracia, *La resistencia silenciosa*, p. 23.
9. J.P. Fusi, *Un siglo de España. La cultura* (Madrid: Marcial Pons, 1999), p. 125.
10. C.P. Boyd, *Historia Patria. Política, historia e identidad nacional en España: 1875–1975* (Barcelona: Pomares-Corredor, 1997), p. 223.
11. Fusi, *La cultura*, p. 125.
12. S. Juliá, *Historia de las dos Españas* (Madrid: Taurus, 2004), pp. 409–62.
13. Pere Ysàs, *Disidencia y subversión. La lucha del régimen franquista por su supervivencia, 1960–1975* (Barcelona: Crítica), pp. 3–5.
14. It is necessary to point out that Juliá, *Historia de las dos Españas*, does not identify the emergence and development of these currents of critical thought towards Franco's regime with the failure of official culture. Nevertheless, considering the importance he gives to these events it seems reasonable to infer that they considerably weakened what could be called the cultural bases of Francoist discourse.
15. Notable among the party organizations would be the Women's Section, the Youth Front and the Spanish University Union (SEU). Among the organizations linked to the Church it is worth mentioning the lay organizations of Catholic Action, with its 'specialized movements' such as the Workers' Brotherhood of Catholic Action (HOAC), the Workers' Catholic Youth (JOC) and the University Youth of Catholic Action.
16. J.P. Fusi, 'Para escribir la biografía de Franco', *Claves de Razón Práctica* 27 (1992), p. 14.
17. P. Muñoz has for instance convincingly shown that the view of women defended by the Francoist regime was prevalent from the 19th century and only partially changed during the brief period of the Second Republic: 'The ideas of women as different beings, weak and needing protection, which found an excellent source of authority in religion and later on in science was not exclusive to the most conservative and ultramontane politicians; it was the general sentiment of nineteenth-century bourgeois society'. See P. Muñoz López, *Sangre, amor e interés. La familia en la España de la Restauración* (Madrid, Marcial Pons, 2001), pp. 208–9.
18. Well documented in Juliá, *Historia de las dos Españas*, pp. 358–66 and 396–401.
19. If the first aspect was expressed in such regulations as the 1956 Judicial Review Control Law and the 1958 Administrative Procedure Law, the second aspect had its principal expression in the 1959 Economic Stabilization Plan.
20. About the propagandistic use of these and other dates of celebration see R.R. Tranche and V. Sánchez-Biosca, *NO-DO. El tiempo y la memoria* (Madrid: Cátedra/Filmoteca Española, 2000), pp. 202–18.
21. A. Cazorla Sánchez, *Las políticas de la victoria. La consolidación del Nuevo Estado franquista (1938–1953)* (Madrid: Marcial Pons, 2000), p. 224.
22. Aguilar, *Memory and Amnesia*, Chapter 2.
23. I am grateful to the historian Miguel Martorell for this information regarding Alfonso Paso. For more about the anecdotes mentioned here consult http://www.alfonsopaso.com/.
24. Quoted in J. Ginzo and L. Rodríguez Olivares, *Mis días de radio. La España de los 50 a través de las ondas* (Madrid: Temas de Hoy, 2004), p. 252.

25. Quoted in Ginzo and Rodríguez Oliverares, *Mis días de radio*, p. 260.
26. I have extensively analysed this lawmaking process in *El poder y la palabra. Prensa y poder politico en las dictaduras. El régimen de Franco ante la prensa y el periodismo* (Madrid: Biblioteca Nueva/UNED, 2001), pp. 156–72.
27. About the implementation of the 1966 Press Law and its indirect effects see Chuliá, *El poder y la palabra*, pp. 172–219.
28. Extracted from the film *Good Night, and Good Luck* (2005), directed by George Clooney and produced by Warner Independent Pictures.

10
The Spanish Church: Change and Continuity

William J. Callahan

During the three decades that have followed the death of Franco and the beginnings of the transition to democracy, the topic of the relationship of the Catholic Church to the regime has received and continues to receive extensive study. General works, monographs, personal memoirs and the publication of documents have provided detailed information and informed analysis about the political, social and religious role of the Church, especially during the Franco regime's later history between 1960 and 1975.[1] Although we know more about civil–ecclesiastical relations and the internal life of the Church for the period than we did 25 years ago, discussion and controversy still revolve around certain issues such as the role of Pope Paul VI who, while encouraging a spirit of reform among the bishops, also seemed disposed, on occasion, to conclude a new concordat with the regime in spite of the objections of the hierarchy and a majority of the clergy. The long-term impact of the Second Vatican Council (1961–65) on the internal life of the Church has also caused ongoing debate, as has the reworking of civil–ecclesiastical relations between 1976 and 1978 along lines first explored, if tentatively, during the late Franco period. To what extent was there continuity or decisive change? Or was there, rather, a constantly shifting balance between continuity and change depending on specific circumstances at different times?

'National Catholicism'

The alliance between Church and State forged during the Civil War (1936–39), once so apparently triumphant, proved no more enduring than the regime itself. The term 'National Catholicism' often used to describe the close ties between Church and State has been the object of considerable discussion between those who interpret it as little more than a thin cover disguising a mutually advantageous arrangement for the parties involved to those who believe that it provided the regime with ideological justification.[2] Whatever the respective merits of this debate and whatever the strengths and weaknesses of 'National Catholicism', it is now clear, thanks to the perspective of time, that it was a temporary phenomenon and, increasingly as time passed, an anachronism within the Catholic world just as Franco and Salazar were within the democratic framework of Western Europe during the 1960s and early 1970s.

Spain's first modern political revolution carried out by the liberal Cortes of Cádiz (1810–13) continued the tradition of absolute monarchy by recognizing Catholicism as the religion of the State. Although the official relationship of the Church to successive nineteenth-century and early twentieth-century governments was often difficult, it survived intact until the separation of Church and State proclaimed by the republican constitution of 1931. During the Civil War, the clergy supported the rising against the Republic for the most part. Bishops, priests and activist lay people expected that the new regime of General Franco would restore the financial, educational and other benefits lost in 1931. In fact, the regime went further than a simple restoration of old privileges. Taken as a whole the advantages possessed by the Church under Franco were the most generous the institution had enjoyed since the waning days of absolute monarchy (1824–33). The government provided a subsidy for the salaries of the clergy and the maintenance of church fabrics through the *culto y clero* appropriation in the national budget. An analysis of ecclesiastical revenues (1970) shows that the Church received substantial additional funding from a variety of government ministries and other official bodies.[3] The Church also had a free hand in the establishment of schools, while the State required students in both public and private schools to attend religion classes. The number of students in church primary and secondary schools increased by four times during the history of the regime with much of the expansion occurring during the 1960s. By the mid-1970s, nearly two million students were enrolled in Catholic schools.[4] Until 1970, the government provided little financial support to these schools, but an education law approved in that year provided generous funding, although with some strings attached. The Church enjoyed other privileges. Bishops sat in the regime's unrepresentative parliament and received military honours on certain occasions, while members of the clergy occupied a wide range of official positions on censorship boards, in the education bureaucracy or in the State-controlled labour syndicate system.

In spite of these advantages, the apparent solidity of 'National Catholicism' in a Spain 'splendidly consolidated in its Catholicism', according to the papal nuncio in 1953, was less firm than these enthusiastic words suggested.[5] There is no convincing evidence that the strategy of 'religious reconquest' carried on for years after the end of the Civil War with the full support of the State succeeded in penetrating a working-class long alienated from the Church. At the level of civil–ecclesiastical relations, the hierarchy was fully aware of its debt to Franco, but from the beginning of the regime relations were not always as smooth as government and church authorities pretended. There were periodic skirmishes, hidden for the most part from public view, over official censorship to which most church publications were subject until 1966. The hierarchy viewed the only political group permitted by the regime, the Falange and its successor, the National Movement, with suspicion because of their pretensions to dominate government, their ambitions to exert greater control over education at the expense of the Church and their hostility toward Catholic workers' associations operating under the protective umbrella of Acción Católica Española.[6] During the 1950s, the sympathy of activist laity and clergy in the Basque provinces and Catalonia for the cause of regional autonomy became more intense, especially in the Basque provinces. The protest movement culminated in 1960 when 339 priests of the dioceses of Vitoria, Bilbao and San Sebastián published an open letter to their bishops that constituted nothing less than a frontal attack on the very principles of 'National Catholicism'.[7] The Basque priests called attention to 'the contradiction existing between Catholic doctrine with respect to the human person and its lack of fulfilment by a regime that calls itself Catholic'.[8]

During the 1950s, new currents of thought began to surface among Catholic laity, especially through the Conversaciones Católicas, a periodic conference which began to question, albeit cautiously, some of the principles of 'National Catholicism'.[9] In addition, during the 1940s and 1950s, new theological ideas began to penetrate the closed and rigid world of clerical education, although slowly and incompletely.[10] An important demographic shift became apparent by the early 1960s among the clergy as nearly 40 per cent of diocesan priests were between 24 and 44 years of age, thereby forming new clerical generations that had not personally experienced the Civil War.[11] The undercurrents of discontent and dissatisfaction present in some sectors of Spanish Catholicism during the 1950s did not form by any stretch of the imagination

a coherent movement of change within the Church. But their very existence on the eve of the meeting of the Second Vatican Council in 1961
suggested that, however tentatively, the winds of change were in the air.

The beginnings of change

The future of 'National Catholicism' was not particularly rosy in 1960,
although few anticipated the dramatic impact of the work of the Second
Vatican Council on the Spanish Church. Virtually all commentators
who have considered the topic agree that the teaching of the Council on
human rights, religious liberty and the role of the Church in a secular,
pluralistic world unleashed a complex movement of change that gradually undermined the assumptions on which the alliance of Church and
State had rested since the Civil War. The Council proved an 'authentic
catalyst' that opened a long period of debate and division among clergy
and laity over civil–ecclesiastical relations and the role of the Church
in society.[12] The election of Pope Paul VI in 1963 brought to the papal
throne a pope intent on moving the Spanish Church into the modern
world.[13] The regime was unenthusiastic about the new pope, who, as a
cardinal, had criticized in discreet fashion the government's record on
human rights.

Within the rigidly hierarchical organization of the Church during
the early and mid-1960s, the role of the bishops was crucial for any
prospect of change. Although they dutifully accepted the decisions of
the Council, they were caught by surprise by its direction and unsure
of how to implement conciliar recommendations in their dioceses.
This was scarcely surprising. Appointed for the most part before the
Civil War or during the 1940s, by 1961 the bishops formed an elderly
episcopal cohort presiding over an increasingly younger clergy. They
remained attached to official confessionality and were keenly aware of
the abundant financial and other benefits derived from the Church's ties
to the regime. Even at this time the bishops did not form a monolithic
block with a clear strategy. At the Council, a minority of Spanish bishops,
the so-called 'Twelve Apostles', vigorously supported reforming initiatives, while in 1965, a small episcopal delegation headed by Cardinal
Bueno Monreal of Seville called on Franco and urged him to give the
country 'a modern configuration, politically speaking, along the lines
of European democracies'.[14] Moreover, there was a certain fluidity in
episcopal mentalities that manifested itself in surprising ways. Bishop
Antonio Pildain, a harsh critic of the regime's syndical monopoly and
its patronage rights over episcopal appointments, opposed, for example,

the 1967 Law on Religious Liberty because it went too far in his judgment, while two younger prelates, Casimiro Morcillo, named Madrid's first archbishop in 1966, and his auxiliary bishop, José Guerra Campos, once regarded as relatively progressive, moved in a resolutely conservative direction during the late 1960s.[15]

As a result, the hierarchy did not speak with one voice on a number of crucial issues. Indeed, one progressive Catholic has described its policies during the late Franco period as an 'uninterrupted series of small advances, [and] tactical retreats'.[16] The hierarchy's 1966 decision to assert total control over Catholic workers' associations, thereby provoking mass resignations and undermining the foundations of Acción Católica Española, on the grounds that these organizations had abandoned their religious purpose in favour of social and political action moved in the opposite direction in 1969 when the bishops severely criticized the regime's proposed syndical law because it did not sufficiently represent or protect the interests of workers.[17] But during the same year, on the occasion of the rededication of the monument to the Sacred Heart at the Cerro de los Angeles, the bishops praised Franco for his participation in 'an act agreeable to God and the Church'.[18]

The response of clergy and laity

By 1969, episcopal attitudes began to change. This occurred for two reasons. First, as a result of the Second Vatican Council, bishops were now required to resign their positions at the age of 75, thereby, in the Spanish case, creating numerous vacancies given the advanced age of many prelates. Second, in 1967 Paul VI named Luigi Dadaglio as papal nuncio to carry out the renovation of the Spanish hierarchy in the spirit of the Council. Virtually all commentators on the state of the Spanish Church at this time agree that the role of Dadaglio was critical for the remaking of the hierarchy. This is not to suggest that the nuncio pursued a single-minded plan to create a specific block of reforming bishops. He had to operate within the give and take of the official patronage system at a time when the government was becoming more and more worried about the political reliability of the Church. On occasion, the appointment process sent out mixed signals. The appointment of a moderate reformer, Cardinal Vicente Enrique y Tarancón to the archbishopric of Madrid in 1971, for example, was followed by the naming of the more conservative Marcelo González Martín to the primatial see of Toledo. But on balance, the 42 new bishops appointed during the tenure of Dadaglio were more open to change than their elderly predecessors and, not surprisingly given the age of Franco, increasingly concerned about the Church's and the country's future when the dictator passed from the scene.[19]

Renovation of the hierarchy did not occur overnight, but was done 'in a slow and gradual way'.[20] By 1971, a shifting alliance of moderates predominated in the *Conferencia Episcopal Española* (CEE).[21] The appointment of Cardinal Tarancón to the archbishopric of Madrid and his subsequent election to the presidency of the CEE symbolized a significant change in direction. The hierarchy's opposition to the negotiation of a new concordat between the regime and the papacy and its 1973 statement, 'On the Church and the Political Community', showed that the hierarchy now accepted the necessity of political change within a pluralistic society. The 1973 statement explicitly affirmed the right 'of the political community to determine its own constitutional system'.[22]

Although there were many factors behind the hierarchy's gradual move toward the acceptance of change, the role of Cardinal Tarancón proved especially important.[23] It was not so much that he single-handedly orchestrated a party of change among his fellow bishops. But he possessed a spirit of openness, prudence and realism that encouraged a change in direction among his colleagues. He was, of course, subject to criticism from both the 'right' and the 'left' within the Church, the former believing that he had gone too far in promoting a new approach to civil–ecclesiastical relations, the latter that he had not gone far enough. Although supporters of the regime viewed him with hostility by 1973, the fact is that he attempted to avoid confrontation with the civil authorities at a time when severe tensions developed between Church and State. Tarancón was not an advocate of a radical break with the past.[24] Indeed, his support for change in civil–ecclesiastical relations rested on the idea that Spain 'cannot break totally with its history and with its tradition thereby risking the loss of its distinctive personality'.[25] At the same time, however, he possessed a realistic sense that the terms of the relationship between Church and State elaborated by 'National Catholicism' could no longer be sustained.

The regime viewed the evolution of episcopal attitudes and continuing examples of clerical dissent with incomprehension and frustration. In 1972, Franco's close associate, Admiral Luis Carrero Blanco, left no doubt of the extent of official resentment toward a Church that in his view had been saved from destruction by the Nationalist victory in the Civil War. 'No government', he declared in the presence of Franco, 'has done more for the Catholic Church than that of Your Excellency'.[26] The regime initially hoped to resolve the problems in civil–ecclesiastical relations by seeking to negotiate a new agreement with the papacy to replace the concordat of 1953. In spite of occasional hesitation by Pope Paul VI, there was never any possibility that the Vatican and the hierarchy would conclude an agreement 'with a power in bankruptcy', although by 1973 the regime was prepared to abandon official confessionality, the State's patronage rights over episcopal appointments, accord complete liberty of association to Catholic groups of all kinds and provide adequate financial means for the support of the clergy.[27] Between 1969 and 1975 the bishops moved in the direction of favoring political change. But what exactly did they want or not want? They did not favour radical social and economic change. They favoured a process of evolutionary change, a 'a change of regime but not of the system'.[28] And they remained deeply suspicious of the parties of the left. Even Cardinal Tarancón told the CEE in 1974 that the faithful must oppose social and political movements opposed to Christian principles.[29] The bishops were prepared to renounce certain official privileges, such as representation in parliament and the patronage rights of the government over episcopal appointments. But they were anxious to avoid open conflict with the regime, although the government's actions against Bishop Antonio Añoveros Bilbao in 1974 for making a statement allegedly in support of Basque separatism threatened the unimaginable, a formal break between an officially Catholic State and the Church. The government's decision to place Añoveros under house arrest and to consider sending him into exile caused Cardinal Tarancón, president of the CEE, to draft a document of excommunication against any officials involved in such actions, even though he believed that Añoveros had gone too far in his statement. The role of Franco as the affair unfolded is not entirely clear. But, in the end, when the cabinet sought his approval for vigorous action against the bishop of Bilbao, Franco reacted strongly against the initiative on the grounds, according to Cardinal Tarancón, that 'a Government that clashes with the Church is a Government that falls'.[30] In spite of Franco's late intervention, the Añoveros case provided a powerful example to all sectors of the Church that little was to be expected from the regime of the ill and aged dictator. The hierarchy's willingness to renounce certain privileges did not extend, however, to areas that the Church deemed essential to its interests, such as the survival of its subsidized school system and financial assistance for the support of the clergy.

The bishops did not operate, of course, within an ecclesiastical vacuum. During the 1960s and early 1970s, they were under constant pressure from the rank and file of the clergy, many of whom were far in advance of the hierarchy on the critical question of Church–State relations. To be sure, a clerical minority of 6000 priests gathered in the *Hermandad Sacerdotal del Clero*, founded in 1969, resolutely opposed ecclesiastical reform and any change in the Church's official status. But between 1966 and 1969, a wave of clerical effervescence swept through the clergy that took the form of protests of different kinds. The causes of what Guy Hermet has called this clerical *fronde* were varied.[31] Some originated in concerns with human rights, others with social justice and still others with nationalist concerns in the Basque provinces and Catalonia.[32] But taken as a whole, they showed the existence of deep discontents among many priests with the regime, the Church's identification with it and the failure of the bishops to move more rapidly and decisively in the realm of civil–ecclesiastical relations.

By and large, the bishops were unhappy with these repeated manifestations of clerical dissent, but they were forced to take them into account for two reasons. First, the heavy handed repression employed by the regime against some priests in the form of fines, arrest and imprisonment could not be ignored.[33] The bishops found themselves, recalled Cardinal Tarancón, 'between a rock and a hard place. They could not justly defend those priests who ... deserved punishment. But they could not admit that the civil authority ... could take action against priests'.[34] The emergence of this official anticlericalism by the authorities of a legally Catholic State forced the bishops to view civil–ecclesiastical relations from a more critical perspective than before and forced them, as time passed, to defend their priests more vigorously whatever episcopal reservations about the conduct of their clergy in specific cases.

Second, the hierarchy recognized that it could not afford to ignore the opinions of the clergy on important questions affecting the internal life of the Church and its relations with the regime. Father Martín Patino, a close associate of Cardinal Tarancón, has maintained that had not 'those responsible for the Spanish Church' paid attention to the reforming impetus of the Second Vatican Council, there would have been an 'explosion within the Catholic community'.[35] The wave of discussion and debate that swept through clergy and laity in Spain following the Vatican Council proved impossible to contain from the hierarchy's perspective. By 1970, the bishops recognized that a serious attempt had to be made to listen to their clergy's concerns. Various surveys of clerical opinion were undertaken, while in an unprecedented move, the hierarchy agreed to the convocation of a Joint Assembly of Bishops and Priests.

The Assembly opened on 23 September 1971 and operated on the radical principle, for the Church at least, of equality in voting among the clerical representatives whether bishops or ordinary priests. There is considerable debate about the long-term impact of the Assembly whose recommendations the bishops could or could not follow as they saw fit. But the Assembly sent shock waves through the principles of 'National Catholicism' by rejecting the ideology of division promoted by the regime since the Civil War and by calling upon the hierarchy to speak out about 'those situations and events which affect the human rights of the community'.[36] These declarations and others were, in the opinion of Cardinal Tarancón, an 'authentic bomb' for the Franco regime because they constituted 'the first public act of the Spanish Church in which it called into question the intimate connection between the Church and the Regime'.[37]

The role of the laity during the regime's last decade and a half is more difficult to assess. The Second Vatican Council intended the laity to play a larger role within the Church and urged bishops to develop closer relations with lay people and the lower clergy through a consultative process. In Spain, some efforts were undertaken in this direction but in an episodic, sometimes contradictory way, as in 1966 when the bishops' preemptive strike against the leadership of Catholic workers' organizations provoked mass resignations from Acción Católica Española and demoralized the movement that had long been the most important lay organization within the Spanish Church. But there is no doubt that the Second Vatican Council contributed to the creation of a more open, questioning spirit among some priests and lay people, and there was little the bishops could do about it. Progressive theologians and various lay organizations forming what has been called a 'parallel Church', raised uncomfortable questions about the Church's ties to the regime. The 'parallel Church' did not form a coherent and unified movement of change, but its components, ranging from 'base communities' inspired by Latin American liberation theology to Christians for Socialism openly questioned the privileges enjoyed by the Church, including the financial and educational advantages to which the hierarchy remained attached even as the bishops accepted the necessity of substantial revision in civil–ecclesiastical relations. The bishops lacked a clear idea about how to deal with the effervescence and enthusiasm generated by such movements and by the Vatican Council itself. Some prelates recognized that something new and vital was happening within the Church. Others were unconvinced, fearing that such ideas and initiatives threatened episcopal authority. Such a high level of emotion and enthusiasm among priests and lay people inspired by the Council could not last indefinitely. Indeed, there were signs of disillusionment following the Joint Assembly of 1971 when many of its recommendations were effectively ignored by the bishops. In any event, the renewal of the hierarchy by Pope John Paul II beginning in 1978 moved in a distinctly conservative direction, thereby creating new conflicts over the application of conciliar principles within the Spanish Church. Moreover, the wave of optimism that swept through large segments of clergy and laity began to recede as signs of crisis appeared in the form of declining seminary enrollments and indications of declining religious practice, especially among young people.

By 1975, a majority of the hierarchy, clergy and laity accepted the necessity of political change and a substantial revision in civil–ecclesiastical relations. But there was no political consensus on a strategy to achieve these objectives other than a determination of the bishops through the CEE to safeguard what they saw as the Church's vital interests in whatever political order would emerge following Franco's disappearance. When these arrangements were worked out during the period of transition and in the years following, the Church more or less achieved its objectives, at least in the realm of clerical finances and education. There were, to be sure, areas where this was not so. The introduction of divorce in 1981 and the subsequent introduction of legislation allowing limited abortion by the Socialist government in 1983 were setbacks for the Church. But, on balance, the Church managed to defend itself exceptionally well, certainly far better than in earlier periods when civil–ecclesiastical relations were substantially redefined, whether between 1834–43, 1868–69, or 1931–33. Or as the Madrid correspondent of *The New York Times* remarked following passage of the 1978 constitution, Church and State were not quite separate, in Spain's new democracy.[38] In the end, both change and continuity were present in civil–ecclesiastical relations during the later Franco period and the early years of democratic Spain, but, on balance, there was perhaps more continuity than change.

Notes

1. Detailed bibliographical references for this period can be found in the important works of G. Hermet, *Les catholiques dans l'Espagne franquiste*, 2 Vols. (Paris: Foundation Nationale des Sciences Politiques, 1981); V. Cárcel Ortí, *Pablo VI y España: Fidelidad, renovación y crisis, 1963–1978* (Madrid: Biblioteca de Autores Cristianos, 1997), pp. 1009–34; G. Redondo, *Política, cultura y sociedad en la España de Franco, 1939–1975: La configuración del*

192   *The Spanish Church*

Estado español nacional y católico, 1939–1947 (Pamplona: Ediciones Universidad de Navarra, 1999), pp. 1057–104. There are also useful recent bibliographies in: A. Brassloff, *Religion and Politics in Spain: The Spanish Church in Transition, 1961–1996* (London/New York: Palgrave Macmillan, St. Martin's, 1998), pp. 167–75; F. Lannon, *Privilege, Persecution and Prophecy: The Catholic Church in Spain, 1875–1975* (Oxford: Oxford University Press, 1987), pp. 258–68; J. Andrés-Gallego and A.M. Pazos, *La Iglesia en la España Contemporánea*, 2 Vols. (Madrid: Encuentro Ediciones, 1999).

2. R. Gómez Pérez, *El franquismo y la Iglesia* (Madrid: Rialp, 1986), p. 15 and F. Amoveri, *Stato cattolico e chiesa fascista in Spagna* (Milan: Celuc, 1973), p. 14, dismiss the term as virtually meaningless, a view shared in some measure by F. Urbina, 'Formas de vida de la Iglesia de España, 1939–1975', in F. Urbina et al., *Iglesia y sociedad en España, 1939–1975* (Madrid: Editorial Popular, 1977), p. 119. A. Álvarez Bolado, on the other hand, has argued for a more sophisticated interpretation of the term in two works: *El experimento del nacional catolicismo, 1939–1975* (Madrid: Edicusa, 1976) and *Teología política desde España: del nacional-catolicismo y otros ensayos* (Bilbao: Desclée de Brouwer, 1999). A. Botti has also maintained that National Catholicism formed an elastic, complex ideology that was less a coherent system of thought than a mentality with ideological characteristics. *Cielo y dinero: El nacionalcatolicismo en España, 1881–1975* (Madrid: Alianza Editorial, 1992), p. 141.

3. J. Castellà-Gassol, *De donde viene y donde va el dinero de la Iglesia española?* (Barcelona: Editorial Dirosa, 1975), pp. 28, 54–8.

4. 'Número de alumnos de los centros católicos por cursos, 1977–1987', Oficina de Estadística y Sociología de la Iglesia, *Estadísticas de la Iglesia Católica, 1989* (Madrid: EDICE, 1989), p. 282.

5. Quoted in F. Blázquez, *La traición de los clerigos en España: Crónica de una intolerancia, 1936–1975* (Madrid: Editorial Trotta, 1991), p. 107.

6. For conflicts over censorship during the 1950s, see the memoir of J. Iribarren, *Papeles y memorias: Medio siglo de relaciones Iglesia-Estado, 1936–1986* (Madrid: Biblioteca de Autores Cristianos, 1992), pp. 149–74. For the constant behind-the-scenes battles with the Falange, see the key work of J. Tusell, *Franco y los católicos: La política interior española entre 1945 y 1957* (Madrid: Alianza Universidad, 1984), third and fourth parts, and for the struggle over Catholic workers' associations, notably the *Hermandades Obreras de Acción Católica* (HOAC) and the *Juventud de Obrera Católica* (JOC), see J. Castaño Colomer, *La JOC en España, 1946–1970* (Salamanca: Ediciones Sígueme, 1978), pp. 49–118 and A. Murcia Santos, *Obispos y obreros en el franquismo* (Madrid: Ediciones HOAC, 1995).

7. P. Iztueta Armendariz, *Sociología del fenomeno contestario del clero vasco, 1940–1975* (Zarautz: Elkar, 1981), pp. 147–57. For Catholic resistance to the regime in Catalonia during the 1940s and 1950s, see the work of J.M. Piñol, *El nacionalcatólicme a Catalunya i la resistencia, 1926–1966* (Barcelona: Edicions 62, 1993), pp. 137–50 and Joan Casañas, *El progressime catolic a Catalunya, 1940–1980: Aproximació històrica* (Barcelona: La Llar del Llibre, 1989).

8. 'Carta de 339 curas vascos a sus obispos', 30 May 1960, in J. Domínguez, ed., *Organizaciones obreras cristianas en la oposición al franquismo, 1951–1975* (Bilbao: Mensajero, 1985), p. 63.

9. See, for example, the essays of participants in C. Santamaría et al., *Catolicismo español: Aspectos actuales* (Madrid: Ediciones Cultura Hispánica, 1955) and the work of J.M. Román Fuentes, *La autocrítica religiosa en el catolicismo contemporáneo* (Madrid: La Milagrosa, 1968).

10. J.I. Tellechea Idigoras, *Tapices de la memoria: Historia clínica 279.952* (San Sebastián: Caja Guipuzkoa, 1991), pp. 120–5; J. Domínguez, *Enseñanza católica para una generación* (Madrid: Editorial Popular, 1979), p. 81.

11. Hermet, *Les catholiques*, p. 46; S. Petschen, *La Iglesia en la España de Franco* (Madrid: Sedmay Ediciones, 1977), p. 99.

12. J.M. Piñol, *La transición democrática de la Iglesia católica española* (Madrid: Editorial Trotta, 1999), p. 232.

13. The fundamental work on Paul VI and Spain is the magisterial study of V. Cárcel Ortí, *Pablo VI y España*, cited above.

14. Piñol, *La transición democrática de la Iglesia católica española*, p. 37. Quoted in A. Hernández, 'El viraje de la Iglesia', *Diario 16*, 14 July 1985, suplemento semanal, p. 642.

15. The fluctuating division among the bishops of the late 1960s and early 1970s have been intelligently studied by J. Chao Rego, *La Iglesia en el franquismo* (Madrid: Ediciones Felmar, 1976), pp. 303–13.

16. Piñol, *La transición democrática de la Iglesia católica española*, p. 395. J.J. Ruíz Rico has observed that during the 1960s the strategy of the Church was not as straightforward as could be supposed. Neither shifts forward nor retreats were lacking. Nor were internal disputes among sectors of the ecclesiastical system missing. See *El papel político de la Iglesia católica en la España de Franco, 1936–1971* (Madrid: Editorial Tecnos, 1977), p. 184.

17. Antonio Murcia's well-documented analysis of the hierarchy's initiative in 1966 is highly critical of its action, in *Obreros y obispos en el franquismo*, Chapters 5–7. Bishop José Guerra Campos, a leading participant in the measures taken against Catholic workers' associations has defended his role in *Crisis y conflicto en la Acción Católica Española y otros organos nacionales de apostolado seglar desde 1964* (Madrid: Ediciones ADUE, 1989), pp. 25–39. Controversy over the question continues. See, for example, the analysis, sympathetic to the hierarchy, in Andrés-Gallego and Pazos, *La Iglesia en la España contemporánea*, Vol. 2, pp. 157–8. A former active member of ACE, Enrique Miret Magdalena, has taken a different view, arguing that the bishops took action because, under pressure from the government, 'they wished a Catholic Action which would not clash with the Franco regime': *Luces y sombras de una larga vida: Memorias* (Barcelona: Planeta, 2000), p. 339.

18. Cincuentenario de la Consagración de España al Corazón de Jesús, 25 May 1969, in J. Iribarren, ed., *Documentos colectivos del episcopado español, 1870–1974* (Madrid: Biblioteca de Autores Cristianos, 1974), pp. 441–2.

19. Chao Rego, *La Iglesia en el franquismo*, pp. 212–13.

20. Cárcel Ortí, *Pablo VI y España*, p. 323.

21. Hermet, *Les catholiques dans l'Espagne franquiste*, Vol. 2, p. 381, and Chao Rego, *La Iglesia en el franquismo*, pp. 314–15, have studied the complex divisions among the bishops during this period.

22. 'Sobre la Iglesia y la comunidad política', 23 January 1973, in J. Iribarren, ed., *Documentos de la Conferencia Episcopal Española, 1965–1983* (Madrid: Biblioteca de Autores Cristianos, 1984), p. 265.

23. There is an extensive literature dealing with the role of the cardinal. His own extensive recollections of this time, *Confesiones* (Madrid: PPC Editorial, 1996) provide abundant references to his interpretation of the key events of the period. Several useful articles and some of the cardinal's sermons, pastoral letters and publications can be found in S. Grisolía et al., *Homenaje al Cardenal Enrique y Tarancón* (Valencia: Generalitat Valenciana, 1997). Also useful is the collection of articles by several authors: *Al servicio de la Iglesia: Homenaje al Cardenal Tarancón en su 75 aniversario* (Madrid: Narcea, 1984). A highly favourable biography of the cardinal is J.L. Martín Descalzo, *Tarancón: El cardenal del cambio* (Barcelona: Planeta, 1982).

24. R. Gómez Pérez has argued that the bishops hoped that arrangements with the regime could be made for a 'friendly separation' of Church and State. See *Política y religión en la España de Franco* (Barcelona: Dopesa, 1976), p. 309.

25. Quoted in R. Díaz-Salazar, *El capital simbólico: Estructura social, política y religiosa en España* (Madrid: Ediciones HOAC, 1988), p. 56.

26. Quoted in Chao Rego, *La Iglesia en el franquismo*, pp. 217–18.

27. J.M. Cuenca Toribio, *Relaciones Iglesia-Estado en la España contemporánea, 1833–1985* (Madrid: Alhambra, 1985), p. 127; Hermet, *Les catholiques dans l'Espagne franquiste*, Vol. 2, p. 39.

28. Ruíz Rico, *El papel político de la Iglesia católica en la España de Franco*, p. 234.

29. Brassloff, *Religion and Politics in Spain*, p. 73.

30. Quoted in Martín Descalzo, *Tarancón: El cardenal del cambio*, p. 217.

31. Hermet, *Les catholiques dans l'Espagne franquiste*, Vol. 2, p. 310.

32. See, for example, the study of J. Crexell on the demonstration of Catalan priests in 1966 which was violently broken up by the police, *La 'manifestació' de capellans de 1966* (Montserrat: Abadía de Montserrat, 1992).

33. See the account of the harassment to which the progressive theologian and canon José María González Ruiz was subject by the police and the courts, *Memorias de un cura: Antes de Franco y después de Franco* (Málaga: Editorial Mirimar, 1995), pp. 122–7.

34. Enrique y Tarancón, *Confesiones*, pp. 272–3.

35. J.M, Martín Patino, 'La Iglesia en la sociedad española', in Juan Linz, et al., *España: Un presente para el futuro*, 2 Vols. (Madrid: Instituto de Estudios Económicos, 1984), Vol. 1, p. 155.

36. 'Ponencia primera: conclusiones', in Secretariado Nacional del Clero, *Asamblea Conjunta Obispos-Sacerdotes* (Madrid: Biblioteca de Autores Cristianos, 1971), pp. 172–3.

37. Enrique y Tarancón, *Confesiones*, pp. 469 and 489.

38. 'Spanish Church, State: Not Quite Separate', *The New York Times*, 12 November 1978.

11
The Origins of Democratic Support in Post-Franco Spain: Learning to Be a Democrat under Authoritarian Rule?

Mariano Torcal

According to some scholars, the support of the majority of citizens for democratic rule constitutes a bedrock of stability for any new democratic regime. In their well-known book on the topic, Linz and Stepan (1996, pp. 5–6) maintain that a new democratic regime is consolidated when it becomes the only 'game in town', which implies that it enjoys, among other things, the majority support of its citizens. Support for democracy or democratic legitimacy in Spain, as in many other new democracies, only pertains to citizens' beliefs that democratic politics is the most appropriate (indeed, the only acceptable) framework for governance.[1] It has been demonstrated that the new Spanish democratic political regime has enjoyed high levels of democratic support from the very outset, although this support has coexisted with high levels of political disaffection (lack of political trust) and changing and unrelated levels of satisfaction with its functioning (Maravall 1984, 1995; Montero and Torcal 1990; Gunther 1992; Morán and Benedicto 1995; Montero et al. 1997). But how was this high level of democratic support created and how can we explain its stability over time?

Many scholars have attributed this high level of democratic support in Spain to the attitudinal change resulting from the process of modernization that occurred during the 1960s and the last part of the Francoist regime, in which there was a resurgence of Spanish civil society and the re-emergence of 'Democratic Spain'. This attitudinal change not only facilitated the democratic transition, but, according to the literature, also made it unavoidable (López Pintor 1982: p. 90; 1987; Pérez Díaz 1993: pp. 4–5 and 40–6; Edles 1995: p. 248). In this chapter, I dispute the idea that democratic support was created during the non-democratic Franco regime and attempt to demonstrate that the high levels of democratic support that Spaniards display today are mostly the result of an 'adult re-socialization process' that produced an important aggregate attitudinal change. This attitudinal change occurred among Spaniards in a very few years and it produced not only an increase in the general level of demo-cratic support, which has remained stable since,[2] but, more importantly, it also gave way to unconditional or diffuse democratic support.

This type of unconditional support is the only support that can produce an attitudinal 'safety area', making it immune to daily politics, economic and political crises, and the general performance of the system; it is the only kind of support that can contribute to the final consolidation of new-found democracies. When this type of support is present among citizens in new democracies, we can consider an 'attitu-dinal consolidating effect' to have taken place completing the process of democratic consolidation. Spain today enjoys high unconditional levels of democratic support. This majoritarian unconditional support for democracy among Spaniards can be observed empirically in the fact that this democratic support is not only high, but more importantly, it no longer depends on an individual's ideological and party preferences and/or economic and regime performance evaluations; this new-found autonomy for democratic support has produced an attitudinal 'safety area' for the new Spanish democracy (see also Maravall 1995).

I will also analyse the attitudinal changes which resulted from the politics of consensus that was so prevalent during the Transition and the process of democratic consolidation (López Pintor 1987: pp. 106–7; Montero and Torcal 1990: p. 42; Gunther 1992: pp. 51–61). In other words, this attitudinal change depended on the nature and evolution of the regime-founding coalition during the Transition and the period of democratic consolidation as well as on the absence of the 'regime issue' from election campaigns during the same period of change and uncertainty.

The creation of support for democracy and its consequences for new democracies

A wide range of hypotheses have been put forward to explain how support for democratic regimes is sustained and, to a lesser extent, generated. On the whole, these hypotheses can be divided into three categories or types: socio-cultural explanations, macro or micro-economic and social explanations, and political explanations. Advocates of the socio-cultural theories maintain that as a society modernizes, its citizens tend to give more support to democratic systems and to moderate their political positions (Lipset 1960: pp. 78–9). Another socio-cultural explanation stems from the systemic tradition developed by Easton and Dennis (1969: p. 5), who argued that the degree of support for a political regime is determined by a long and complex process that depends on the success of the agents of socialization 'in producing children who acquire positive sentiments towards it'. It can be seen, there-fore, that the distinguishing characteristic of these explanations is their preference for explanations involving long-term processes of economic, social, and cultural change.

Macro and micro-economic and social explanations for democratic support focus on the importance of the economic and social results of democratic regimes. According to the proponents of these interpreta-tions, the stability of citizens' support for a democratic regime depends on their assessment of government performance and its economic and social achievements. In this case, citizens' expectations of constant economic growth, its distributional effects, and general prosperity will increase the potential for declining democratic support (Przeworski 1991: p. 26; Mishler and Rose 1999: pp. 94–7).

Political explanations for the creation and stability of democratic support, in contrast, highlight the importance of much more imme-diate processes, which are endogenous to the ongoing functioning of the political system (Przeworski 1991: pp. 31–3, 95). Some of the proponents maintain that a decline in support for a regime may be due to factors such as the character of its party system (Powell 1982: pp. 74–110), governmental instability (Schmitt 1983; Harmel and Robertson 1986), or the nature of the governments resulting from the changing parlia-mentary majorities and electoral results (Nordlinger 1972; McRae 1974; Lijphart 1977, 1999; Boix 2005). The second type of political explana-tion focuses on the role of the political opposition and the inclusiveness of the regime-founding coalitions (Linz 1978: pp. 27–49). Finally, one group of scholars has recently maintained that approval of democracy depends on its ability to guarantee the rule of law and basic political rights (Diamond 1999; Bratton and Mattes 2001; Rose and Mishler 2002).

The findings regarding the creation and stability of democratic support are thus very contradictory. This is partly because an important number of the interpretations are concerned with the question of how to sustain support for long-established democratic regimes instead of with the creation of democratic support in new democracies. With the excep-tion of the literature on political opposition in inter-war Europe, the political explanations put forward in the studies of democratic support mentioned above are mostly based on the analysis of cases of representative democracies that have existed for half a century or more, that is to say, democracies in which citizens only have experience of democratic politics and who cannot imagine it being replaced by any other type of regime. The problem with generalizing from these results is, of course, that citizens of new democracies do have direct or indirect experience of different political regimes (Diamond 1999). In contrast to those who have only known democratic institutions, they have accumulated experience of at least one other type of political regime, which serves as a point of reference when it comes to evaluating the recently re-established system (Di Palma 1990). This support for the regime in new democracies is, thus, the result of a comparison with other types of regime (Rose and Mishler 1996: p. 53). Democratic support in new democracies could solely reflect, therefore, an individual rational decision based on the evaluation of regimes from preceding experiences. However, the relevant question is to establish how this rational calculation produces an unconditional support that leaves this support for the new regime relatively immune to the functioning of the system, its social and economic results, or the electoral support given to different political options.

It is logical, and somewhat tautological, to argue that the degree of support for the new regime depends on the rejection of the preceding non-democratic one; in fact, although they are not the same thing,[3] the rejection of the previous regime, and hence, approval of the present system, vary simultaneously. This is because both are, I argue here, partially the product of individual experiences of the previous and current regimes, but this simultaneous variation of democratic support and non-democratic regime rejection mostly reflects an attitudinal change springing from the essentially individual political experience of the transition to, and consolidation of, the new democracy (Rose and Mishler 1996: p. 50); a change in which the most important political and social actors and elites play a leading role. The absence, or failure, of an attempt to politicize the issue of the approval of the preceding regime and/or the new one by significant political actors is the main explanation for the existence of this attitudinal change. In other words, the inclusive nature of the regime-founding pact and the omission from the political agenda of the regime issue during the years of transition and consolidation might foster the rapid attitudinal change that produces high levels of democratic support (and rejection of the preceding regime) and the emergence of unconditional democratic support. When high unconditional support is present, the 'attitudinal consolidating effect' is complete and the attitudinal 'safety area' is in place.

The existence of some sort of elite settlement or convergence (Burton et al. 1992) for the new regime might foster the presence of this attitudinal 'safety area', but it is not sufficient for an attitudinal change to take place. That is to say, the presence of exclusionary regime-founding pacts or the lack of any political convergence might lead those sectors of the ideological spectrum which were reluctant to support a regime that could represent a threat to their interests to leave the new regime not only without their support, as has occurred many times in the past, but more importantly, without the attitudinal 'safety area' in place. A necessary condition for this attitudinal change to take place is the failure of any attempt to politicize the 'regime issue' by any major or significant political actors, which depends, as I said before, on the presence of an inclusive regime-founding pact and the absence of the regime issue from the agenda of the most significant political actors.

Obviously, the protagonists of the Transition were not at complete liberty when it came to fostering, creating, and recreating citizens' rejection of the preceding regime as well as support for the new one. Rather, the possibilities for producing the attitudinal change not only depended on the existence of a regime-founding pact or the elite's desire to separate the regime issue from the political agenda, but also, to a large extent, both were highly influenced by the legitimizing discourse of the previous regime, by citizens' perception of the previous regime's successes and failures, and the reasons for, and the nature of, its collapse. All these factors conditioned the levels of support for the outgoing regime, setting a structure of opportunities for some political actors to make the regime issue part of the agenda at the outset of the transition to democracy and during its consolidation. The legacies of non-authoritarian rule, thus, condition the possibility of a foundational democratic pact and of a consensual return to political competition, as well as the extension of support for the new regime among all the partisan and ideological positions. This reduces the incentives for major political actors to make the regime issue part of the political agenda in competing for citizens' electoral support.

Therefore, the presence or absence of a foundational regime pact and the politics of the transition to democracy and its consolidation (which are also conditioned by the nature of the legitimating discourse and the success of the preceding non-democratic regime) determine the existence or otherwise of the attitudinal change that completes the 'attitudinal consolidating effect'. That said, I do not deny the influence on the creation of unconditional democratic support of other transnational factors such as the democratic legitimacy discourse dominant in the international arena – what has been termed the triumph of the 'democratic ethos' or 'democratic *Zeitgeist*' – or the effect, in the case of Southern Europe, of the prospect of integration into the European Union (Pridham 1995: pp. 166–203; Linz and Stepan 1996: pp. 113 and 140–1). However, the actual building of majoritarian unconditional support for democracy among all citizens, regardless of their political preferences and ideological positions, depends on national politics, especially during periods of major political change and uncertainty (Weil 1994: pp. 104–6). This idea concerning the importance of national politics is not new (Rose and Mishler 1996: p. 50; Teorell 2002). What is novel in my argument is the idea that politics produces the rapid and instrumental rational attitudinal change that generates not only higher democratic support but also unconditional democratic support.

Twenty-five years of democratic support in Spain

Levels of democratic support in Spain over the last 25 years have remained high and substantially stable, with almost only monotonic increments. It is true that the economic and political situation has varied considerably during this period and that these have been reflected in important fluctuations in the evaluations, but support for democracy appears to have been remarkably immune to these fluctuations.

In striking contrast to the high rates of economic growth and growing individual prosperity during the last decade and a half of Franco's authoritarian regime, the transition to and consolidation of democracy took place amidst successive economic crises provoked by the 'oil crises' of the 1970s. As was the case in the rest of the industrialized world, Spain's recession peaked in 1981–82, when unemployment reached 20 per cent of the labour force (García Delgado 1990). After a period of economic transition, the Spanish economy, in contrast, expanded rapidly during the mid-to-late 1980s. While the base level of unemployment remained the highest in Western Europe, overall levels of affluence rose considerably. A third period came with the sudden, acute recession that began in the early 1990s, when unemployment rose to over 23 per cent. The climate of economic crisis was most acute in 1993, but it started to improve substantially, giving way to the present new period of prosperity and growth. Figure 11.1, which represents graphically the annual evolution of economic conditions as measured by GNP growth, unemployment, and the rate of inflation, shows this evolution clearly.

The political situation also fluctuated considerably during this period. The *Unión de Centro Democrático* (UCD) (Union of the Democratic Centre)

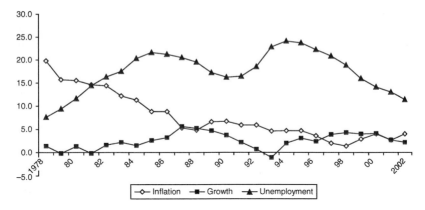

Figure 11.1 Economic conditions in Spain, 1978–2002 (annual data)
Source: *Economie Européene*, 1995, Tables 3, 10, and 26; Anuario El País, Madrid, 2002; Eurostat and INE (Anuario Estadístico 2002).

government headed by Adolfo Suárez was given much of the credit for the remarkable success of the transition to democracy. This enabled the Prime Minister to capitalize on the wave of satisfaction after the ratification of the new constitution in December 1978 by calling for early elections in March 1979. Yet shortly afterwards, popular support for the UCD government collapsed; the weak and divided minority UCD governments were considered to be incapable of resolving the challenges posed by the economic crisis, increasing terrorist violence, and an inconsistent regional policy (Gunther 1986: pp. 433–92). It was widely feared at the time that the inefficacy of the UCD government was seriously undermining the original legitimacy accorded to the democratic system. This diagnosis was summed up in the term *desencanto* (disenchantment), which referred to the disillusionment that emerged in the wake of the high expectations generated earlier in the transition from authoritarianism. It was generally thought that this *desencanto* was threatening the consolidation of the new regime. These fears were dispelled, however, after the 1982 general elections, which brought the Socialist Party (*Partido Socialista Obrero Español*) (PSOE) to power with a majority mandate and facilitated the recovery of the economy.

By the late 1980s, Spain had the second highest rate of economic growth in Europe, inflation had fallen significantly, and the highly stable socialist government had achieved notable successes in both foreign and domestic affairs. Political problems appeared again in the late 1980s and especially in the early 1990s. Political opposition to the government increased, trade unions called for general strikes, a succession of political scandals involving party funding began, cases of corruption involving senior figures in the socialist administration increased, and crimes committed in the fight against ETA terrorism were revealed (Wert 1996: pp. 113–51). All of this coincided with a sudden and severe economic crisis. Economic recovery in the mid-1990s and the electoral victory of the conservative Popular Party (*Partido Popular*) (PP) in 1996 marked the departure from the preceding political situation. From 1996 to 2000, the political situation was stable, lacking important political scandals in comparison with the preceding legislature, while a stable cabinet was formed by the PP with the support of the Catalan nationalist party coalition (*Convergencia i Unió*) (CiU) and the Canary Islands' regionalist party coalition (*Coalición Canaria*) (CC) in parliament. Economic growth during this same period was outstanding (far above the EU average) with unemployment reduced to previously unseen levels. In 2000, the PP obtained the absolute majority in the Spanish parliament for the first time since democracy was re-established.

Spaniards' evaluation of the political and economic situation responded to these events and phases. As can be seen in Figure 11.2, the level of satisfaction with the *economic* situation co-varies with the assessment of *political* conditions and both closely parallel the changing circumstances outlined above.[4] As would be expected, dissatisfaction with the economic situation was most acute precisely at the peak of the two recessions and improved at the end of the recession, with the

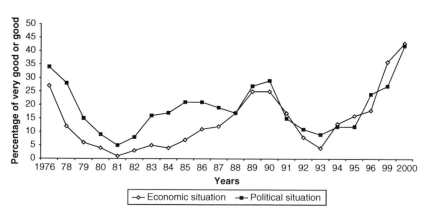

Figure 11.2 Evaluations of the political and economic situation in Spain, 1976–2000
Source: For 1976–1986, 1999, and 2000, CIS; for 1987–1996, cires surveys.

return to prosperity reaching very high levels at the end of the 1990s. The political situation followed exactly the same pattern. This could be the result of improvements in the economic situation or of pure coincidence in the timing of improvements in the political situation. What is important here is the correspondence between the different phases and periods of the political and economic situation and their evaluation by the public. In fact, a recent time series analysis of the relationship between the state of the economy and aggregate assessments by the public has shown that people are able to accurately assess the state of the economy (Maravall and Przewroski 1998: p. 20).

How did support for democracy evolve during this same period? Did democratic support evolve in the same way as citizens' evaluations of the political and economic situation? It seems clear that political discontent with the functioning of the democratic system, an attitude clearly related to and conditioned by dissatisfaction with the incumbent government (Gunther, Montero and Torcal 2007), is the only attitude that presents serious oscillations in response to the different political and economic crises of the system; whereas support for democracy seems more stable and appears not to be influenced by the economic and political situation and by citizens' evaluation fluctuations over time. Figure 11.3 shows that the indicator of political discontent evolves and fluctuates in line with assessments of the economic and political situation.[5] The figure confirms that this

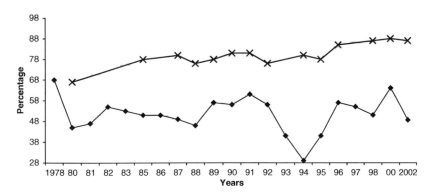

Figure 11.3 Political discontent with democratic functioning and support for democracy in Spain, 1978–2002

Source: 'Satisfaction with functioning', Temporal series of the Eurobarometer 1974–1994, Eurobarometers 43, 48, and 49, CIS (study 2218 and 2107), and DATA (the formulation was somewhat different 'Democracy enables problems solution'). For Democratic Support CIS, except 2002, 'Values Systems of the Citizens and Socio-Economic Conditions – Challenges from Democratization for the EU-Enlargement'.

attitude mostly relates to the economic and political situation and the incumbent authorities and shows how this is related to party support (political discontent). Spaniards apparently do not find it easy to distinguish between their evaluation of the incumbent government, economic conditions, the efficacy of democracy as a problem-solver, and their satisfaction with the way democracy is functioning. However, Spanish citizens appear to have no difficulty in differentiating these views from their support for democracy. Except for a sudden and significant increase at the very beginning of the 1980s, which I will discuss later, support for democracy has only increased monotonically, despite fluctuating opinions of the economic and political situation and despite variations in the economy. Between 1985 and 2000, 76–88 per cent of Spaniards regarded democracy as the most desirable political regime. Furthermore, as other scholars have shown, this support for a democratic regime was hardly conditioned by partisan and ideological options. For instance, only a small percentage of conservatives declare their preference for authoritarian options (Maravall 1984: p. 121; Montero and Torcal 1990: p. 53). Alternative legitimacy in favour of authoritarianism and loyalty to Franco has never constituted a threat to democracy in Spain, even during the acute political crises and corruption scandals of 1994 and 1995 (Morlino and Montero 1995: pp. 236–7).

I have, therefore, shown that levels of attitudinal support for democracy have both remained quite constant and were unaffected by the economic crises of the early 1980s and 1990s, the widespread discontent with the UCD government before its 1982 electoral collapse, the scandals which beset the socialist government in the years leading up to its electoral defeat in 1996, or the political stability and marked economic growth that took place during the last legislature under the conservative government of Aznar. These findings highlight two basic points: first, that attitudes related to system functioning are strongly related to the evaluation of the economic and political situation, good indicators of an incumbent government's performance and 'partisanship'; second, that basic support for democracy is relatively autonomous, in both theoretical and empirical terms, from political discontent, that is to say, from perceptions of system inefficacy and general dissatisfaction with the functioning of democracy.

Generations and politics in Spain

In order to examine the possible reasons for the emergence and evolution of democratic support, we must study their patterns of change and continuity, generation by generation. In other words, we must ascertain whether certain *political generations* reflect characteristically different levels of democratic support and look at how these differences reflect particular patterns. But before tackling the results I shall briefly outline my longitudinal or generational analysis and the way in which I have grouped the political generations in Spain.

Longitudinal or generational analysis

In order to detect the existence of different political generations with respect to democratic support, I will carry out a longitudinal or generational analysis using transversal survey data collated over a number of years. This kind of analysis can detect three different effects that explain attitudinal continuity or change: the cohort, the period and age effect.

The presence of cohort effects reflects the influence of past political events on current levels of democratic support. Pure period effects demonstrate how volatile this attitude can be and its lack of connection to past political events. Age effects reflect the effect of ageing on the presence of democratic support. These different effects can be detected using two procedures: first, by specifying a model, and second, by simple visual analysis of figures. This last one is easier to follow and interpret, but it does not always capture the presence of cohort effects since they normally appear mixed up with cross-generational fluctuations in opinion resulting from a specific political event (period effect). On other occasions, life cycle effects can be confused with the presence of a cohort effect, as some attitudes, despite their varying proportions in the different generations, tend to converge across all the generations as they grow older. On the other hand, modelling is a more complete and reliable procedure, but involves more technical difficulties that are not easy to resolve. Therefore, as well as presenting the figures, I have included some very simple regression models in order to detect these effects.

In addition to the presence of the three aforementioned effects and their hybrids, there are other important factors that should be sought in a cohort analysis. When a generational effect is detected, we must try to ascertain what the inter-generational differences are. If the inter-generational differences are constant but *quantitatively small*, we can conclude that these are political attitudes with considerable inter-generational continuity, and we can therefore not expect cultural change to occur as a result of inter-generational replacement (the natural replacement of older generations by younger generations). On the other hand, if the differences between generations are both constant and *quantitatively greater*, we can conclude that there are significant inter-generational differences due to different political experiences among generations and, as a result, natural inter-generational replacement will be the driving force behind attitudinal and cultural change (Jennings and Niemi 1975: p. 1318; Jennings and Niemi 1981: pp. 7–9 and 117–24).

Political generations in Spain

In studies of attitudinal change, the cohort limits are normally fixed by date of birth in order to reflect different historical events (Ryder 1965; Mason and Fienberg 1985: p. 12). As we know, cohort analysis has often been used in studies of attitudinal change and continuity, but discrepancies over fixing the cohort limits have been a constant bone of contention. Not only is this due to differences in defining the cohort limits in accordance with the political events that may have influenced the various generations, but it is also due to disparities in setting the basic age of socialization. In this study, I have focused mainly on the stage of 'political maturity' (17–25 years old) because this period is characterized by a greater openness to the impact of socialization through non-primary political agents, with the role of the family and school relegated to second place. In this study, I have set the cohort limits on the basis of two criteria: the socialization period between the ages of 17 and 26; and the main economic, social, and political events of Spain's recent history. This has resulted in the creation of six different cohorts.[6]

Five of the six cohorts will be used for this analysis. The youngest generation (the *democracy* generation) has not been included for two reasons: first, because of its similarity with the previous generation (the *transition* generation), which made it more difficult to visualize; second, and more importantly, because this generation is still in the process of being formed, with new members being incorporated during the period analysed. There are no attitudinal data available for this generation in the early studies because its members had not yet come of age, which has prevented their inclusion in the equation models. Nevertheless, this first generation is very similar to the second in virtually all respects.

Political generations and support for democracy

The presence of generational or period effects in Spaniards' democratic support could be identified visually (Figure 11.4) or by the estimation of an equation (11.1), although both represent exactly the same reality. The variables included in the equation are dummy variables and they should be interpreted by taking as a reference point the oldest generation

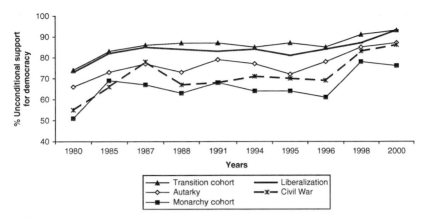

Figure 11.4 Cohorts and support for democracy in Spain, 1980–2000
Source: CIS studies 1,237, 1,461, 1,695, 1,788, 1,984, 2,107, 2,154, 2,218, 2,309, and 2,384.

Equation (11.1) Model of period and cohort effects on support for democracy

---

$\hat{Y} = 65.2 + 19.2 \times C_2 + 17.1 \times C_3 + 10 \times C_4 + 4.5 \times C_5 - 11.6 \times P_1 - 0.8 \times P_2$
$\quad\;\;(0.000)\quad\;\;(0.000)\quad\;(0.000)\quad(0.004)\quad\;(0.000)\quad\;\;(0.647)$
$+3.2 \times P_3 - 0.2 \times P_4 + 1.8 \times P_5 + 0.8 \times P_6 - 0.6 \times P_7 + 9.4 \times P_9 - 11.2 \times P_{10}$
$\;(0.079)\quad\;(0.919)\quad\;(0.306)\quad\;(0.647)\quad\;(0.731)\quad\;(0.000)\quad\;(0.000)$
R^2: 0.94

Variables in the models: C_2 = Cohort 2 (*transition*), C_3 = Cohort 3 (*liberalization*), C_4 = Cohort 4 (*autarky*), C_5 = Cohort 5 (*Civil War*), P_1 = Period 1 (1980), P_2 = Period 2 (1985), P_3 = Period 3 (1987), P_4 = Period 4 (1988), P_5 = Period 5 (1991), P_6 = Period 6 (1994), P_7 = Period 7 (1995), P_9 = Period 9 (1998), P_{10} = Period 10 (2000).

Reference variables: Cohort 6 (*monarchy*) and Period 8 (1996).

(*monarchy*) for the cohort variables and the year 1996 for the period variables. A positive and statistically significant coefficient for the cohort variables means that support for democracy is higher on average for that specific cohort. A positive and significant coefficient for the period means that in this specific year or period democratic support increased significantly with respect to the year 1996. A non-significant coefficient means that there is no variation for that specific year (for period effects) or generation (for the cohort variables). A coefficient of 10 for one of the cohort variables in the equation means that there is a 10 per cent difference between the support given by this specific cohort and the oldest one, which is the reference category. If we want to know the relative contribution of each generation to the increase in aggregate democratic support, we have to subtract the value of the coefficient of interest of the cohort from the value obtained by the preceding cohort.[7]

The analysis of support for democracy by cohorts reveals a clear cohort effect with a general pattern: the younger a cohort, the more it supports the democratic regime. This is confirmed visually in Figure 11.4 or statistically in equation (11.1). The latter shows that all the cohort coefficients are statistically significant in contributing to the increase in democratic support. However, it is important to note that all generations profess majority support for the democratic regime (over 60 per cent), including those that are least in favour (the value of the constant in equation (11.1) is 65.2). This means that inter-generational differences in the level of democratic support have had proportionally very little impact on Spaniards' current levels of democratic support. As I will discuss below, this is due to an important, dramatic, and rapid attitudinal change that took place mainly during the Transition. Finally, just three period effects seem to be statistically significant, one at the beginning of the series in 1980 (P_1 with a decrease of 11.6) and two at the end, 1998 (P_9 with an increase of 9.4) and 2000 (P_{10} with a decrease of 11.2).

Admittedly, we can observe some gradual yet conspicuous changes between the generations in terms of support for the new regime. As the coefficients of equation (11.1) show, there is a moderate increase between each generation and the reference generation (the oldest, or *monarchy* generation). The most significant contribution among all generations to the aggregate increase of democratic support comes from the third or *liberalization* generation (C_3–C_4 = 17.1–10 = 7.1), followed by the fourth or *autarky* generation (C_4–C_5 = 10–4.5 = 5.5), the fifth or *Civil War* generation (C_5–reference = 4.5), and then stabilizing with the *transition* generation, with an average increase of 2.1 points over the previous generation (C_2–C_4 = 19.2–17.1 = 2.1). Given that the average difference between the youngest and oldest generations is 19.2 per cent (65.2 per cent for the *monarchy* generation[8] and 84.4 per cent for the *democracy* generation[9]), we can see that the contribution of the third and fourth generations (the protagonists of the modernization and liberalization period during the Francoist regime) to the increase in democratic legitimacy is only 36 per cent of the total contribution of all cohorts (the contribution of these two generations to the increase in democratic support are 7.1 and 5.5 per cent, respectively, with a total of 12.6 per cent, which only represents 36 per cent of the total contribution of all generations to the increase in democratic support). This means that the contribution of these two generations of the modernization period in Spain is not distinctly important. All generations have contributed somewhat to the increase in democratic support.

There are three possible explanations for the observed generational contributions to the increase in support for the new regime. The first, which we discussed previously, concerns Pérez Díaz's argument about the importance of the resurgence of civil society following the economic and social transformations of the 1960s (see also López Pintor 1982; Edles 1995). The second, a little more political, is that the differences in support for the regime among these two generations simply reveal the changes that took place in the legitimizing discourse of the Francoist regime: during the first phase, the Civil War and the regime that followed were presented as an essential 'crusade of saviours' against the nation's enemies, whereas the second phase saw this discourse take a back seat, with priority now given to exalting the peace and prosperity induced by the regime (Aguilar 1996). Finally, the third theory states that the evolution of legitimacy through different generations also reflects the political events that have influenced each generation, in addition to the changes in the regime's legitimizing discourse and the developments of the 1960s.

As I have said, the difference between the first and last generation is around 19 per cent, whereas the difference between the third generation (*liberalization*) and the fourth (*autarky*) is only 7.1 per cent (subtracting coefficients 17.1 and 10). On the other hand, the *autarky* generation's contribution to the change is 10 per cent with respect to the reference generation (see coefficient) and 5.5 per cent with respect to the preceding generation (*Civil War*). If the first two aforementioned theories were correct (i.e. the change in the legitimizing discourse regarding the Civil War and Francoism and the re-emergence of civil society), then the third generation (*liberalization*) would be the main source of increased support for the regime. In fact, this generation's contribution constitutes less than half the inter-generational differences observed for regime support. The greatest proportion of attitudinal change is in fact due to the influence of all the other political generations (just over 12 per cent). This means that support for the democratic regime is conditioned to a certain extent by the diverse pre-adult political experiences of all six generations, not only the fourth generation. The older generations' direct experience of the Second Republic and the Civil War, and experience of the recent Transition, also contributes to this change since the different levels of support for the regime with respect to the previous or successive generations are also significant. On the whole, they have all contributed in some way to creating political generations that now express greater support for the democratic regime than their predecessors.

This conclusion can also be seen in the evaluations of the authoritarian regime. Evaluations of Franco and of the authoritarian experience may yield much more polarizing results among Spaniards (McDonough et al. 1994: p. 356; McDonough et al. 1996: pp. 735–59), but these evaluations are linked with support for the current democratic regime. Inter-generational differences in evaluations of the authoritarian regime and Franco occur both between the fourth (*autarky and post-war*) and the third (*liberalization*) generations and between the third and the second (*transition*) generations.[10]

But this does not mean that support for democracy is purely an effect of socialization that took place in the past. On the contrary, support for democracy, although conditioned by socialization, is mostly the product of an instrumental decision taken by the great majority of Spaniards. First, I argue here that support for democracy mostly originated during the Transition; this is why older generations also profess majority support for the democratic regime (around 65 per cent on average). Note also that the constant in the equation is very high: support for democracy reaches 65.2 per cent, which cannot be explained by the variables in equation (11.1) (cohorts and period). This means that inter-generational change has little impact on majority support for the democratic regime.

This confirms that the current levels of support for democracy took place some time during the transition to democracy and, I argue, it was due to a rapid attitudinal change produced during that short period. By the end of the previous regime, Spaniards did not profess great support for the latter, but neither were they committed democrats. It was more a case of a 'great, silent majority' whose priority values were peace, justice, and order, with democracy much lower down the list (Instituto de Opinión Pública 1967; López Pina and Aranguren 1976: pp. 73–94). As Aguilar suggests (López Pintor 1982: pp. 85–6; Aguilar 1996: p. 349), this was the greatest socializing achievement of Francoist propaganda. The legitimizing discourse and the new political symbols of the second phase of Francoism affected all Spaniards by changing the way they saw the regime; but they failed, as Aguilar has argued, to legitimize the authoritarian regime. The legitimizing discourse and symbols of the last years of Francoism have also failed to leave a very distinctive impact on the democratic support of the new regime; other generations have also contributed substantially to the current levels, and, more importantly, current support is mostly the product of a rapid change during the Transition and, to a lesser degree, the consolidation of the new regime. However, I would like to point out that the construction of current democratic support might have been facilitated precisely by the main political actors' instrumental use of the legitimizing symbols and discourses constructed and used during the second period of Francoism to emphasize the achievements of peace and prosperity of the regime. Along with the fact that the Transition itself was smooth and peaceful, the rapid and instrumental attitudinal change we have observed was partly possible due to the importance given by the protagonists of the Transition and of the subsequent consolidation of democracy to the maintenance of these achievements. The legitimacy of the current democratic system was built upon the socializing base of Francoism and the symbols it generated, but the attitudinal change took place not before the Transition but during it. As we can see in a survey in which Spaniards were asked how political decisions should be made, the percentage preferring 'decisions to be made by those elected by the people' rose from 53 per cent in 1966 to 56 per cent in January 1976 and 78 per cent just a few months later, in May of that year. Yet between 1976 and 1982, this percentage only rose to 79 per cent (López Pintor 1982: p. 153). In fact, as early as 1978, 77 per cent of Spaniards already identified themselves as unconditional democrats.[11] This change in attitude in just five months shows why inter-generational change is responsible for only a small proportion of the high levels of democratic legitimacy.

It is also important to note, as Morlino and Mattei (1998: p. 1757) have pointed out, that in 1985, just after the consolidation of the regime had taken place in Spain, the percentage of 'neo-democrats or converted' (citizens who supported the new regime but who also had a positive view of the Francoist regime) was 46.9 per cent, whereas 'pure democrats' (those supporting the regime but who also rejected the Francoist regime) was only 31.1 per cent. This is another clear symptom of the presence of an instrumental and rapid attitudinal change that took place during the Transition and its consolidation in Spain.

The instrumental-rational construction of the majoritarian support for democracy in Spain can also be observed in its evolution over time. Despite its dominant stability during 20 years, I should also point out that support for democracy reveals two points of substantial increase: one between 1980 and 1985 and one after 1996 (this can clearly be seen in the magnitude and significance of the regression coefficient of period effects 1 (P_1), 9 (P_9), and 10 (P_{10}) – 1980, 1998, and 2000, respectively – in Equation (11.1)).[12] The first increase appears to reflect the final stage of the construction of democratic legitimacy during the consolidation of the new regime and it might have been triggered as well by the coming to power of the Socialist Party. The slight attitudinal change that occurred during this period with respect to democratic legitimacy even affected those generations of Spaniards who were rather less inclined to accept the new regime as a result of their pre-adult political experiences and it constitutes a clear symptom of the culmination of the already mentioned 'attitudinal consolidating effect'. The second increase (1998 and 2000) is important too and has also affected all the generations, but mostly the citizens on the right of the ideological spectrum.[13] This might be due to the coming to power of the conservative PP for the first time since democracy was re-established. Thus, majoritarian support for democracy in Spain, although conditioned by the political past, is mostly a rational-instrumental creation.

Testing the unconditional democratic support of Spaniards

To confirm the presence of an 'attitudinal consolidating effect' due to the politics of the Transition and democratic consolidation in Spain, I propose a model with unconditional democratic support, measured by a dichotomous variable, as the dependent variable for three points in time: 1980, 1995 and 2000.[14] This model includes a set of independent variables to measure the impact of different alternative theories for democratic support:

$Ln\,(P_j/1-P_j) = \beta_{0j}\alpha_j + e.$ *previous regime$_j$* $\beta_{1j} +$ *ideology$_j$* β_{2j}

$+ i.$ *distance$_j$* $\beta_{3j} + reg.$ *functioning$_j$* $\beta_{4j} + personal\ econ.$ *situation$_j$* β_{5j}

$+ general\ econ.\ eval_j$ $\beta_{6j} + achievement\ of\ democratic\ ideals_j$ β_{7j}

$+ frequency\ of\ political\ discussions_j$ $\beta_{8j} + gender_j$ $\beta_{9j} + education_j$ β_{10j}

$+ trust_j$ $\beta_{11j} + internal\ efficacy_j$ $\beta_{12j} + external\ efficacy_j$ β_{13j}

$+ cohort1_j$ $\beta_{14j} + cohort2_j$ $\beta_{15j} + \cdots + cohort\ n_j$ $\beta_{nj} + e$

where $Ln\,(P_j/1-P_j)$ is the probability of supporting the democratic regime.

The reasons behind the inclusion of most of the variables in this model are somewhat self-explanatory, although those variables central to our argument require some brief discussion. The inclusion in the model of an evaluation of the previous regime is very important in order to control the effect of the impact of this variable in predicting current democratic support. Gender, cohort, education, social trust, and frequency of political discussion are included in order to estimate the lasting effect of different political, social, cultural, and economic socializing experiences in the levels of democratic support. Variables such as regime functioning and evaluation of the personal or general economic situation are included to test the impact of purely economic instrumental democratic support and the connection between democratic support and the economic performance of the regime. Finally, evaluation of the achievement of certain democratic ideals is included in order to test the possibility that the rule of law and a general ability to guarantee basic political rights have an important predictive capacity in explaining democratic support (see Diamond 1999; Bratton and Mattes 2001; Rose and Mishler 2002).

The inclusion of ideology and ideological distance in the model deserves greater attention since they are essential variables for capturing the impact of the 'consolidating effect'. As discussed earlier, in many countries, the 'rules of the game' in the past included the political exclusion of, or collective action against, one sector or another of the population and their political representatives. This can leave an attitudinal legacy, traceable through the impact of ideology on support for the democratic regime. If the attitudinal change and the resulting consolidating effect take place in a new democracy, this relationship can be reduced or diminished. In Spain in 1980, soon after the end of the Transition, the correlation coefficients between ideology and support for democracy of all generations were still high and negative (see Table 11.1), confirming that, for all political generations, left-wing Spaniards tended to identify themselves as more committed democrats

Table 11.1 Relation between ideology and support for democracy by cohort in Spain, 1980 and 2000 (the figures represent the correlations between ideology and support for democracy)

Cohort	1980	1995	1996	2000
Cohort 1 (*democracy*)	Not yet formed	−0.19**	−0.13**	−0.09**
Cohort 2 (*transition*)	−0.36**	−0.27**	−0.07	−0.12**
Cohort 3 (*liberalization*)	−0.43**	−0.24**	−0.17**	−0.04
Cohort 4 (*autarky*)	−0.39**	−0.23**	−0.01	−0.07*
Cohort 5 (*Civil War*)	−0.33**	−0.34**	−0.39**	−0.07
Cohort 6 (*monarchy*)	−0.30**	−0.30*	−0.24**	0.00

Source: CIS studies 2154, 2218, and 2384.
*Significant at $p < 0.05$; **significant at $p < 0.01$.

than those on the right. This tendency accords, once again, with Spain's political history. While both the left and the right have adopted semi-, if not overtly, disloyal stances with respect to democracy, the left has nonetheless always shown a greater commitment to establishing and defending representative democracy than the right, especially during and after the Francoist regime. The gap between left- and right-wing Spaniards is particularly pronounced in the third political generation, which came of age during the period of *liberalization*, when the left completely dominated the opposition to the Francoist regime and struggled to replace it with a democracy. Hence, as can be seen in Table 11.1, the closest correlation between ideology and support for democracy is found precisely in this generation. Nonetheless, it should be emphasized that the relationship between ideology and support for democracy is very strong in all the generations. This finding shows that while a major attitudinal shift did take place during the Transition, the indelible marks of Spain's past are still visible in Spaniards' political attitudes. The attitudinal change was not yet complete and the 'attitudinal consolidating effect' not fully present either.

These marks, however, have faded as a result of the passage of time under democracy, or, to be more precise, as a result of the actively pro-democratic discourse that all the significant political actors from across the ideological spectrum, with the partial exception of the Basque country, have adopted since the return to democracy. But more importantly, the results observed in Table 11.1 highlight again the effect of the coming to power of the conservative PP, teaching most conservatives that anyone could obtain power with the present 'rules of the game'. Between the discourse and the arrival of the PP in government, even the most right-wing extremists have become supporters of democracy. Part of the attitudinal change in support of democracy among Spaniards that sustained what I have called the 'attitudinal consolidating effect' was instrumental in nature. Hence, Table 11.1 also shows that in 1995, after 18 years of democracy, the correlation between ideology and support for democracy is much weaker in the first generation socialized under democracy, and even more strikingly, it has become significantly weaker in the second, third, and fourth generations. This was the effect of almost two decades of democracy, even at a time when the right had yet to win a general election or hold power in democratic Spain. In fact, the data for 1996, drawn from a survey conducted just three months after the electoral victory of the conservative PP, shows a further substantial weakening of the correlation between legitimacy and ideology. Only the oldest two generations, those of the *monarchy* and the *Civil War*, remained immune to the socializing effect of the functioning of democracy (and the moderating discourse of the main political actors). Data collected in the year 2000 confirms this trend, and after four years of conservative rule, and just after obtaining the absolute parliamentary majority in March of 2000, even the most conservative of the oldest generations have become convinced democrats. It would seem, therefore, that the dramatic political events that shaped these generations' political socialization have left a lasting mark on their level of democratic support for the new regime, a mark that the present democratic system has been unable to remove.

All of this suggests three conclusions. First, that despite the enormous attitudinal change regarding support for democracy that took place during the Transition, the political past of Spanish society, marked by the struggle between the 'two Spains', can also be seen in the greater presence of a 'democratic ethos' among left-wing citizens than among those on the right. Second, and as a result of this, in the early years of the new democracy, ideology was an important factor that had a similar influence on the degree of support for democracy professed by citizens from all generations, despite the great attitudinal transformation that took place during the Transition. Third, this analysis shows that the functioning of democracy has led to a qualitative, rather than a quantitative, change in Spaniards' support for democracy (which was already high in 1978 and has increased little since then). Almost 20 years of democracy have eliminated the influence of ideology and diminished the influence of the preceding regime in determining citizens' unconditional support for democracy (McDonough et al. 1998: pp. 43–53).

Estimating the model for the presence of an attitudinal consolidating effect

As I have shown in the preceding pages, the year 1980 displays the lowest level of democratic support since democracy was re-established in Spain. The level of support was very high, but not majoritarian, since only 67 per cent of Spaniards expressed unconditional support. This might be due to the lack of a complete attitudinal change and the absence of a full 'attitudinal consolidating effect'. Perhaps, the attitudinal change that was underway was stopped short by political circumstances following the approval of the Spanish constitution. This was a period of substantial political and economic turmoil. Popular support for the UCD government was rapidly collapsing and the weak and divided minority UCD governments were considered to be incapable of resolving the challenges posed by the economic crisis, increasing terrorist violence, and an inconsistent regional policy (Gunther 1986: pp. 433–92). The important attitudinal change may have occurred by then, but the process of creating majority unconditional democratic support was not complete. If my diagnosis is correct, the estimation of the model should be able to show that ideological (party) preferences, the variables measuring respondents' personal material situation, and their assessment of the functioning of democracy, along with variables measuring the socializing legacies of the past, contain the capacity to predict the level of support. These results, if inserted into this type of analysis, would provide a good indication that the attitudinal change that gave way to majority unconditional democratic support was incomplete in 1980.

The results of the estimation of the model for Spain with the 1980 survey data, displayed in Table 11.2, are exactly as predicted, displaying an unfinished 'attitudinal consolidating effect'. Rejection of the preceding regime[15] was one of the best predictors of support for democracy in 1980; however, the respondents' ideology was still more powerful (the left tended to support democracy much more). Another sign of the lack of completion of the attitudinal change is the very minor impact of cohorts 3 and 4 (*liberalization* and *autarky*, respectively), already observed in the preceding section above. Nevertheless, there were signs that the major attitudinal change had already taken place. The absence of any relation between democratic support and the variables measuring respondents' personal material situation, their assessment of the functioning of democracy or government in the midst of the political and economic crisis shows that a significant attitudinal 'safety area' for democracy already existed. Similarly, there are no relationships between indicators that measure indirectly the impact of different socialization experiences, with the exception of the very weak relation between the gender and the frequency of political discussions during childhood. Social trust has some impact on democratic support, but it is very low, which demonstrates that cultural heritage is not responsible for the level of support for democracy. Finally, the value of the constant and the model's scant, albeit significant, explanatory power, also point to the presence of the consolidating effect in explaining the origin of support for democracy in 1980.

However, in 1995 and in 2002, as can be seen from the estimation of a very similar model with survey data from these years (Table 11.3), the attitudinal change was completed and the 'attitudinal consolidating effect' was fully present. In 1995, the evaluation of the previous regime constitutes, along with ideology, the best predictor of the level

Table 11.2 Model to explain support for democracy in Spain, 1980 (only statistically significant logistic regression coefficients)

	Coefficients	Odds ratios	First difference probabilities (1)
Independent variables			
E. previous regime (2)	−0.50**	0.60	0.25
Ideology	−0.50**	0.61	−0.82
I. distance			
Regime functioning (3)			
Personal econ. situation			
General econ. evaluation			
Achievement of democratic ideals: freedom	n.i.		
Achievement of democratic ideals: equality	n.i.		
Socialization variables			
Frequency of political discussion during childhood	0.23**	1.26	0.16
Gender	0.34*	1.40	0.09
Education			
Cohort 2 (*transition*)	Reference		
Cohort 3 (*liberalization*)	0.68*	1.97	0.10
Cohort 4 (*autarky*)	0.67*	1.95	0.03
Cohort 5 (*Civil War*)			
Cohort 6 (*monarchy*)			
Social trust	0.57**	1.76	0.09
Constant	3.63**		
Chi-square of model	225.3** (d.f. 16)		
−2 log likelihood	766.42		
R^2 Nagelkerke	0.33		
(N)	(1026)		

Source: CIS, Study 1,237.
** Significant at $p < 0.01$; * significant at $p < 0.05$.
(1) This column shows the difference between the estimated probability, when the independent variable is at its lowest value and the others remain constant at the mean, and the same probability when the value of the independent variable is at its highest value. This is known as the first difference.
(2) I have used family's side in Civil War as a proxy.
(3) This year the question was: 'When Franco died people felt a lot of uncertainty as to what could happen in the country. Do you think that things have got better or worse than you expected?'

of support for democracy (with first differences of –0.4 and 0.4, respectively). Ideology, however, lost predictive capacity in comparison with 1980. This result is probably due to ideological depolarization with respect to support for the democratic regime, which, as discussed

218

Table 11.3 Model to explain support for democracy in Spain, 1995 and 2002 (only statistically significant logistic regression coefficients)

	1995			2002		
	Coefficients	Odds ratios	First difference probabilities (1)	Coefficients	Odds ratios	First difference probabilities (1)
Independent variables						
Evaluation of Franquism	−0.92**	0.34	−0.41	−0.83**	0.44	
Ideology	−0.18**	0.84	−0.44	−0.14*	0.87	
I. distance						
Regime functioning (2)						
General econ. evaluation	0.19*	1.21	0.11			
Personal econ. situation						
Achievement of democratic ideals: freedom (3)	0.34**	1.38	0.16			
Achievement of democratic ideals: equality (4)				0.26*	1.30	
Socialization variables						
Frequency of political discussion during childhood	n.i			n.i		
Gender						
Education	0.11**	1.12	0.15			
Cohort 1 (*democracy*)						
Cohort 2 (*transition*)						
Cohort 3 (*liberalization*)						
Cohort 4 (*autarky*)						

Cohort 5 (*Civil War*)		—	—	—
Cohort 6 (*monarchy*)	Reference	—	—	Reference
Social trust	n.i.			
Constant	3.84**			2.64*
Chi-square of model	391.7** (d.f. 16)			143.35** (d.f. 19)
−2 log likelihood	1938.6			513.95
R^2 Nagelkerke	0.24			0.29
(N)	(2339)			(807)

Source: For 1995, CIS Study 2154 and for 2002, 'Values Systems of the Citizens and Socio-Economic Conditions – Challenges from Democratisation for the EU-Enlargement.'

*Significant at $p < 0.05$; **significant at $p < 0.01$.

(1) See Table 11.2 for an explanation.
(2) In 1995, respondents were asked if 'they think that democracy works well or badly'. In 2002, people were questioned about improvements in the general, as well as their personal, economic situation since the 1980s.
(3) In 1995, respondents were asked if individual freedom had improved over the last 10 years. In 2002, they were questioned if they considered that freedom of speech was guaranteed in Spain.
(4) In 1995, respondents were asked if social inequalities had improved over the last 10 years. In 2002, they were questioned about the level of existing social equality in Spain.

extensively before, took place over the course of the 15–22 years that separated these two surveys from 1980. Otherwise, the results are similar to those in 1980, except in two important aspects. First, with the passage of time under democracy, the legitimacy of the system became more closely related to the overall (not personal) material situation and an evaluation of the regime's political achievements. Over time, Spaniards seemed to become convinced also of the overall benefits of democracy, including the most reluctant sectors and generations, as a result of the efficient functioning of rules that guarantee the fairness of the game and the political rights of major political actors (see also Miller et al. 1997). While these variables still have nothing like the predictive capacity of ideology or the evaluation of the previous regime, they nonetheless show a significant correlation in relation to support for the regime. It is important to take this into account when trying to understand the potential reduction of the attitudinal 'safety area' which gives uncondi-tional support to a regime once a democracy has been established and consolidated. Second, education – one of the socialization variables – is now found to be significant, a finding that does not accord with the expected results.

The analysis of 2002 survey data confirms the observed trend and, more importantly, the central hypothesis (see also Table 11.3): an increasing disappearance of the ideology effect and the lack of any effect of the variables measuring the impact of different socializing experi-ences – except discussions of politics in the family during childhood. We can also see that the political performance evaluation variables (achieve-ment of the democratic ideals) are weak, but increasingly important, as noted in the 1995 data.

Conclusion

In short, the creation of majoritarian unconditional support for the democratic regime in Spain took place mostly during the Transition and expanded during the consolidation process. This attitudinal change is the result of a combination of political factors (mostly the appearance of an inclusive regime-founding political pact and the absence of the 'regime issue' from the political agenda and party competition) that emerged during these years, although it is also based upon the opportun-ities created by the political heritage of non-democratic rule. This first and rapid attitudinal change took place during the Transition and could not completely bury the political struggle between the right and left that had long polarized Spain's political history, but reduced its impact considerably. Moreover, the subsequent functioning of the democratic system during the consolidation process and the discourse of the main actors from across the political spectrum favoured and completed this attitudinal shift. As a result of this phenomenon, which unfolded during the transition to and consolidation of democracy, generational effects played a very secondary role in generating democratic legitimization. This secondary role of generations includes a limited degree of divergence between the generation of the *liberalization period* (1960–70), late Francoism (1970–75), and the rest. In general, socialization variables do not explain much of the increasing levels of democratic support. We have also seen here that the variables relating to respondents' evaluation of their economic personal situation show virtually no correlation with support for democracy. This was particularly true in the early years of the new democratic regime, as the attitudinal 'safety area' created by unconditional support for democracy was already great and the 'attitudinal consolidating effect' was already in place.

Acknowledgement

I would like to express my gratitude to Sunnee Billingsley for her helpful comments on the previous draft of this chapter. Many thanks also to the European Commission for the funding of the project 'Values Systems of the Citizens and Socio-Economic Conditions – Challenges from Democratisation for the EU-Enlargement' and to the Spanish Ministry of Science and Technology.

Notes

1. According to Linz (1978: p.16; 1988: p. 65), support for democracy may be considered to be 'the belief that, in spite of shortcomings and failures, the political institutions are better than any others that might be established'.
2. Despite what other scholars have argued (Justel 1992; McDonough et al. 1998), this attitudinal change took place only for democratic support and not for other civic attitudes, resulting in an important presence of 'disaffected democrats' or 'critical democrats' (Montero et al. 1997).
3. However, as has been argued, support for the new regime and approval of the preceding non-democratic one are not exactly opposite sides of the same coin and the latter does not constitute a precondition for democratic support (McDonough et al. 1998: pp. 50–1). Some people might positively value the experience of the non-democratic regime and consider it as a necessary step towards modernity and progress at that time, while giving total support to the current democratic regime (Linz and Stepan 1996: pp. 144–6).
4. The questions were the following: 'Generally speaking, would you consider that the current political (economic) situation is very good, quite good,

not good or bad (neither good nor bad?), quite bad or very bad?' Positive evaluations in the figure include 'very good' and 'quite good'.

5. The data in Figure 11.3 was collected using the satisfaction with functioning questions included in the CIS and Eurobarometer surveys ('In general, are you very satisfied, somewhat satisfied, not very satisfied or not satisfied at all with the way democracy is working in Spain?'), but between 1978 and 1983 a question regarding whether 'democracy permits the solutions of Spaniards' problems' was used.

6. The oldest cohort (6th, the generation of the *monarchy*) is made up of those born in 1914 or earlier, who in 1977 (the year of the first democratic election) were 63 years old or more. Members of this generation reached 17 years of age before 1931, which means that they became young adults during the reign of Alfonso XIII, experienced the dictatorship of Primo de Rivera, his fall from power, and the arrival of the Second Republic. The next cohort (5th, the *Civil War* generation) is composed of those born between 1915 and 1923, who reached 17 years of age between 1932 and 1940. This generation experienced their period of political maturation during the Second Republic, the Civil War, and the beginning of the post-war period. The following cohort (4th, the *post-war or autarky* generation) includes those born between 1924 and 1943, who reached 17 years of age between 1941 and 1960. Members of this generation therefore entered into the stage of adult political socialization during the difficult post-war period, enduring a period of severe economic depression and harsh political repression. The third generation (3rd, generation of the *liberalization*) includes those born between 1944 and 1957, who reached 17 years of age between 1961 and 1974. In other words, these people matured politically while the Francoist regime was in the liberalization process and in the midst of the economic development of the 1970s. The second cohort (2nd, *transition* generation) is made up of those born between 1958 and 1965, who reached 17 years of age between 1975 and 1982, maturing politically during the process of political change and consolidation of the new regime, which culminated with the coming of the socialists to power. Finally, the first cohort (1st, the *democracy* generation) includes those born in 1966 and after, who reached the age of 17 in 1983 and who were socialized within a democracy and with the socialists in power.

7. For instance, if we want to know the contribution of the youngest generation (*transition* or C_2), we need to subtract the coefficient of that cohort variable 19.2 from the coefficient obtained by the preceding one (*liberalization* or C_3), 17.1. Total 2.1.

8. This figure is obtained from the constant in equation (11.1) since *monarchy* is the reference variable.

9. This figure is also obtained from equation (11.1), constant + coefficient 19.2 of C_2, *transition* cohort.

10. Sixty-four per cent of the second generation has a very negative or negative evaluation of Franco and Francoism, whereas these percentages are reduced to 52 per cent for Franco and 49 for the regime in the third generation, and 45 and 42 per cent for the fourth generation. The differences between the evaluations of the other generations only vary between 1 and 3 per cent. The questions for this 1991 CIRES study of political culture were: 'After

these five years, what is your opinion of the Franco regime? (very positive, positive, neither positive nor negative, negative, or very negative)'; and 'In your opinion, how would you evaluate the job done by Franco as head of state? (very positive, positive, neither positive nor negative, negative, or very negative)'.

11. According to Linz and others, 77 per cent of Spaniards declared that, 'Democracy was the best political system for a country like ours', and only 15 per cent disagreed with this statement. See Linz et al. (1981, pp. 627–9).

12. The reference point in this regression is 1996. This is why 1980 has a significant and negative coefficient, and 1998 and 2000 a positive and significant one.

13. In 1995, the proportion of people supporting democracy unconditionally in the right (9, 10) and centre-right positions (7, 8) was 49 and 65 per cent, respectively. However, these percentages increased in the year 2000 to 88 and 84 per cent. The difference in support for democracy between the extreme left and right was 39 per cent in 1995, whereas this number had been reduced to only 10 per cent in the year 2000. The difference in the centre-right position had been reduced from 25 per cent to only 6 per cent. Data collected from studies 2154 and 2384 of the CIS Data Bank.

14. The value '1' represents unconditional support for democracy and '0' the other options.

15. For this survey, I have used the side that the respondent's family sympathized with in the Civil War. Respondents were not asked about their assessment of the political regime in this year, but this variable can be considered a valid, albeit imperfect, proxy, since they are highly related.

References

Aguilar, P., *Memoria y olvido de la Guerra Civil española* (Madrid: Alianza, 1996).

Bratton, M. and R. Mattes, 'Support for Democracy in Africa: Intrinsic or Instrumental?', *British Journal of Political Science*, 31 (2001), pp. 447–74.

Boix, C., 'Constitutions and Democratic Breakdowns', working paper no. 222 (Madrid: Juan March Center for Advance Studies, 2005).

Burton, M., R.P. Gunther and J. Higley, 'Introduction: Elite Transformation and Democratic Regime', in J. Higley and R.P. Gunther, eds, *Elites and Democratic Consolidation in Latin America and Southern Europe* (Cambridge: Cambridge University Press, 1992).

Diamond, L., 'Political Culture', in L. Diamond, ed., *Developing Democracy Toward Consolidation* (Baltimore, MD: The Johns Hopkins University Press, 1999), pp. 161–217.

Di Palma, G., *To Craft Democracies. An Essay on Democratic Transitions* (Berkeley, CA: University of California Press, 1990).

Easton, D. and J. Dennis, *Children and the Political System* (New York: McGraw, 1969).

Edles, L.D., 'Rethinking Democratic Transition: A Culturalist Critique and the Spanish Case', *Theory and Society*, 24 (1995), pp. 355–84.

García Delgado, J.L., *Economía española de la Transición y la Democracia, 1973–1986* (Madrid: CIS, 1990).

Gunther, R.P., 'El colapso de la UCD', in J.J. Linz and J.R. Montero, eds, *Crisis y cambio: Electores y partidos en la España de los ochenta* (Madrid: Centro de Estudios Constitucionales, 1986), pp. 433–92.

Gunther, R.P., *Politica y cultura en España* (Madrid: Centro de Estudios Constitucionales, 1992).

Gunther, R., J.R. Montero and M. Torcal, 'Democracy and Intermediation: Some Attitudinal and Behavioural Dimensions', in R. Gunther, J.R. Montero and H.-J. Puhle, eds, *Democracy, Intermediation and Voting on Four Continents* (Oxford. Oxford University Press, 2007), pp. 29–74.

Harmel, R. and J.D. Robertson, 'Government Stability and Regime Support: A Cross-National Analysis', *Journal of Politics*, 48 (1986), pp. 1029–40.

Instituto de Opinión Pública, 'Cuestiones de actualidad política', *Revista Española de Opinión Pública*, 9 (1967), pp. 185–227.

Jennings, M.K. and R.G. Niemi, 'Continuity and Change in Political Orientations: A Longitudinal Study of Two Generations', *American Political Science Review*, 69 (1975), pp. 1316–35.

Jennings, M.K. and R.G. Niemi, *Generations and Politics. A Panel Study of Young Adults and their Parents* (Princeton, NJ: Princeton University Press, 1981).

Justel, M., 'Edad y cultura política', *Revista Española de Investigaciones Sociológicas*, 58 (1992), pp. 57–96.

Lijphart, A., *Democracy in Plural Societies* (New Haven, CT: Yale University Press, 1977).

Lijphart, A., *Democracies: Patterns of Majoritarian and Consensus Government in Twenty-One Countries* (New Haven, CT: Yale University Press, 1999).

Linz, J.J., *The Breakdown of Democratic Regimes. Crisis, Breakdown and Reequilibration* (Baltimore, MD: The Johns Hopkins, 1978).

Linz, J.J. and Stepan, A., *Problems of Democratic Consolidation. Southern Europe, South America, and Post-Communist Europe* (Baltimore, MD: The Johns Hopkins University Press, 1996).

Linz, J.J., M. Gómez-Reino, D. Vila and F.A. Orizo, *Informe sociológico sobre el cambio político en España, 1975–1981* (IV Informe FOESSA, Vol. I) (Madrid: Euromérica, 1981).

Lipset, S.M., *Political Man. The Social Basis of Politics* (Baltimore, MD: The Johns Hopkins University Press, 1960).

López Pina, A. and E.L. Aranguren, *La cultura política de la España de Franco* (Madrid: Taurus, 1976).

López Pintor, R., *La opinión pública española: Del franquismo a la democracia* (Madrid: Centro de Investigaciones Sociológicas, 1982).

López Pintor, R., 'El impacto del autoritarismo en la cultura política. La experiencia española en una perspectiva comparada', in *Política y Sociedad. Homenaje a Francisco Murillo Ferrol* (Madrid: Centro de Investigaciones Sociológicas, 1987).

Maravall, J.M., *La política de la Transición*, 2nd ed. (Madrid: Taurus, 1984).

Maravall, J.M., *Los resultados de la democracia* (Madrid: Alianza, 1995).

Maravall, J.M. and A. Przeworski, 'Political Reactions to the Economy: The Spanish Experience', working paper no. 127 (Madrid: Centro de Estudios Avanzados en Ciencias Sociales Juan March, 1998).

Mason, W.M. and S.E. Fienberg, eds, *Cohort Analysis in Social Research. Beyond the Identification Problem* (New York: Springer Verlag, 1985).

McDonough, P., S. Barnes and A. López Pina, 'The Nature of Political Support and Legitimacy in Spain', *Comparative Political Studies*, 27 (1994), pp. 349–80.

McDonough, P., S. Barnes and A. López Pina, 'The Growth of Democratic Legitimacy in Spain', *American Political Science Review*, 80 (1996), pp. 735–60.

McDonough, P., S. Barnes and A. López Pina, *The Cultural Dynamics of Democratization in Spain* (Ithaca, NY: Cornell University Press, 1998).

McRae, K., ed., *Consociational Democracy* (Toronto: McClelland and Steward, 1974).

Miller, A.H., V.L. Hesli and W.M. Reisinger, 'Conceptions of Democracy Among Mass and Elite in Post-Soviet Society', *British Journal of Political Science*, 27 (1997), pp. 157–90.

Mishler, W. and R. Rose, 'Five Years After the Fall: Trajectories of Support for Democracy in Postcommunist Europe', in P. Norris, ed., *Critical Citizens. Global Support for Democratic Governance* (Oxford: Oxford University Press, 1999), pp. 78–101.

Montero, J.R. and M. Torcal, 'La cultura política de los españoles: Pautas de continuidad y cambio', *Sistema*, 99 (1990), pp. 39–74.

Montero, J.R., R.P. Gunther and M. Torcal, 'Democracy in Spain: Legitimacy, Discontent, and Disaffection', *Studies in Comparative International Development*, 32, 3 (1997), pp. 124–60.

Morán, M.L. and J. Benedicto, *La cultura política de los españoles. Un ensayo de reinterpretación* (Madrid: CIS, 1995).

Morlino, L. and F. Mattei, 'Old and New Authoritarianism in Southern Europe', in S.U. Larsen, ed., *Modern Europe After Fascism 1945–1980s* (Boulder, CO: Columbia University Press, 1998), pp. 1752–74.

Morlino, L. and J.R. Montero, 'Legitimacy and Democracy in Southern Europe', in R.P. Gunther, P. Nikiforos Diamandouros and H.-J. Puhle, eds, *The Politics of Democratic Consolidation. Southern Europe in Comparative Perspective* (Baltimore, MD: The Johns Hopkins University Press, 1995), pp. 231–60.

Nordlinger, E., *Conflict Regulation in Divided Societies* (Cambridge: Center for International Affairs, 1972).

Pérez Díaz, V.M., *The Return of Civil Society: The Emergence of Democratic Spain* (Cambridge: Harvard University Press, 1993).

Powell, G.B., *Contemporary Democracies: Participation, Stability, and Violence* (Cambridge: Harvard University Press, 1982).

Pridham, G., 'The International Context of Democratic Consolidation: Southern Europe in Comparative Perspective', in R.P. Gunther, P. Nikiforos Diamandouros and H.-J. Puhle, eds, *The Politics of Democratic Consolidation. Southern Europe in Comparative Perspective* (Baltimore, MD: The Johns Hopkins University Press, 1995), pp. 166–203.

Przeworski, A., *Democracy and the Market* (Cambridge: Cambridge University Press, 1991).

Rose, R. and W. Mishler, 'Testing The Churchill Hypothesis: Popular Support for Democracy and Its Alternatives', *Journal of Public Policy*, 16 (1996), pp. 29–58.

Rose, R. and W. Mishler, 'Comparing Regimes in Non-Democratic and Democratic Countries', *Democratization*, 9, 2 (summer 2002), pp. 1–10.

Ryder, N.B., 'The Cohort as a Concept in the Study of Social Change', *American Sociological Review*, 30 (1965), pp. 843–61.

Schmitt, H., 'Party Government in Public Opinion: A European Cross-National Comparison', *European Journal of Political Research*, 11 (1983), pp. 353–75.

Teorell, J., 'Popular Support for Democracy in Russia: A Cross-Temporal Comparison', paper presented at the conference 'Consolidation in New Democracies' (Uppsala University, 8–9 June 2002).

Weil, F.D., 'Political Culture, Political Structure, and Democracy: The Case of Legitimation and Opposition', in *Research on Democracy and Society*, Vol. 2 (Greenwich: Jai Press, 1994), pp. 104–6.

Wert, J.I., 'Sobre cultura política: Legitimidad, desafección y malestar', in J. Tussell, E. Lamo de Espinosa and R. Pardo, eds, *Entre Dos Siglos. Reflexiones sobre la Democracia Español* (Madrid: Alianza, 1996), pp. 113–51.

12
The United States and Spain: From Franco to Juan Carlos

Charles Powell

Introduction: Spain and the 'third wave'

In his seminal work, *The Third Wave. Democratization in the Late Twentieth Century*, published in 1991, the political scientist Samuel P. Huntington set out to explain why some 30 countries in Europe, Asia and Latin America experienced transitions from non-democratic to democratic political systems between 1974 and 1990. In his view, this third wave of democratizations (the first and second being those which had taken place worldwide in 1828–1926 and 1943–62, respectively) could be attributed to five global factors which had emerged in the 1960s to 1980s: (i) the deepening legitimacy problems of authoritarian systems in a world where democratic values were widely accepted, the dependence of those regimes on performance legitimacy, and the undermining of that legitimacy by military defeats, economic failures, and the oil shocks of 1973–74 and 1978–79; (ii) the unprecedented global economic growth of the 1960s, which raised living standards, increased education, and greatly expanded the urban middle class in many countries; (iii) the striking changes in the doctrine and activities of the Catholic Church manifested in the Second Vatican Council in 1963–65 and the transformation of national churches from defenders of the status quo to opponents of authoritarianism and proponents of social, economic, and political reform; (iv) changes in the policies of external actors, including in the late 1960s the new attitude of the European Community towards expanding its membership, the major shift in US policies beginning in 1974 towards the promotion of human rights and democracy in other countries, and Gorbachev's dramatic change in the late 1980s in Soviet policy towards maintaining the Soviet empire; and (v) 'snowballing' or demonstration effects, enhanced by new means of international communication, of the first transitions to democracy in the third wave in stimulating and providing models for subsequent efforts at regime change in other countries.[1]

This wave approach, though useful in encouraging us to look for commonality in democratization processes in countries that might otherwise appear very different from one another, has been criticized for the empirical problems it raises. As far as the Spanish experience is concerned, it is generally agreed that a number of European actors, such as the European Community, the Council of Europe, certain individual states (most notably Germany), transnational (though essentially European) political organizations (such as the Socialist International), political parties, trade unions, and party foundations played a significant role in undermining the Franco regime and paving the way for democratization, as Huntington acknowledged in the fourth of the factors mentioned above.[2] This chapter will examine whether 'the major shift in US policies beginning in 1974 towards the promotion of human rights and democracy in other countries' identified by this author had a comparable effect on events in Spain, as some of those responsible for US foreign policy at the time have repeatedly claimed.[3]

Cold War legacies

Although in the wake of the Spanish Civil War the United States was initially as ill-disposed towards the Franco regime as the major European democracies, the outbreak of the Cold War prompted a change of heart which led to the signing of a crucial bilateral agreement in September 1953, whereby Washington was granted the use of a network of air bases, naval stations, pipelines, and communications facilities in exchange for military aid worth around $600 million and economic assistance to the tune of some $500 million. The agreement, which went a considerable way towards alleviating the post-war isolation imposed on the dictator on account of his former association with the Axis powers, was also of considerable strategic importance to the United States, given the access the bases provided to the Eastern Mediterranean and the Middle East. Washington would no doubt have preferred to link Spain to the West more permanently via NATO membership, but stumbled repeatedly on Scandinavian, Dutch, Belgian, and British opposition to Franco's authoritarian regime, notwithstanding the fact that the equally dictatorial Salazar had become a founding member of the Alliance in 1949. Inevitably, President Dwight D. Eisenhower's visit to Madrid in December 1959 came to symbolize both Franco's acceptance as a respectable friend and ally by the world's leading superpower and the confirmation of his regime's stability and endurance.

President John F. Kennedy was rather less enthusiastic about his nation's ties with Franco than his predecessor, but as he had announced in his inaugural speech, he was willing to 'pay any price, bear any burden, meet any hardship, support any friend, oppose any foe to assure the survival and the success of liberty', and this included the renewal of the Madrid agreements in 1963. Nevertheless, from the 1960s onwards, Washington was increasingly torn between the need to guarantee continued access to these valuable military facilities and the desire to support a gradual evolution away from authoritarianism in Spain. Thus, as early as 1965, the US Embassy in Madrid claimed to be grappling with 'the problem of achieving a transition from the Franco regime to a stable succeeding government with a minimum disturbance to public order and the economic structure, and hopefully in a manner conducive to the gradual application of liberal democracy and social justice in a form suitable to the Spanish framework'.[4] However, given the priorities dictated by the Cold War, under President Lyndon B. Johnson (1963–68) the Administration generally kept a low political profile, though Ambassador Angier Biddle Duke (1965–68) did not shy away from discreet contacts with regime dissidents and even outright opponents. Nevertheless, US diplomats in Madrid remained anxious not to upset Franco unnecessarily: in late 1968, for example, they succeeded in preventing an official visit to Washington by his rival the Bourbon pretender, Don Juan, on the grounds that it was unwise to meddle in the succession debate.[5]

President Richard M. Nixon (1969–74) was more interested in Spanish affairs than his predecessor and held Franco's statesmanship in considerable esteem.[6] When the bases agreement came up for renewal once again in 1968, the Spanish government initially called for the removal of the Torrejón Air Base near Madrid as a way of applying pressure on Washington in the hope of obtaining further military aid and an assurance of a full military commitment to Spain's defence. Under growing pressure from the Senate over Vietnam, Nixon was not in the mood to be generous to Franco, however, and Madrid's original request for $1 billion was finally scaled down to $50 million in military aid and $25 million in credit. This paved the way for a new five-year agreement in August 1970 and an official Nixon visit to Spain in October, even though his national security adviser, Henry Kissinger, would later acknowledge that at the time 'the post-Franco transition was a subject too delicate for even the most oblique allusion'. This was perhaps just as well, as both the 77-year-old Franco and a jet-lagged Kissinger dozed off during their only meeting, leaving the president to chat amiably with Foreign Minister Gregorio López Bravo. Curiously, Nixon's main concern was that the crowds lining the streets of Madrid should be larger than those that had turned out in 1959 to greet Eisenhower, a president whom he both respected and envied. According to Kissinger, Franco was 'able to assuage Nixon's unease over unfavourable comparisons with Eisenhower's reception by commenting sagely that once crowds exceeded several hundred thousand the only problem was to announce some plausible figure'.[7]

Nixon was at least able to meet Juan Carlos, whom the dictator had finally appointed his successor in July 1969 and who impressed him very favourably. Alarmed by Franco's physical condition, and partly at the suggestion of Lord Mountbatten, Juan Carlos' second cousin once removed, in January 1971 the President invited the Prince to an official week-long visit to the United States that was to prove a turning point in the Administration's strategy towards post-Franco Spain. In the Oval Office, the President advised the future king that, after Franco's death, his first priority must be law and order and that he should not concern himself about reforming the political system until stability had been guaranteed. He also urged him not to worry about presenting an image as a liberal and a reformer, but rather to play on his youth, dynamism, and amiability, as this would suffice to project the message that things would change once he was in the driving seat. The President confirmed his earlier favourable impression of the Prince, though he was not entirely convinced that he would be able to 'hold the fort after Franco's death'. Nevertheless, George Landau, the country director for Spain at the State Department, told a British diplomat in Washington that the visit had been arranged so as to 'express American confidence in the Prince not only in the context of US–Spanish relations, but also as the best bet in securing the internal stability of Spain after Franco'.[8]

Following this visit and partly at the Prince's instigation, in February 1971 Nixon sent the deputy director of the CIA, the Spanish-speaking General Vernon Walters, on a secret fact-finding mission to Madrid, which included an interview with the dictator. The President hoped to persuade Franco to hand over to the future king while he was still alive and fully in control – 'only you, Mr. President, are in a powerful enough position to tell him this', Mountbatten had pleaded with him – but the dictator reassured Walters that 'the succession would be orderly' and insisted that 'there was no alternative to the prince', while expressing complete confidence in the latter's ability to handle the situation after his death. Despite an official State Department denial, in July 1971 the Washington Post reported that the Administration was waging a low-key campaign to convince Franco to hand over to Juan Carlos as soon as possible and during that year a number of high-ranking US officials travelled to Spain to make this point, though to no avail. Given Franco's reluctance to stand down, the Nixon administration hoped he would at least appoint a powerful prime minister, who would then oversee the transition from his dictatorship to the monarchy after his demise.[9]

In his memoirs, Kissinger, Secretary of State from September 1973, would later claim that America's contribution to Spain's evolution during the 1970s was 'one of the major achievements of our foreign policy'.[10] According to his somewhat clichéd view of the past, 'encouraging a democratic Spain after Franco would be a complex challenge in the best of circumstances' as there was 'no precedent in Spanish history for change that was moderate and evolutionary, not to say democratic rather than radical and violent'. The former Harvard professor was of the opinion that 'Spain's history had been marked by an obsession with the ultimate, with death and sacrifice, the tragic and the heroic. This had produced grandiose alternations between anarchy and authority, between chaos and total discipline. Spaniards seemed able to submit only to exaltation, not to each other'. Spain on the eve of Franco's death was 'as if suspended, waiting for a life to end so that it could rejoin European history'.

According to Kissinger, during the final years of the Franco regime the US Administration had been faced with the choice of having to 'ostracize and oppose the existing regime or, while working with it, to extend our contacts and therefore our influence for the post-Franco period' and had opted for the latter course of action. Washington 'saw no sense in a confrontation with an aged autocrat whose term of power was clearly ending, a confrontation that would stimulate the proverbial Spanish nationalism and pride'; furthermore, international ostracism 'ran the risk of making Spain a prisoner of its own passions'. The Secretary of State's high opinion of the United States' ability to cultivate 'moderate elements in Spanish government and society' is rather overstated, however. Robert C. Hill, Nixon's first ambassador to Madrid (1969–72), was generally pragmatic, as is revealed by an embassy cable informing Washington in early 1970 that while 'mission officers will not reject opportunities to obtain the views of disaffected elements', they would 'make no special effort to cultivate them'.[11] Whenever in doubt, however, the embassy went out of its way not to antagonize the Spanish authorities: in May of that year, for example, Hill acted in collusion with the government to prevent a delegation of moderate opposition figures, led by José María de Areilza, from presenting Secretary of State William Rogers, who was on an official visit to Madrid, with a document opposing the renewal of the bases agreement. This was in sharp contrast to the policy pursued by the German Embassy, which encouraged moderate opposition leaders to meet Foreign Minister Walter Scheel in Madrid in April 1970.[12] Hall's successor, Horacio Rivero (1972–75), the first Hispanic to reach the rank of admiral in the US Navy, was a committed cold warrior who surprised even members of the Franco establishment with his enthusiasm for the regime and his dislike for its opponents.[13] Significantly, it was only after his departure in November 1974 that an assistant deputy secretary of state was able to meet moderate opposition leaders during a visit to Madrid later that year.[14]

If anything, developments in Spain's vicinity in the early 1970s augmented its already considerable geo-strategic value to the United States and hence Washington's reluctance to meddle in domestic affairs. Above all, the world economic crisis triggered by the 1973–74 oil shock increased the importance of the Straits of Gibraltar, since most Middle East oil reached Western Europe and the United States via the Suez Canal and the Mediterranean. In October 1973, the Yom Kippur War highlighted the importance of Spain's bases, even though the Franco government, anxious not to antagonize its Arab allies, forced US aircraft in transit to Israel to refuel in the air. Shortly afterwards, the collapse of the Portuguese dictatorship following the military coup of 25 April 1974 seriously threatened to undermine NATO's southern flank, prompting Washington to press for Spanish membership with renewed vigour. Several months later, at the opposite end of the Mediterranean, the Cypriot crisis resulted in the collapse of the Greek military dictatorship, which was succeeded by a government which saw in NATO a symbol of US military support for the defunct Junta. Additionally, the conflict over Cyprus led Washington to impose an arms embargo on Turkey, which retaliated by threatening to buy weapons from the Soviet Union. Finally, during these years the French and Italian communist parties steadily improved their electoral performance to the extent that many in the West came to see their participation in future coalition governments as inevitable. As Kissinger himself would acknowledge, 'the Administration did not believe that with the Middle East in turmoil and our other bases in the Mediterranean in jeopardy we could afford to abandon the Spanish bases and compound the impression of a global American retreat'.

Events within Spain and the Franco regime also discouraged the US Administration from adopting a more vigorous policy of democracy promotion. In June 1973, the dictator finally appointed his loyal alter ego, Admiral Luis Carrero Blanco, who was also a staunch ally of the United States and a committed cold warrior, president of the government, a decision that was well received in Washington. Barely six months later, however, his spectacular assassination by the Basque terrorist organization ETA raised fresh doubts about the country's political future. Kissinger, who had recently visited Madrid to negotiate the forthcoming renewal of the bases agreement and was one of the last people to see him alive, became increasingly despondent about the possibility of a peaceful succession. The Secretary nevertheless insisted that, out of respect for Franco, Vice President Gerald Ford, who had only recently been appointed following Spiro Agnew's resignation, should attend the admiral's funeral, something Nixon readily agreed to. Inevitably, the Spanish press did not fail to contrast his presence with the total absence of senior European dignitaries.

Although Carrero Blanco's death was almost universally perceived as a decisive blow to plans for the continuity of the Franco regime after its founder's death, it does not appear to have had much impact on the Nixon Administration's overall policy towards Spain. The admiral's successor, Carlos Arias Navarro, was largely uninterested in foreign policy, but valued Spain's special relationship with the United States. This became evident in July 1974, when Franco's health deteriorated to the extent of forcing him to stand down as Head of State for a few weeks, leaving Prince Juan Carlos to take his place. Undeterred by Franco's illness and determined as ever to guarantee access to their military facilities in Spain, only days later Washington pressed ahead with the signing of a joint declaration of principles which would pave the way for the subsequent renewal of the bases agreement. Prince Juan Carlos was of course happy to guarantee existing relations with the United States, but was also understandably reluctant to endorse a document that he was not responsible for, but for which he might nevertheless be held accountable after Franco's death.

Nixon's political demise in August 1974 as a result of the Watergate scandal and his replacement by President Ford resulted in an overall increase in Kissinger's influence over US foreign policy, but this was not immediately apparent with regard to Spain. Seemingly oblivious to Franco's increasingly precarious health and the changes his death would undoubtedly bring with it, Ford initially planned to replace Ambassador Rivero, who resigned in August 1974, with Peter M. Flanigan. The latter was a controversial banker and former assistant to the President for International Economic Affairs, whose father had been a vocal supporter of Franco in the 1930s. In view of the doubts subsequently expressed about him by the Senate Foreign Affairs Committee, however, in November Flanigan himself asked the president to withdraw his name, enabling an outstanding career diplomat, Wells Stabler, who had served as deputy assistant secretary of state for European Affairs, to take his place. Stabler had the added advantage of having worked closely with Kissinger in the past.

The United States and democratization

Given its excellent relations with the Franco regime, it is perhaps pertinent to enquire whether the United States had any substantive interest in a change of regime in Spain. On the one hand, it was reasonable to expect future democratic governments to become increasingly demanding when it came to renewing the crucial bases agreement, as was indeed to be the case. At the same time, however, a democratic Spain would finally be able to join NATO, thereby strengthening the southern European flank which so obsessed Kissinger. Similarly, it would also become eligible for European Community membership, something the United States had always advocated, even against its own economic self-interest. As a State Department memorandum argued in August 1974, 'it is our objective to favor and work for Spain's closer integration with the West, both because of the strategic importance of the country, and in order to provide an anchor to its domestic stability in the post-Franco period ... it is in our long-term interest to use what influence we have, in Spain and in the other European countries, to move along the rapprochement between Spain and the rest of Western Europe, particularly in NATO'.[15]

As both Kissinger and Stabler have acknowledged, however, on the eve of Franco's death the top priority for the US Administration was not democratization, but rather the renewal of the bases agreement, which was due to expire in September 1975. This determination to secure a military presence in Spain regardless of the political price paid caused concern and dismay in some West European capitals. In May 1975, German Chancellor Helmut Schmidt reminded Ford that the Franco era was obviously coming to an end, in view of which 'we should be encouraging those we hope will govern after Franco; that means we must deal not only with those who are in power now'. Ford objected that the renewal of the bases agreement was of vital importance to the West, including Germany, to which Schmidt replied that 'so that you can be sure of your bases and your special strategic ties with Spain you should talk about it with tomorrow's rulers as well'.[16] Ford was unimpressed, however, and visited Spain later that month, ignoring his own ambassador's advice to the contrary. By then, Stabler was advising the Secretary of State in favour of postponing the signing of a new agreement until after Franco's death, but to no avail.[17]

Prior to the visit, Kissinger sent the President a lengthy memorandum explaining the situation in Madrid as seen from Washington. The Secretary acknowledged that 'younger Spaniards are less and less willing to acquiesce in the more repressive features of the authoritarian regime installed by Franco' and rightly predicted that 'many observers in and out of Spain will be inclined to view your visit... as an attempt to prop up Franco and his system'. Nevertheless, the President's presence in Madrid was fully justified by 'our political/military interest in a pro-Western Spain which allows us to use certain important bases to support our forces elsewhere in Europe and the Mediterranean'; most importantly, 'we want to be able to renew our bases agreement... and we also want to continue this defence cooperation after Franco goes', though he was aware of the fact that 'many Spaniards view the US base rights in Spain as more important to the US than Spain' and that 'some see them as an embarrassing symbol of US support for Franco'. This led the Secretary to conclude, somewhat implausibly, that 'we should strengthen our existing ties with the present leadership, particularly with regard to defence cooperation, while avoiding excessive identification with Franco'.[18]

Looking to the future, in Kissinger's view 'the prospect for the succession after Franco is reasonably good in the short term but less certain thereafter. Juan Carlos and (Prime Minister) Arias would probably enjoy reasonably broad acceptance at the outset, though not much active support... over the longer term, the success of the post-Franco leadership will hinge on their ability to steer a careful course between pressures to loosen controls and rightist insistence on preserving the status quo. The fragmented clandestine opposition parties, including the active Spanish Communist Party (PCE), would probably not be able by themselves to force government changes but would try to take advantage of problems as they arose... ' This generally sanguine view relied heavily on his perception of 'the deterrent role of the Spanish military, which appears united and disposed to accept political change and has generally wanted to stay out of politics, but would be disposed to intervene if a serious threat to law and order developed or if a radical left-wing regime seemed about to come to power'. Given that 'the odds are against a radical upheaval in Spanish political life during the twilight and succession periods', Kissinger was not unduly concerned about the consequences of Franco's death for US policy, though he acknowledged that future governments would be 'much more susceptible to popular pressure than Franco needed to be, and there are certainly sectors of Spanish opinion – not all on the left – which favour reduced dependence on the US in defence and other areas'.

In his memorandum to the President, the Secretary also argued that 'we should signal our desire to continue these cooperative relations with the post-Franco leadership, with a view to developing a broad consensus on the value of US–Spanish relations which includes leaders in and out of government'. In keeping with this spirit, and in an attempt to improve Ford's standing in the eyes of Spaniards hostile to the regime, Ambassador Stabler sought and obtained Kissinger's approval for a brief meeting between the President and moderate opposition leaders, but when the Madrid government raised objections, the Secretary quickly backed down.[19] Years later, Stabler readily admitted that this had been a mistake; had Washington insisted, the Spanish government would probably have allowed the meeting to take place and this would have been 'a signal – though a very minor one – that we did have some view about relations with the opposition'.[20] Worse still, Ford's visit coincided with the declaration of a state of emergency in the Basque country, decreed by the Spanish government to deal with an outbreak of severe unrest. The President was at least careful to spend considerably more time with Juan Carlos than with Franco during his visit, thereby giving some indication of the Administration's priorities. Nevertheless, in October 1975, at the height of a major international campaign against the regime triggered by the execution of five anti-Franco activists convicted for terrorist killings, and only weeks before the dictator's death, the United States pressed ahead regardless and signed a pre-agreement for the renewal of the lease on the military bases. In marked contrast, the major European democracies withdrew their ambassadors from Madrid in protest.[21]

The US Administration's determination to guarantee Spain's stability did not always militate against the cause of democratization, however. In early October 1975, news reached Madrid that King Hassan II of Morocco was planning a 'green march' of half a million volunteers to take over the Spanish Sahara, a territory it had long since claimed. With Franco on his deathbed and the Portuguese Revolution very much on his mind, Prince Juan Carlos feared that an armed conflict with Morocco might divide the army and destabilize an already fragile political situation at home.

He therefore turned to Kissinger, who agreed to intercede with Hassan II and other Arab leaders, as well as with the French President, Valéry Giscard d'Estaing. This allowed Juan Carlos to travel to the Saharan capital of El Aaiún to address his fellow army officers, promising them a negotiated withdrawal rather than a dishonourable retreat. Hassan II was true to his word and called off the march in early November, thereby strengthening Juan Carlos's standing in the eyes of the army and even many regime diehards.[22] In spite of the above, it would appear that the US Administration did less than it might have done to discourage the King of Morocco from adopting a belligerent attitude towards the Saharan question at a time of acute political uncertainty in Spain.

Sensing that Franco's death was now imminent, in early November 1975 Kissinger wired Stabler a fresh set of instructions.[23] In this highly revealing text, the Secretary reminded the ambassador that 'the basic US objective in Spain remains that of strengthening our broad political and security relationship with a Spain more closely linked to the Atlantic community'. At the same time, Washington favoured 'evolutionary political changes on terms acceptable to the people of Spain and leading toward a more open and pluralistic society'. Although Kissinger supported 'no particular political solution or party within the broad range of democratic thought', he anticipated that 'the transition will be in the hands of essentially conservative people' and did not hide the fact that 'we would view communist participation in a future Spanish government as an unhealthy development which would inevitably damage ties with us and the institutions of Western Europe'. In short, 'the US will play a stabilizing and supportive role, and counsel against any efforts to press for faster changes which might force the process beyond realistic limits and risk severe reactions'.[24] The State Department was nevertheless anxious that this role should not be misinterpreted, a matter openly addressed in a memorandum prepared for Vice President Nelson Rockefeller, who later attended the dictator's funeral on Ford's behalf: 'many Spaniards have come to believe that the United States Government has been willing to accept Franco because of our overriding interest in protecting our bases in Spain. With Franco gone, they may be concerned that we will somehow seek to discourage political change. The Communists in and out of Spain can be expected to keep pushing their line that we and the Spanish right are collaborating to preserve Francoism without Franco'.[25]

Kissinger's telegram accepted that the US Embassy in Madrid 'must have continuing but discreet contacts with opposition groups, including those reasonably moderate groups now forced to operate illegally', but 'all contacts with the opposition should be monitored carefully in order to avoid leaving the impression that we would favour any particular party'. Indeed, since his arrival in Spain Ambassador Stabler had gradually established contact with leaders of the non-Communist opposition, including Felipe González, who had been elected leader of the Socialist Party (PSOE) in October 1974. However, although the Communist Party (PCE) was undoubtedly the largest and best organized opposition group at that stage, the Administration refused to have any formal dealings with it. In keeping with this position, the above-mentioned State Department memorandum prepared for the vice president argued that 'one indispensable element will be to legalize most of the opposition parties, excluding the communists and other non-democratic groups. While some opposition groups will probably be reluctant to accept overtures from the government if the communists remain illegal, most would eventually be persuaded to take part in electoral and other reforms with concrete political benefits'. This was precisely the – ultimately unsuccessful – strategy later adopted by the King's first government under Arias Navarro during the first six months of 1976.

The decision as to who should represent the United States at Franco's funeral and the future king's proclamation several days later is highly revealing of the Administration's policy towards Spain overall. When the matter was first raised by Ambassador Rivero in the summer of 1974, he had advised that the President himself attend both ceremonies. A year later, the State Department suggested that the US delegation be led by a senior member of the cabinet, but Ford finally decided in favour of Vice President Rockefeller. Significantly, unlike the major European democracies, the US Administration was represented at the same level both at Franco's funeral and at Juan Carlos' proclamation ceremonies. As a result, the Vice President found himself in the company of the likes of Imelda Marcos and General Augusto Pinochet at the former, but was joined at the latter by the Duke of Edinburgh, German President Walter Scheel and French President Giscard d'Estaing, amongst others. To the very end, the United States sought to invest in the future without distancing itself from the past, a policy whose subtlety appears to have been lost on most Spaniards.[26]

In spite of his outspoken support for the young monarch, Kissinger, strongly influenced by events in Portugal and the electoral advance of the Communist Party in Italy, remained highly sceptical as to the long-term prospects for democracy in Spain, and greatly resented external pressure in favour of rapid regime change. In December 1975, he reassured foreign minister Areilza: 'I want you to know you won't be under pressure from the United States. You know there must be some evolution, but you are doing it'. His European colleagues would 'take no responsibility if it blows up and they won't help you', he warned him and added, 'if Americans press you, if they are State Department, let me know; if they are not State Department, ignore them'. Indeed his advice to his Spanish counterpart a month later could be summed up in two words: 'Go slowly!' Not surprisingly, perhaps, Areliza soon came to the conclusion that Kissinger was 'a man of many doubts and little hope'.[27]

In particular, the Secretary of State remained unenthusiastic about the legalization of the Communist Party, an issue that had come to dominate the domestic Spanish political debate. In January 1976 he reminded Manuel Fraga, the new Minister of the Interior, that the Communist Party was illegal in West Germany and was clearly relieved to hear that he had no intention of legalizing it in Spain. Two months later the Irish Prime Minister, Garret FitzGerald, who had recently seen Areilza, told Kissinger this was a mistake, because 'it is important to defeat communists, not to suppress them', but to no avail. In June, the Secretary told Areilza frankly that 'we won't say anything if you insist on legalizing the Communist Party, but we won't be too unhappy if you decide to postpone the decision several years'. Responding to media claims that the Administration sought to veto Communist participation in the first elections, later that month the State Department declared that, while this was purely an internal affair, 'in our judgement it would be absurd to make legalization of a party dedicated to authoritarian principles a litmus test as to whether or not democratization is taking place'. Absurd or not, this was precisely the view held by a majority of Spaniards at the time. In spite of this, according to a senior US diplomat in Madrid, 'our contacts with the Communists were only at the level of a junior or middle-grade officer in the political section and with Communists who were not members of the party's central committee'.[28]

US policy after Franco

As the available diplomatic correspondence makes abundantly clear, at the time of Franco's death Kissinger's top priority was the renewal of the bases agreement, but at least he was willing to assist King Juan Carlos and his reformists in their efforts to make this more palatable to Spanish public opinion. Although the young monarch had inherited a Prime Minister, Carlos Arias Navarro, who was lukewarm about undertaking substantial reforms, he had also secured the appointment of a foreign minister who was firmly committed to the establishment of democracy in Spain. Areilza insisted on raising the existing executive agreement over the bases to the status of a treaty, which required the approval of the US Senate, so as to underline Washington's recognition of the fact that it was no longer dealing with a dictatorship, but with a democracy- in-the-making. In spite of serious doubts concerning Arias Navarro's ability to further democratization, Kissinger allowed Areilza to convince him of the benefits of a new Treaty of Friendship and Cooperation, which was duly signed in January 1976.[29] This 'excellent gift for the Monarchy', as Areilza described it, paved the way for Juan Carlos's highly successful visit to Washington in June 1976, in the course of which he committed himself to a Western-style parliamentary monarchy in a speech to a joint meeting of the US Congress which has come to be regarded as a turning point in Spain's transition to democracy. Although doubts had been raised about this process in the Senate Foreign Affairs Committee, partly in response to the highly favourable impact of the King's visit the Treaty was ratified later in June and came into force in September 1976.

Prior to this state visit, Kissinger wrote a lengthy memorandum for President Ford analysing developments in Spain in some detail.[30] The Secretary made no bones about the fact that 'our purpose in the visit is to demonstrate our full support for the King as the best hope for the democratic evolution with stability which will protect our interests in Spain'. Juan Carlos, he argued, 'recognizes that, if the monarchy is to survive, he must not become just another participant in the political process. To avoid becoming a captive of any faction of a figurehead, he must project a broader image, above politics in a partisan sense but visibly committed to changes broadly acceptable to Spain's evolving society. He also recognises that the fate of the monarchy restored by Franco depends on the success of the democratic evolution. It will require skill, determination and cool nerves to walk this narrow line, and there is not yet sufficient evidence to determine whether the King has these qualities'.

The Secretary also acknowledged that 'there has been considerable foreign and domestic criticism of Prime Minister Arias' cautious approach, and it may well be that certain opportunities to assert positive leadership were lost in the first days and weeks after Franco's death', but in his view 'the Government has in practice managed to chart a middle course, staying clear of the die-hard reactionaries opposed to any significant change even if not satisfying the left oppositionists who call for a complete break with the past'. This was an interpretation few Spaniards would have shared: indeed Juan Carlos himself had told *Newsweek* in April that Arias Navarro was 'an unmitigated disaster'. Whatever the case, Kissinger himself acknowledged that one of the purposes of the visit was to 'bolster the King's confidence in himself and to strengthen his resolve', something it undoubtedly achieved: on returning to Madrid, in early July 1976 he finally took the decision to remove Arias Navarro and replace him with a young, relatively unknown though up-and-coming reformist, Adolfo Suárez, who was to become the key figure in the subsequent democratizing process. If the point of the visit, as Kissinger's memorandum had claimed, was to 're-affirm our support for the King and thus to strengthen his influence', it was a spectacular success. Ironically, Areilza had hoped the visit would also improve his own chances of succeeding Arias Navarro, but it may well have been his undoing; as Kissinger would later tell one of the monarch's closest advisers, Manuel Prado, they had been 'absolutely shocked' by the way Areilza treated Juan Carlos in Washington: 'Ford would ask a question and the Foreign Minister would answer it for the king'.[31]

In the run-up to the November 1976 US presidential elections, both Ford and Kissinger inevitably paid less attention to events in Spain, just as King Juan Carlos's efforts were beginning to bear fruit. Nevertheless, the Secretary appears to have approved of the progress made by Suárez under the young monarch's guidance. As to the latter, in December 1976 he told Prado that 'I don't wish to sound condescending, but I am really very impressed with him, and I was not so at the beginning'. (The admiration seems to have been mutual: that same month Juan Carlos asked a senior State Department official to tell Kissinger that 'he not only has a friend but a King-friend'.) Curiously, though, he was still of the opinion that Arias Navarro was 'a rather decent man' and 'probably very good for the transition period'. His views on the future of the PCE were also unchanged. In September, at a meeting with leading West European diplomats, he had expressed the opinion that 'the practical point is whether they are more dangerous in or out', but when Sir Michael Palliser, a permanent under secretary at the Foreign Office, pointed out that 'some people in Spain who are non-Communists but leftwing will see it as a touchstone of whether Spain is moving toward liberalization', he had quickly agreed that 'if that is the case, they should do it'. His conversation with Prado in December was unusually frank in this regard:

> as the Secretary of State, I have to tell you that from our point of view the legal position of the communist party has to be a Spanish decision. It is not ours to take, and it is not one on which we can comment. But speaking as a political scientist, my judgement is that to the greater degree that you can have your system evolve internally

before the changes take place, the better off you will be. Let matters
begin to sort themselves out. Let the system stabilize itself. But I don't
think you need the communist party to do it. If I were the King, I
wouldn't do it. You show your strength by not doing it. You will have
a completely normal spectrum of political opposition and opinion
without it. The left may yell, but they will yell anyway.

On a more pragmatic note, he concluded: 'As far as I'm concerned, the
decision you take should be whichever decision gives you the stablest
government. You will simply have to weigh the pros and cons to see
where the balance lies. Personally, I cannot shed tears over a party which
declares all other parties illegal'.[32]

President Ford's successor, the reformist Democrat Jimmy Carter,
appears to have adopted a somewhat more flexible stance towards
Communism in Western Europe generally, an attitude which may have
tempered earlier US opposition to the legalization of the PCE. In January
1977, his Secretary of State, Cyrus Vance, told Suárez's deputy prime
minister that he advocated legalization on the grounds that 'icebergs
are more dangerous when they are submerged', though he was still
in favour of excluding the Communists from the first elections. José
Manuel Otero Novas, a senior official whom Suárez had entrusted with
the delicate task of mediating with the major opposition groups at a
time when they were still illegal, came to the conclusion that senior US
diplomats in Madrid – including ambassador Stabler – were generally far
more in favour of legalizing the Communist Party than their political
masters in Washington. Whatever the case, the Prime Minister soon
concluded that without the PCE the first elections would not be seen as
fully democratic either in Spain or in Western Europe and pressed ahead
with legalization in April 1977. This may partly explain the rather cool
reception awarded to him by the Carter Administration during his first
official visit to Washington later that month, even though it was widely
acknowledged at the time that Suárez would win the June elections, the
first held in Spain since 1936. Surprisingly, in May Vice President Walter
Mondale turned down the US ambassador's suggestion that he should
meet a group of opposition leaders (excluding the Communists) during
an official visit to Madrid. As pollsters had been predicting for some
time, in the June 1977 elections the PCE fared rather badly, obtaining a
mere 9 per cent of the vote.[33]

Given Washington's overriding concern for Spain's stability and its
long-standing support for the King, the Carter Administration's lack
of enthusiasm for Suárez is more than a little surprising. In order to

bolster his image at home and abroad, the Prime Minister was keen to visit the United States officially prior to the June 1977 elections, but the State Department initially turned him down. This left Juan Carlos no alternative but to send a personal emissary to plead with the White House, which reconsidered its position. Stabler, however, was mortified to learn that Suárez had only been awarded a half-hour interview and insisted on a formal luncheon as well. The White House initially agreed to this, but changed its mind when they discovered he spoke no English; in the end, President Carter was with Suárez and his party for little over an hour. According to Stabler, the latter 'went away frankly a little irritated with what he thought was not exactly support'; although he remained in office until early 1981, Suárez never returned to Washington on an official visit. Understandably, the ambassador would later reflect that 'if we took the view that we supported Spanish democracy, then we ought to have followed through so that people involved believed we supported them'.[34]

Conclusion

The behaviour of successive US Administrations towards Spain during the twilight years of the Franco regime and beyond is revealing both in terms of shedding light on some of the unintended legacies of the Cold War and the dilemmas of democracy promotion as a foreign policy goal. In his *Third Wave*, Huntington acknowledged that Nixon and Kissinger had 'espoused a realpolitik approach to foreign policy', but argued that 'in 1974 the tide began to move in the other direction'. As we have seen, however, there is little evidence of this with regard to Spain, even after Nixon's replacement by Carter. It is thus probably not unfair to conclude that Washington did not contribute significantly to the undermining of authoritarianism, and played only a modest role in promoting democratization, essentially through its support for Juan Carlos.[35]

Overall, it would appear that US governments favoured a very gradual transition process which would respect the existing balance of power in southern Europe and, in particular, their continued access to Spanish military bases; in Kissinger's words, the goal was 'democratic evolution with stability'.[36] As a result, domestic Spanish opinion, which had generally perceived the United States as one of Franco's closest allies, later saw Washington as a somewhat lukewarm supporter of democratization during the transition proper. As Kissinger had foreseen, this partly explains why US bases continued to be tainted by their association with the Franco era long after his demise, a situation which eventually forced the departure of the US Air Force from Torrejón following the renegotiation of the treaty in 1988.[37] Indeed, the history of US bases in Spain, Portugal, and the Philippines has led one author to conclude that 'engaging authoritarian leaders by striking basing deals with them has done little for democratization in those states because these leaders know that, at bottom, US military planners care more about the bases' utility than about local political trends'. As a senior US diplomat serving in Madrid in 1974–78 observed, 'the security relationship itself (would) be more soundly based for the long term if founded on a democratic consensus than if derived from the will of one man'. This advice, however, was only rarely followed by decision-makers in Washington during the twilight years of the Franco regime and beyond, thereby undermining the future standing of the United States in the eyes of many Spaniards.[38]

Notes

1. Samuel S. Huntington, *The Third Wave. Democratization in the Late Twentieth Century* (Norman: University of Oklahoma Press, 1991), pp. 45–6.
2. See C. Powell, 'International Aspects of Democratization: The Case of Spain', in Laurence Whitehead, ed., *The International Dimensions of Democratization. Europe and the Americas* (Oxford: Oxford University Press, 1996), pp. 285–314.
3. This question is also addressed in Angel Viñas, *En las garras del águila. Los pactos con Estados Unidos, de Francisco Franco a Felipe González (1945–1988)* (Barcelona: Crítica, 2003), pp. 424–8.
4. National Archives at College Park (Maryland), Record Group 59. Central Foreign Policy Files, Subject Numeric Files, 1964–66, Box 2664, POL 13-10 Spain–POL 17 Spain. Aerogram A342 from the United States Embassy in Madrid to the State Department, 20 November 1965.
5. NACP. RG 59. Central Foreign Policy Files, Subject Numeric Files, 1967–69, Box 2490, POL 14 SP-POL 15-1 SP. Telegram from the United States Embassy in Madrid to the United States Mission in NATO, 15 November 1968.
6. Richard Nixon, *RN. The Memoirs of Richard Nixon* (New York: Grosset & Dunlap, 1978), p. 248.
7. Henry Kissinger, *White House Years* (Boston, MA: Little Brown & Co, 1979), pp. 930–2; Laureano López Rodó, *El principio del fin: Memorias III* (Barcelona: Plaza & Janés, 1991), pp. 84–5; Vernon A. Walters, *Silent Missions* (New York: Doubleday, 1978), pp. 570–1.
8. Charles Powell, *Juan Carlos of Spain, Self-Made Monarch* (London: Palgrave Macmillan, 1996), pp. 50–2; Philip Ziegler, *Mountbatten* (New York: Knopf, 1985), p. 204; Crowe (Washington) to Thomas (FCO), 4 February 1971, FCO9/1455, WSS3/304/1; Lopez Rodó, *Memorias III*, p. 147; Walters, *Silent Missions*, pp. 551–2.
9. Walters, *Silent Missions*, pp. 555–6 and pp. 570–1; *The Washington Post*, 28 July 1971; Stanley Payne, *The Franco Regime 1936–1975* (Madison, WI: University of Wisconsin Press, 1987), p. 574.
10. Kissinger, *White House Years*, pp. 930–2.

11. NACP. RG 59. Central Foreign Policy Files, Subject Numeric Files, 1970–73, Box 2597, POL 5 SP–POL 12 SP. Aerogramme A114 for United States Embassy in Madrid to State Department. 'Impact of Youth and the US National Interest. Mission Youth Program', 4 January 1970.

12. José María de Areilza, *Crónica de libertad* (Barcelona: Planeta, 1985), pp. 150–5 and 103–4.

13. Samuel Eaton, the deputy chief of mission at the Madrid Embassy from 1974 to 1978, has described Rivero as 'a man of the Right, identified with the now-fading Franco tradition', who was nevertheless 'a far better ambassador for his time than those who decided he should leave would admit'. Samuel D. Eaton, *The Forces of Freedom in Spain, 1974–1979. A Personal Account* (Stanford, CA: Hoover Institution Press, Stanford University, 1981), p. 119.

14. Wells Stabler, 'The View from the US Embassy', in Hans Binnendijk, ed., *Authoritarian Regimes in Transition* (Washington, DC: Center for the Study of Foreign Affairs, 1987), p. 193.

15. Memorandum (Briefing Papers on Spain and Portugal) from the State Department to Brent Scowcroft, 20 August 1974, Spain (1), Box 12, National Security Adviser. PCF-EC, GFL.

16. Helmut Schmidt, *Men and Powers: A Political Retrospective* (London: Cape, 1990), pp. 167–8. For a similar exchange between Kissinger and the Irish prime minister, see Garret FitzGerald, *All in a life* (London: Papermac, 1992), p. 180.

17. Telegram from the US Embassy in Madrid to the State Department, 26 May 1975. Spain–State Department Telegrams to SECSTATE-NODIS(1) Box 12, National Security Adviser. PCF-EC, GFL.

18. President Ford's visit to Madrid 31 May–1 June 1975, from the Secretary of State to the President, NACP, RG59, Briefing Books, 1958–1976, E.5037, Box 217.

19. Secret, Memorandum of Conversation, 28 May 1975, NACP, RG 59. Department of State Records. Records of Henry Kissinger, 1973–77. Box 13. Misc documents, telegrams, etc. from 1975.

20. In the ambassador's view, 'there was no real reason to have a presidential visit. It wasn't a question of shoring up the Franco regime because there was no need to do so. During and after the visit a great many Spanish friends asked me, "Why did you have to do this? What did you gain from it?" If we thought we had gained something important with regard to the bases, that simply wasn't true. That visit achieved absolutely nothing at all, except, again from Franco's point of view, to indicate that Spain's big friend was rallying around'. Stabler, 'The View', pp. 193–5.

21. Defence Secretary James Schlesinger admitted that Madrid had threatened to block the renewal of the agreement if Washington issued pleas for clemency, as the major European democracies had done. *Time*, 13 October 1975.

22. Kissinger would later tell the Spanish foreign minister: 'if you had gotten involved in a war in the Sahara, it would have been a disaster'. Secret, Memorandum of Conversation, 25 January 1976, NACP, RG 59. Records of the Department of State. Office of the Counselor, 1955–77. Box 3. HS Chron-Official January–March 1976.

23. Telegram from the Secretary of State to the embassy in Madrid, 1 November 1975. 'Spain-State Department Telegrams from SECSTATE-EXDIS', Box 12, National Security Adviser. PCF-EC, GFL.

24. After seeing the US ambassador on 9 December 1975, the new foreign minister, Areilza, concluded that 'the United States wants the democratization of the political system, but true to their traditional pragmatism, without being unduly eager, demanding or impatient. Above all they want us to avoid the path followed by Portugal'. José Maria de Areilza, *Diario de un ministro de la monarquía* (Barcelona: Planeta, 1977), pp. 14–15.

25. Vice President's Mission to Spain, November 1975, from the State Department, E.5037, Box 231, NACP.

26. The State Department's confidential memorandum for Vice President Rockefeller explained that 'our objective in attending these ceremonies is to convey our sympathy on the death of a strong leader and to provide reassurance that we seek even closer relations with the new leadership'. Vice President's Mission to Spain, November 1975, from the State Department, E.5037, Box 231, NACP.

27. Secret, Memorandum of Conversation, 16 December 1975, NACP, RG 59. Records of the Department of State. Office of the Counselor, 1955–77. Box 3. HS Chron-Official October–December 1975; Areilza, *Diario de un ministro*, pp. 65–6.

28. Secret, Memorandum of Conversation, 25 January 1976, NACP, RG 59. Records of the Department of State. Office of the Counselor, 1955–77. Box 3. HS Chron-Official January–March 1976; Confidential, Memorandum of conversation, March 18, 1976, NACP, RG 59, Records of the Department of State. Office of the Counselor, 1955–77. Box 9. POL 2 Ireland; Areilza, *Diario de un ministro*, p. 196; Eaton, *The Forces of Freedom*, pp. 116–17 and 128.

29. Secret, Memorandum of Conversation, 16 December 1975. NACP, RG 59. Records of the Department of State. Office of the Counselor, 1955–77. Box 3. HS Chron-Official October–December 1975.

30. Memorandum for the President, RG 59, Executive Secretariat Briefing Books, 1958–1976, E. 5037, Box 241.

31. Secret, Memorandum of Conversation, 2 December 1976. NACP, RG 59. Department of State Records. Records of Henry Kissinger, 1973–1977. Box 19. NODIS Briefing Memos. 1976.

32. Secret, Memorandum of Conversation, 28 September 1976. NACP, RG 59. Records of the Department of State. Office of the Counselor, 1955–77. Box 6. Quadripartite Memcons February 1976; Secret, Memorandum of Conversation, 2 December 1976. NACP, RG 59. Department of State Records. Records of Henry Kissinger, 1973–1977. Box 19. NODIS Briefing Memos. 1976; Telegram from the Madrid Embassy to the Secretary of State, 14 December 1976, Spain-State Department Telegrams to SECSTATE-NODIS(3), Box 12, National Security Adviser. PCF-EC, GFL.

33. Alfonso Osorio, *Trayectoria política de un ministro de la Corona* (Barcelona: Planet, 1980), p. 280; José Manuel Otero Novas, *Nuestra democracia puede morir* (Barcelona: Plaza, 1987), p. 28.

34. Stabler, 'The View', pp. 196–7.

35. Significantly, there are barely any references to Spain in Tony Smith, *America's Mission. The United States and the Worldwide Struggle for Democracy in the Twentieth Century* (Princeton, NJ: Princeton University Press, 1994).

36. See also Alfred Tovias, 'US policy Towards Democratic Transition in Southern Europe', in Geoffrey Pridham, ed., *Encouraging Democracy. The International*

Context of Regime Change in Southern Europe (Leicester: Leicester University Press, 1991), p. 176.

37. According to a confidential, unpublished study carried out by Louis Harris International in June 1976, only one in ten Spaniards approved of US bases in Spain. Tellingly, only 13 per cent of those polled said they 'trusted the US completely', as opposed to 23 per cent who said this of Germany.

38. A. Cooley, 'Base Politics', *Foreign Affairs*, 84, 6 (November/December 2005), p. 80. Eaton, *The Forces of Freedom*, pp. 116–17. According to a poll conducted in mid-2006, 46 per cent of respondents still believed the US was responsible for the survival of the Franco regime. *El Mundo*, 30 July 2006.

13
The Franco Dictatorship: A Bifurcated Regime?

Edward Malefakis

One of the most obvious features of the Franco dictatorship is that it lasted for a very long time. If we count from the last days of September 1936, when his military colleagues granted him full dictatorial powers, until his death in November 1975, Franco ruled Spain for 39 years, almost six times as long as the only other Spanish dictatorship, that of Miguel Primo de Rivera (September 1923 to January 1930). In comparison with the interwar dictatorships of Eastern Europe, Franco's lasted seven, eight, nine and even ten times as long as they did, with the sole exception of the Horthy regime in Hungary, which continued for slightly more than half the time that Franco's did. The longevity of the Mussolini regime was also roughly half that of the Francoist. As for Hitler, his malevolent reign survived for 12 years, less than a third of the time that Franco's dictatorship did. In the whole of European history, in fact, only one personal dictatorship has been comparable in duration, that of his neighbour and close contemporary, Salazar, which lasted a few months more or less than Franco's did, depending on what date we choose to mark Salazar's assumption of full powers. The only European dictatorships whose durability clearly surpassed Franco's were not personal autocracies, but the institutional dictatorship of the Communist party in Russia, as well as, by a slight margin, the institutional dictatorships established by the force of Soviet arms in Eastern Europe in the late 1940s.

What we have noted in connection with the longevity of dictatorships in Europe can be applied with almost equal force to the rest of the world. In Latin America, for example, personal dictatorships that managed to stay in power for half or more of the time that Franco did are not as scarce as in Europe. Although Perón dictated affairs in Argentina for only ten years, Trujillo managed to do so for 31 years. The tyrannical dynasties of the Stroessners, Duvaliers and Somozas were also able to oppress their people for three decades or more. And there is, of course, a personal dictatorship that has clearly beaten Franco's record – that of Fidel Castro which, as of January 2007, has been in power for 48 years. In Asia, the Middle East and Africa, the situation has not been as radically different as one might expect. Mobutu, Bokassa and Saddam Hussein tyrannized their respective countries for approximately half as long as Franco ruled Spain. But once again, only the institutional dictatorships of the Communist Party in China and North Korea have lasted longer.

The very simple point that I want to make must be clear by now. The durability of the Franco dictatorship is historically exceptional, especially within the context of Europe but also within that of the world in its entirety. A second and even more important characteristic of the regime is that it changed radically over the course of its long career. At first sight, this might seem self-evident. Of course, one says, having survived for so long, the Franco dictatorship was bound to change greatly, particularly since it coincided with a period of unprecedented transformation in every aspect of life in the world as a whole. But as a moment of thought will reveal, the correlation between longevity and innovation is not so straightforward, and at times may not exist at all. The best example in Europe is the Salazar regime. It lasted for as long as the Franco regime did, but transformed itself far, far less. The Castro dictatorship in Cuba is another example. Although it has now lasted almost a decade longer than Franco's did, it has been far more homogeneous. In fact, in the whole of world history, there has never been a personal dictatorship which has changed as much as Franco's did. Nor has it happened in the Communist dictatorship of North Korea, even though this underwent a generational leadership change and has now entered its seventh decade. Only the party dictatorships of the Soviet Union and especially of Communist China rival or surpass the Franco regime in this respect. But in both cases, the great transformations could not begin until the founders of the dictatorships had died. To appreciate the singularity of what happened in Spain one would have to imagine that Stalin himself had carried out the gigantic changes instituted after his death by Khrushchev, Brezhnev and Gorbachev, or that Mao Zedong had ordered the even more extraordinary reforms introduced after his death by Deng Xiaping and his successors in China.

We are faced, in short, with a truly unique historical case, one which is worth examining not only for the impact it had on Spain but also because of its complexity and intellectual fascination. How and why did the dictatorship change so profoundly while remaining under the same leader? How could something that started out as the bloodiest peacetime regime in Europe's history, which executed perhaps 50,000 persons during its first five years in power, change so much that, during its last 15 years, the yearly average of executions was less than one person, that is to say less than it was in Texas and several other states in the USA?[1] The same question arises in relation to imprisonments. From a regime which during its early years confined proportionately some 30 times as many persons in its concentration camps as Hitler did in 1938, before the start of World War II, the prison population in Spain by the 1960s had fallen to proportionately much less than that of the United States and was approaching the average for the European Union?[2] The administrative transformation of the regime was almost as spectacular as that of its punitive policies. The incompetent and corrupt administrative structure of the 1940s, infamous for its wilful ignorance, inefficiency and wastefulness of State resources as well as for the pilfering, bribery, nepotism and cronyism it encouraged, had evolved by the 1960s and 1970s into a highly professionalized administrative corps recruited by meritocratic measures. Cronyism and corruption had become not much, if at all, greater than is customary in most governmental bureaucracies.[3]

The effects of this administrative transformation manifested themselves most spectacularly in the economy. The huge economic retrogression of the 1940s, probably unmatched in scale in any European nation which was not at war, gave way after 1961 to the celebrated Spanish economic miracle. The change in labour relations was also impressive. During the 1940s and early 1950s, participation in strikes was so dangerous that these hardly ever took place. By the beginning of the 1970s, there were more strikes in Spain than in any other of the 25-odd OECD members except for Great Britain and Italy.

The cultural change was equally spectacular. During its early years, the Franco regime had spent hardly anything on education, but by the 1970s, and for the first time in Spanish history, more money was budgeted for education than for the armed forces.[4] This fact reflects an even more surprising one. The Franco regime, which originated in the army and throughout its first decade probably had closer ties with the military than any other dictatorship except for that of Chiang Kai Shek in China, by its final decade had stopped being truly militarist. How could it continue being so when, despite its massive propaganda campaigns during the 1940s for creating a Spanish empire in Africa, Franco decided on three separate occasions after 1955 to peacefully de-colonize African territories already held by Spain when he took office?

To summarize, the Francoists, aside from having precipitated the Civil War by their insurrection of 18 July 1936, imposed a brutal, inept and corrupt government on Spain during their first years in power. Thus they were almost exclusively responsible for creating the miserable, retrograde, Spain of the 1940s and early 1950s. History will never pardon them for this, just as it will never forgive the crimes of Hitler, Stalin, Mao, Trujillo and other nefarious twentieth century dictators.

It is easy to assign responsibility for the tragic Spain of mid-century, but who and what deserve credit for its positive subsequent evolution? Did it occur because of or despite the Franco regime? Were its principal causes regime policies or structural factors? To what extent did it depend on international developments that were beyond the control of any national government? Could it have occurred had Spain not been situated in Europe, both geographically and culturally? These are some of the questions that must be answered if we are to arrive at a satisfactory evaluation of the Franco regime as a whole. They have been generating controversy among historians for the past quarter century. We obviously do not have the space to deal with them adequately here. The predominant interpretative school up to now has been what might be called the 'essentialist'. It believes that Francoism was so deeply impregnated during its early years with authoritarian tendencies of all kinds, from traditionalist to fascist, that it could never rid itself of them. Thus, the changes during the regime's later years were merely cosmetic, and did not alter the nefarious essence of the dictatorship.[5] The other interpretative tendency might be dubbed the 'empiricist'. It maintains that even though early Francoism undoubtedly passed through brief periods of ideological fervour, on the whole it was a pragmatic regime, constantly adapting itself to changing circumstances to guarantee its survival. This school, to which I adhere, recognizes that the positive reforms of the late Franco period were not introduced for altruistic reasons but so as to strengthen the regime, but insists that, whatever their motivation, the reforms were genuine and profoundly altered Spanish society. Neither do we empiricists believe that the Franco regime stopped being dictatorial, as our essentialist critics sometimes imply. There is no doubt whatever that the regime continued to be dictatorial up to its very end, with Franco's death in November 1975. Its repressive nature manifested itself mostly in the form of brief jail sentences and fines imposed by the Tribunal de Orden Público (TOP) (Court of Public Order), a special court system established in 1963 to handle lesser political offenses that had previously been assigned to ad hoc military tribunals.[6] And in the Basque country, the regime applied much harsher policies than in the rest of Spain after 1969, in a tragically counterproductive drive to eradicate the ETA terrorist network.

Moreover, although the Franco regime had long since stopped being a killing machine, a return to its nefarious origins always continued to be a remote possibility. It took worldwide protests, both popular and from the Vatican and other governments, to get the nine death sentences in the Burgos trial of December 1970 commuted. In December 1973, many feared that the regime would avenge the assassination of Prime Minister Luis Carrero Blanco with a widespread attack on its opponents. In March 1974 a young Catalan anarchist was executed on specious grounds. And in September 1975, two months prior to Franco's death, five alleged terrorists who had been tried in military courts were executed in Madrid.

To summarize, flashes of brutality existed in the dictatorship up to its very end, and it continued to impose its will on the population on a daily basis through various non-lethal actions. But its will was no longer united nor easy to determine. During its last two decades, *aperturistas* of various sorts gained strength, both within the ranks of the administration and in society at large. While some wanted only a moderate opening of the regime, others pushed discreetly for complete democracy and full conformity with European socio-political norms. The *aperturistas* were fiercely opposed by the constantly diminishing ranks of extreme Franco loyalists who came to be called the 'bunker' because of their rigidity and the increasing desperation of their position. After Franco's death, the *aperturistas* quickly began to negotiate with those who had formerly been outright opponents of the dictatorship but were now willing to collaborate with regime heretics once these had proved the genuineness of their democratic convictions. Together, under the leadership of the ex-*aperturistas* for the critical first six years, and of the ex-opposition socialists subsequently, these formerly disparate forces were able to carry out perhaps the most successful transition from dictatorship to democracy that the world has ever witnessed.

What conclusions can we draw from all this? First, that the Franco dictatorship definitely was a bifurcated regime, so long as we remember that the bifurcation was not between a dictatorial and a non-dictatorial regime but rather between two different types of dictatorship. Although the demarcation occurred principally between 1957 and 1962, we should also not insist too strongly on there being only two different types of dictatorship. Each of the two major periods had many subdivisions within them. The regime's overall movement was in only one direction, away from what might be called the high degree of abnormality it had developed during the Civil War, through its almost exclusively military origins, as well as through its close association with Fascist Italy and Nazi Germany. Nevertheless, while the regime edged constantly closer to European normalcy, this was not always a linear development. The greatest deviation from such development occurred with the regime's decision after 1969 to wage full-scale war against the ETA terrorist movement, a decision which only served to alienate the Basque population as a whole, and thereby to strengthen ETA. Given that the regime changed so much during its nearly four decades of existence, what kind of overall evaluation does it deserve? Clearly a mixed one, neither overly favourable nor entirely unfavourable. The major achievement of the regime was to preside over the greatest period of economic growth in Spanish history, which in turn produced extraordinary social transformations that established the foundations for Spain's subsequent transition to democracy. It is true that this coincided with and was made possible by the unprecedented economic transformation that was taking place in Europe as a whole. Nevertheless, its effects would not have been as strong in Spain as they were had not the Franco dictatorship, unlike the Salazar regime, for example, not provided an adequate framework within which they could operate. On the other hand, we should never forget that much of the economic growth of the regime's last two decades was merely compensating for the extraordinary economic involution that had occurred during the Civil War as well as during the grim 1940s and very early 1950s. The sad truth is probably that Spain in 1975, when Franco died, was at approximately the same level of socio-economic development as it would have been had he never lived. All the suffering and destruction of the Civil War and of the first two decades of the dictatorship had been for naught. It certainly had not brought a better Spain. But at least the positive features of the regime's last two decades, together with the equally positive ones that occurred in Europe and in the world as a whole, made it possible for Spain's tragic involution, precipitated almost entirely by Franco and his followers, ultimately to be only a parenthesis, however awful, in Spain's history. Evidence of this exists in the speed and completeness with which the Franco regime was forgotten after 1975. No leader or party of importance dared take up his banner, and none of the various splinter groups that did adopt him as their standard ever gained more than a fraction of one percent of the vote in national elections, and all of these groups collectively never won as many as two percent of the ballots. The spiritual heirs of Mussolini, who had done even greater damage to Italy than Franco had done to Spain, were not nearly so severely castigated by the voters. Quite charismatic during the Civil War and its aftermath, Franco remained residually charismatic within Spain until 1975. But another unusual feature of his regime is that his charisma vanished almost completely upon his death. Franco's permanent legacy to Spain is also surprisingly small. There are few, if any, positive features that I can think of. Its most important negative feature is undoubtedly the impetus it gave to the alienation of the Basque country from Spain and to the growth of ETA, both of which have been so harmful to Spanish democracy for the past quarter century, but which may, hopefully, eventually be transcended.

Notes

1. For the repression in Spain, see Santos Juliá, ed., *Víctimas de la Guerrra Civil* (Madrid: Temas de Hoy, 1999).
2. See my article, 'La dictadura de Franco en una perspectiva comparada', in José Luis García Delgado, ed., *Franquismo: El juicio de la historia* (Madrid: Temas de Hoy, 2000), pp. 11–55.
3. Rafael Abella, *La vida cotidiana en España bajo el régimen de Franco* (Madrid: Temas de Hoy, 1996).
4. Richard Gunther, *Public Policy in a No-Party State: Spanish Planning and Budgeting in the Twilight of the Franquist Era* (Berkeley: University of California Press, 1980).
5. The most extreme statement of this essentialist view comes in Michael Richards' *A Time of Silence: Civil War and the Culture of Repression in Franco's Spain, 1936–1945* (Cambridge: Cambridge University Press, 1998).
6. See Juan José del Águila, *El TOP: la represión de la libertad (1963–1977)* (Barcelona: Planeta, 2001).

Notes on Contributors

PABLO MARTÍN ACEÑA is Professor of Economic History at the University of Alcalá. His publications include *Economic Development in Spain Since 1870* (1997), *Monetary Standards in the Periphery* (2000), and *El oro de Moscú y el oro de Berlín* (2001).

WALTER L. BERNECKER is Professor of History at the Erlangen-Nürnberg University, Germany. His publications include *Colectividades y Revolución Social. El anarquismo en la guerra civil española, 1936–1939* (1982), *España entre tradición y modernidad* (1999), and the edited volumes *El precio de la modernización* (1994) and *De la Guerra Civil a la Transición* (1997).

TOM BUCHANAN is University Lecturer in Modern History and Politics at the University of Oxford. He is the author of *The Spanish Civil War and the British Labour Movement* (1991), *Britain and the Spanish Civil War* (1997), *Europe's Troubled Peace 1945–2000* (2006), and *The Impact of the Spanish Civil War on Britain: War, Loss and Memory* (2007), as well as being joint editor of *Political Catholicism in Europe, 1918–1965* (1996).

WILLIAM J. CALLAHAN is Professor of History at the University of Toronto and Fellow of Victoria College. His books include *Church, Politics and Society in Spain, 1750–1874* (1984) and *The Catholic Church in Spain, 1875–1998* (2000).

ELISA CHULIÁ is Senior Lecturer in Political Science at Spain's Open University (the UNED). She is the author of *El poder y la palabra: Prensa y poder político en las dictaduras. El régimen de Franco ante la prensa y el periodismo* (2001).

EDWARD MALEFAKIS is Emeritus Professor of History at Columbia University in New York. His publications include *Agrarian Reform and Peasant Revolution in Spain* (1970), *Southern Europe in the 19th and 20th Centuries: An Historical Overview* (1992), and the editorship of *La guerra de España, 1936–1939* (1996).

SASHA D. PACK is Assistant Professor in History at the State University of New York at Buffalo. He is the author of *Tourism and Dictatorship: Europe's Peaceful Invasion of Franco's Spain* (2006).

CRISTINA PALOMARES is director of the Latin American section at the Fundación para el Análisis y los Estudios Sociales (FAES) in Madrid. She is the author of *The Quest for Survival after Franco: Moderate Francoism and the Slow Journey to the Polls, 1964–1977* (2004).

CHARLES POWELL is Director of the Centro de Estudios de la Transición Democrática Española at the San Pablo-CEU University in Madrid and Deputy Director of the international relations research foundation, the Real Instituto Elcano. His books include *El piloto del cambio: El Rey, la monarquía y la Transición a la democracia* (1991), *Juan Carlos: Self-Made Monarch* (1996), and *España en democracia: 1975–2000* (2001).

PAMELA RADCLIFF is Associate Professor of History at the University of California at San Diego. She is the author of *From Mobilization to Civil War: The Politics of Polarization in the Spanish City of Gijón (1900–1937)* (1996) and the co-editor of *Constructing Spanish Womanhood: Female Identity in Modern Spain* (1999).

ELENA MARTÍNEZ RUIZ is Lecturer in Economic History at Barcelona University. She is the author of a study of the balance of payments in Spain 1940–58 (*El sector exterior durante la autarquía*) (2002) and the co-author of *Los movimientos de oro en España durante la Segunda Guerra Mundial* (2001).

ANTONIO CAZORLA SÁNCHEZ is Associate Professor in History at Trent University, Canada. He is the author of *Desarrollo sin reformistas* (1999) and *La consolidación del Nuevo Estado franquista (1938–1953)* (2000).

MARIANO TORCAL is Senior Lecturer in Political Science at the Pompeu Fabra University in Barcelona. His publications include *Actitudes políticas y participación política en España: pautas de continuidad y cambio* (1995), and, along with Richard Gunther and José Ramón Montero, *Democracy in Spain: Legitimacy, Discontent, and Disaffection* (1997), and *Anti-party Sentiments in Southern Europe* (2001).

NIGEL TOWNSON is Senior Lecturer in the History of Political Thought and Social and Political Movements at the Complutense University of Madrid. Author of *The Crisis of Democracy in Spain: Centrist Politics Under the Second Republic, 1931–1936* (2000), he is also editor of a general history of Spanish republicanism (*El republicanismo en España, 1830–1977*) (1994), three volumes of the work of the Spanish writer and Civil War exile Arturo Barea (2000–2001), and a counterfactual history of modern Spain (*Historia virtual de España, 1870–2004*) (2004).

Index